THE LION HAS WINGS

Blackburn B.20 twin-Vulture engined flying boat. The 'boat' part of the hull could be extended on hydraulic jacks for take-off and landing so as to keep the propellers clear of spray. The prototype was lost in an accident. Production of the second B.20 was abondoned.

The Race To Prepare The RAF For World War II: 1935-1940

L.F.E. Coombs

Airlife
England

First published in the UK in 1997
by Airlife Publishing Ltd

British Library Cataloguing-in Publication Data
A catalogue record for this book
is available from the British Library

ISBN 1 85310 805 7

Typeset by Servis Filmsetting Ltd, Manchester
Printed in England by Butler & Tanner, Frome, Somerset.

Airlife Publishing Ltd

101 Longden Road, Shrewsbury, SY3 9EB, England.

Contents

Airspeed's proposed tandem-engine, twin-boom, two-seat bomber. A number of design offices in the 1930s proposed this layout but few were proceeded with.

ACKNOWLEDGEMENTS

This book would not have been possible without the help of many people and organisations. With the encouragement of editor Richard Riding and Mike Oakey it started life as a series called *The Expanding Years* in *Aeroplane Monthly*. Since then with the invaluable help of many it has, like its alternative title, expanded to embrace more of the technical aspects of the expansion programme.

The verification of facts and much of the essential material of the book depended on the help of the Public Record Office and the RAF Museum records staff, in particular Ray Funnell.

Looming over all, and this is meant in the nicest possible way, is Bill W.T. Gunston whose encyclopaedic knowledge of things aeronautical can always be relied upon to resolve any confusion among facts. I was most pleased when he offered to write the Foreword; particularly as he volunteered to do so before seeing the draft text. He took the trouble to go through the text with a fine toothed pen and made many valuable suggestions. Among fellow writers and historians who gave great help with facts and illustrations are Derek James and Mike Hooks. The former also sorted out conflicting facts concerning Gloster aircraft .

The late Don H. Middleton provided many useful ideas in correspondence over the years: in particular he pointed me toward the many 'paper' aircraft schemed up by Airspeed.

Because radar development played such an important part in the expanding years I consulted the heir to much of the technology in the shape of GEC Marconi where Dr Martin Collier and Roy Rodwell in particular were most helpful in pointing me toward some valuable material. Jill Godsell of DRA, aka The Royal Aircraft Establishment, also helped with illustrations. Peter Ottery provided the important 'black-wing, white-wing' shots to give the 1939 feel to the book. The photographs of Miles aircraft were found for me by Julian C. Temple of the Brooklands Museum and those of Martin Baker by D. Holyland. Dr Mark Nicholls of the Cambridge University Library came up with the required Vickers aircraft visuals. James Goulding helped with untangling information relating to projected fighter aircraft of the late 1930s. Steven Gillard of the Heritage Centre of British Aerospace Brough helped with information on the Botha and the B.20. The in-line engine pictures are there by courtesy of Graham Truscott of Rolls-Royce; the radial-engine illustrations are from John Heaven of Bristol. Alec S. Lumsden helped with information on engines in general. Harry Harvey provided information on Smiths Industries (Kelvin Hughes) equipment. Peter Fitzgerald of the Science Museum helped with illustrations of navigation equipment. Ron Wallace-Clarke along with Laura Hughes of Barr & Stroud provided most of the armament pictures. R. L. Pope of the Duxford Radio Society steered me toward sources of radio and radar equipment illustrations. B.W. Nock of G4BXD and Phil Racher sorted out important facts and illustrations relating to radio and radar sets of the period. Derek Wood, another mine of aviation information, made sense for me of some of the confusing and conflicting accounts of the Graf Zeppelin's ELINT sorties.

Overall the advice of Airlife's managing editor Peter Coles in steering the book from manuscript to print must be acknowledged.

Every effort has been made to avoid errors. Those that occur are down to the author and no other. Omissions are another matter: the best excuse is that there is not enough room to include every aircraft mark and type, system and technological developments in the five years covered by the book.

RAF Pageant at Hendon in 1937: visible, left to right; are Miles Kestrel (prototype of Master) Oxford, Airspeed Queen Wasp, Fairey P4/34 (prototype of Battle), Hawker Henley prototype, Vickers Venom: also the Blackburn Skua prototype next to the DH Albatross civil airliner. (Aeroplane Monthly)

Preface

When in the light of the present we look back on the past our eyes are opened, and we see things that were invisible to contemporaries.

Sir Walter Raleigh

All wars are different

Airforces, like navies and armies, rarely fight a war for which they are equipped and trained.

Once involved in war an airforce usually has to adjust both its tactics and its equipment to meet 'real' as opposed to the 'anticipated' war conditions for which it has prepared.

The Royal Air Force (RAF) from September 1939 onward was no exception. It had to revise, modify and adopt tactics and equipment to match the demands of the air war; albeit they emerged slowly over the first nine months. Fortunately this gave time in which to re-organise and improve before all-out war started. However, one command in particular, namely Coastal, had been virtually operating under war conditions for a year. From day one Coastal Command had to maintain long-range maritime patrols covering all approaches to the British Isles. The personnel and aircraft were stretched to the limit and thoroughly tested under arduous operating conditions.

To some extent Bomber Command also gained real-war experience during the first few months of the war. However, unlike the Coastal squadrons, it was never overstretched. It did not have to sustain a round-the-clock offensive. Bomber Command's greatest tests during the first nine months of the war came when operating in a severe winter in freezing conditions (Whitleys) and the daylight formation attacks (Wellingtons) on the German naval base at Wilhelmshaven. Both highlighted deficiencies and faults in equipment and tactics.

In contrast, Fighter Command was less exposed to the full rigours of air warfare during the opening months of World War Two. The nine months lead in to the full scale air battles and sustained periods of readiness from May 1940 onwards gave valuable time in which to perfect tactics, improve equipment, extend radar coverage and perfect interception control techniques

The author does not subscribe to the modern tendency to add 'British' before RAF. This book is about an airforce that existed before many of its present contemporaries and about events when RAF meant just that and no other.

Wings for the Lion

The title of this book acknowledges the inspiration provided by the memory of Alexander Korda's 1939 film *The Lion Has Wings*. The film is distributed internationally by CTE (Carlton) Ltd who has also given permission for the title of the film to be used for this book. In many ways, despite its inaccuracies, the film presented a useful image of the RAF at the outbreak of the Second World War.

Determination showed on every face: Spitfire pilots ran to their aircraft, took off, and later, like knights of old, were seen closing their cockpit canopies, as if they were visors, on sighting the enemy. Wellington bomber crews flew in formation in daylight. If the film had been made three months later, following the disastrous 18 December raid on Wilhelmshaven, then the bomber sequences might have been very different.

The Lion Has Wings was intended as propaganda

to impress on foreign audiences the potential of the RAF. It was neither 100 per cent fiction based on fact nor 100 per cent a documentary. It was a 'collage' of old propaganda films, old fiction films, newsreels and documentary sequences. Despite its faults, many of those who saw the film in Britain felt a glow of pride and a feeling that all was well in the air.

The film was started just before the war and therefore had to be revised to include a reconstruction of the attack by the RAF on German warships lying off the entrance to the Kiel canal. The fighter control room sequences reflected the real operations rooms: albeit it was implied that information about enemy aircraft tracks came from observer posts and from, to quote the commentator, '. . . all other sources of information' that, presumably, meant radar.

Korda completed the film in two months. The Air Ministry provided access to facilities and squadrons but there was no financial help from public funds. Korda had to pawn his life insurance and those working on the film, including the actors, received only token payments.

Imminence of war

The imminence of war concentrated the minds of both service chiefs and civilian scientists. The five years of expansion and re-equipment of the RAF prior to the end of June 1940 have tended to be overshadowed by the events of late summer 1940 that covered the Battle of Britain and the night battle for London throughout the winter of 1940–41. In retrospect, the RAF of Autumn 1940 was very different from that of 1936 when the expansion scheme got underway. In those five years both men and machines changed: the former acquired new skills and the latter were pushed from the fabric-covered biplane towards the all-metal monoplane era.

Which enemy?

Between 1918 and 1936 the RAF in the United Kingdom had been forced to bide its time and live with the financial restrictions and political attitudes. The Air Staff based its assessment of required strength, in number of aircraft and their types, on different hypothetical wars. One result was the establishment of an airforce that was neither fish nor fowl. It had to be able to perform both offence and defence tasks. It also had to protect the outposts of Empire.

In 1925 the 'enemy' nations included France. Political relations were so strained that the Air Staff was asked to estimate the casualties and damage the French airforce might inflict on Britain. Therefore, figuratively, all eyes were on the nearest coast to the southern shores of England. Squadrons were moved away from the south coast so as to avoid a pre-emptive French strike against airfields. In 1935, with a significant change to the political scene in Europe, the potential enemy became Germany. However, there were few airfields in East Anglia, Lincolnshire and Yorkshire giving the shortest distance to Germany. The exceptions were Martlesham Heath, Felixstowe (seaplane base) and Bircham Newton. Therefore an essential part of the expansion programme was the construction of new airfields; particularly in the eastern counties. Seven new stations with airfields were opened by the end of 1936 and another 14 by the end of 1938 making a total of 89.[1]*

Two concepts of major importance in any study of the expansion of the RAF in the pre-war years are the defendable bomber operating in daylight and fighter control using radar-based information.

Among a host of items, the RAF needed: new guns; new gunsights; better bombs and bombsights; depth charges; new stations and hard runways; new radios; variable pitch propellers, retractable undercarriages and self-sealing fuel tanks; four-engine, long-range bombers with powered turrets; fighters able to fly and fire their eight guns above 15,000 feet.

Luftwaffe

In 1936 Germany was without doubt the 'enemy' in the hypothetical war plans. Under the leadership of Goering, Wever, Milch and Udet, along with the backing of the armaments' industries, the newly constituted *Luftwaffe* was intended to become a formidable force.

On the 7 March 1936 Hitler ordered the army to re-occupy the Rhineland. He gambled on there being no re-action from France, even though his army was weak and the Luftwaffe not at full strength. Compared with the RAF expansion policies, the *Luftwaffe* developed in parallel an entirely different airforce. It concentrated on its role as a support for the army; in doing so neglected the development of long-range heavy bombers.

This book ends on the day the British finally withdrew from France in 1940. It includes, therefore, comment on the technology of air operations during the first ten months of the air war.

* Notes are on page 156.

Airspeed Envoy, military version, from which the Oxford was developed. (Aeroplane monthly)

Chapter One

1935

Volumes have been written on the subject of RAF operations in WWII. Many books have been printed on the different aircraft types. There have been numerous studies of the principal systems and equipment used by the service; such as engines, armament and radar. However less has been written about the upsurge in technology during the years of expansion. The four years leading up to September 1939 were seminal to changes which followed. After September 1939 the RAF went on expanding at an even greater rate.

An upsurge

The British decided to concentrate on getting into production available aircraft types rather than waiting for the next generation to be proved. Of course, that was where those who planned ahead were faced with a virtually insoluble problem. What was the best? Another factor affecting decision making related to the potential theatre of war. Would this be limited to northern Europe or would Britain's overseas possessions be involved. As it happened, the available bomber technology, in respect of range and bomb load, limited sorties from England to an area swept by a radius of about 800 miles.

Histories of the RAF have tended to relegate the immediate pre war years to a lower level of interest. Yet in those years significant changes were made: not only to the types of aircraft in the order of battle but to their equipment. Those changes moved the airforce away from its 1920s–30s, mostly biplane, image. The need to be ready for an all out war within a few years or, later, within a few months accelerated changes and the proving of new technologies.

Metal or fabric?

In 1935, the year in which the first determined effort was made to modernise the RAF, the Air Staff realised that the biplane was no longer an acceptable configuration. They also acknowledged that all-metal structures were preferable. The other important decision related to aircraft engines. 1,000 hp had to be the target. This was the minimum power that would enable an eight-gun, monoplane fighter to achieve an acceptable rate of climb, altitude and top speed: or, in pairs, sufficient power for future fighters; and in fours for the 1940s generation of bombers.

Despite the successful development of stressed-skin metal fuselages and wings, particularly in Germany and the USA, the UK industry was reluctant to give up its metal frame, wooden ribs and formers, fabric-covered, construction technology. One reason being the cost of re-equipping factories for all-metal production. The RAF could have had all-metal, stressed-skin, monoplanes with retractable undercarriages in 1930. That is, if the aviation industry, as a whole, had been able to embrace the new technologies.

At all levels of government, ministry and service, there was a blinkered approach to aviation technology. As Bill Gunston explains so succinctly, British pride dominated rational thinking: British designs were considered the best even though in practice they were rarely as good as comparable aircraft types from Germany and the USA.

Dirigible technology

In 1935 the airforce was five years on from the time when the decision was taken to give up the construc-

Prototype Gloster Gladiator four-gun biplane fighter of 1934. The biplane configuration designed to the limit but with little 'stretch' left for extending its lethality and functions. (Derek James)

tion and operation of large dirigibles. The loss of the R101 had both a psychological and material effect on aviation as a whole. British aviation lost a number of experienced airshipmen in the crash of the R101 on 5 October 1930. However the scorched components of the R101 and the scrapped remains of the sister ship, the R100, represented a number of important advances in materials technology that would be of value to aircraft development in the future. The science of meteorology was also advanced. Until the advent of the large airships, intended for the Empire air route to India, the meteorological department of the Air Ministry had limited resources. However, as airships were very dependent on good forecasting, both the size of the meteorological service and the sciences employed had to be expanded. The new service then became of value to the airforce as a whole.

Germany and the United States did not give up the large airship despite some unfortunate experiences of the US Navy.

Aircraft procurement – policy and procedures

Paramount in the minds of the Air Staff and the government was the choice between going for the best or going for the nearly best. The former would impose excessive demands on production capacity and facilities and would take time. The latter would be ready sooner and the lower standards could be offset by quantity.

The shadow factory scheme, largely based on the car industry, was underway but would take two years in which to get into full production.[1] The decision was taken to concentrate on getting into production available aircraft types rather than waiting for the next generation to be proved. Another factor affecting decision making related to the potential theatre of war. Would this be limited to northern Europe or would Britain's overseas possessions be involved? As it happened, the available bomber

Rolls-Royce Kestrel 12-cylinder supercharged engine which, until the advent of the Merlin, was the principal liquid-cooled engine of the RAF for both bombers and fighters. In its ultimate version, the XXX, fitted to the Master I, its bhp was 720. (Rolls-Royce)

technology, in respect of range and bomb load, limited sorties from England to an area swept by a radius of about 800 miles.

From 1936 onward the new generation of aircraft entered slowly; or more correctly, at a dribble into squadron service: some arriving within only a few months of September 1939; others, the Whirlwind and Beaufort for example, did not make it in time.

The ordering procedure for new types of aircraft in the early 1930s was complicated and time consuming. Firms would be asked to submit designs to the Air Ministry's requirements. The best two or three were then selected and orders placed for an experimental aircraft from each. The best of the experimental aircraft was tested and contract given for six to be built. The six aircraft were then subjected to 'development trials' in a squadron. After the incorporation of modifications and improvements a production ordered was placed. Under the stress of expansion a new procedure was adopted whereby new aircraft were ordered 'off the drawing board'.[2]

Under the revised procurement procedure, outline operational requirements were issued some months before the arrival of a detailed specification. This enabled design offices to prepare feasibility studies that could be quickly adapted to meet the final specification. At a 'mock-up' conference Air Ministry specialists would offer opinions. Another change in the overall procedure for acquiring a new aircraft was a limitation on the tests by the A&AEE Martlesham Heath and delaying armament trials until after the preliminary handling evaluation flights. Even at the risk of putting a 'failure' into full production, service trials were shortened and the number of prototypes reduced.

The Air Member for Supply and Rescarch Dowding (later MRAF Lord Dowding) was not too keen on the new procedure. In some ways he was proved right for there were two notable failures of the system: the Manchester and the Botha; the former delaying the build-up of Bomber Command and the latter failing to perform to specification.[3]

In the 1920s British defence policies were based on the 'no war for another twenty years' concept. However as the twenties ended and even more so in the early 1930s, the 'no war' period was progressively reduced. By 1937 politicians and the Air Staff were thinking along the lines of 'war at least by 1941'. In 1938 war was expected 'tomorrow' and then postponed after the Munich Agreement. Incidentally, 1941 was Hitler's projected 'war' year.

Air Estimates

Successive increases in the Air Estimates from 1928 to 1939 were needed to expand the RAF and to modernise its aircraft and other equipment. In 1928 the figure was over £16 million. In the first year of expansion it was set at £39 million; in the next at over £86 million. Within a year of war it had

Hawker Hind two-seat, day bomber. Note the characteristic extendable radiator of the Hawker series of biplanes in the 1930s. (Peter Ottery)

reached over £100 million and thereafter continued to rise. In 1935 Air Staff policy making was based very much on the power of the bomber and less on the need to defend Britain against a similar bomber attack. In 1932 the prime minister Stanley Baldwin spoke the historic words: 'I think it well for the man in the street to realise that there is no power on earth that can protect him from being bombed . . . The bomber will always get through. The only defence is offence.' Baldwin's pronouncement has to be read against a background of public opinion that was solidly against re-armament.

In 1934 there were two bomber to every fighter squadron. This reflected the Air Staff thinking that the only deterrent to an enemy contemplating an attack on the UK was a strong force of bombers able to inflict a devastating retaliatory blow. This acknowledged Baldwin's warning as well as carrying on the 'bomber' policy of Trenchard's Independent airforce of 1918. At the same time both government and airforce seemed to apply double standards to major decisions. On the one hand it was argued that, even in daylight, a well-disciplined bomber formation could defend itself against attacking fighters. On the other hand England could be defended adequately against bomber attacks. Such ambivalence predicated a significant difference in the quality of aircraft between Britain and its potential enemy. In other words, it was generally believed that fighters and bombers of a potential enemy were well below the standards adopted by the RAF.

The perceived effectiveness of the bomber was to have an important influence on the strength and equipment of the RAF.

Defendable bombers

In 1936 the Air Staff was already committed to the concept of the defendable bomber. All multi-engine bombers prior to that year had one or more gun positions. However, it had been obvious for some years that open cockpit mountings for manually trained guns were rendered useless because of the rush of air. Increasing speeds encouraged the development of power-assisted or fully-powered gun mountings. All the new bombers and ocean patrol aircraft planned for the future were to be defended by guns in power-operated turrets or casemates. Casemate installations, as in the early Wellingtons, were frequently called 'turrets' even though only the guns and sights moved, not the complete enclosure

There is evidence to suggest that in 1936 the Air

What the RAF needed to get away from in 1935. The Vickers Virginia bomber that would not have been out of place over the Western Front in 1918. The air gunner's principal skill was not accuracy but avoiding the extreme cold of the open gun positions.
(Smiths Industries)

Staff did consider that bomber design could sacrifice defensive armament for speed. The theory was advanced that as aircraft speeds increased then the difference between the speed of a bomber and that of a fighter would be marginal. Therefore if a bomber were more like a fighter and had no defensive armament it could outpace or at least keep out of gun range of a pursuing fighter.

The 'undefended' bomber argument was well reasoned. However there were those who considered that were such a bomber produced then its pilots would start to demand some form of tail protection. It would then follow that a rear gun or guns and associated mountings would compromise the fine lines and add to the total drag of the aircraft and so slow it down.

Formation flying

The gun-defended bomber concept depended for its effectiveness on formation flying so that each aircraft could bring cross-fire to bear on any fighters attempting to attack. This theory was put into practice by the US Army Air Force in 1942 during daylight attacks on German targets. To some extent it worked. However any bomber that failed to keep up with the formation was doomed. The RAF placed great faith in daylight formations for bombers. However, the firepower of the 7.7mm guns in each Wellington, Blenheim or Hampden was puny compared with the twelve or more 13mm guns in each Flying Fortress. The RAF's daylight formation attacks were savaged by the *Luftwaffe* during the early months of the war. The Wellingtons, despite their three, powered, twin-gun turrets, were easily forced down: either because of fuel lost from damaged tanks or more directly, in flames, following attacks on the beam where neither the tail nor nose turret could bear and the ventral turret gunner was unsighted for most of the time. The Hampdens were defended originally by only two 7.7mm guns and the Blenheims by only one in an awkward-to-operate powered mounting. Experience in exercises and later in battle soon emphasised the need to at least double the number of defensive guns in both aircraft.

The gun and powered turret lobby exercised by manufacturers was strong in Britain. Vickers Armstrongs, who had long supplied navies with control and power systems for ships' guns, strongly advocated the powered gun turret for aircraft use. As will be noted, they developed the 40mm S gun and a version of the Wellington II with a dorsal turret to be armed with the S gun. This was used to determine the feasibility of a bomber destroyer. The intention being to stand off out of small calibre gun range and use the long-range of the S gun to advantage. However, the question of what happened if a bomber formation was escorted by fighters appears to have been ignored.

Boulton Paul Defiant

At the drawing board stage in 1936 was the Defiant bomber-destroyer fighter. It had no fixed forward-firing guns. All its offensive armament was concentrated in a four-gun powered turret abaft the pilot's cockpit. The Defiant was schemed in advance of a successful radar reporting and fighter control network. It was envisaged that the four-gun turret could be brought to bear on enemy bomber formations. However, this tactic depended on the Defiant being in a favourable position relative to the enemy. That would be difficult to achieve from a standing patrol line unless the line was across the enemy's track and close to his height.

Large bombers

In 1935 the Air Staff decided that the only worthwhile offensive weapon would be large bombers of a size requiring at least 4,000 hp of total engine power. To that end specifications were issued to the aircraft industry. With Germany as the most likely enemy in the future it was hoped to have a fleet of extra large, long-range bombers in squadron service within five years. This was an ambitious programme whose architects deserve great credit.

The performance required of the next generation of bombers after the Whitley and Wellington included such figures as a bomb load of 8,000 lb to be carried for 1,500 miles. The design staffs in the aircraft industry were faced with many new problems. There were few large aircraft designs in the world from which they might receive some guid-

Fairey Hendon night bomber. This, for its time (1930) large twin-engine aircraft had a very thick section wing, poor performance and an insignificant bomb load (1,600 lb). However, it could claim to be the RAF's first monoplane twin-engine bomber. (Derek James)

ance. As it was they had to work in great secrecy. Both the government and the Air Staff were most concerned least the Germans found out about the ideas for extra large bomber designs beginning to emerge as drawings. If the Germans had found out they might have started on a similar programme and not abandoned the Urel (long-range, heavy bomber) project.

Effective technology

In parallel with aerodynamic, structural and engine developments there were over thirty important specific technologies either needing improvement or introducing as new concepts. They were needed in order to maximise the potential of the new aircraft planned to enter squadron service in the second half of the 1930s. As will be explained, many of the essential technologies were either not available or not fully operational by September 1939.

There are many important factors to be considered in any study of the expansion of the RAF in the years leading up to WWII: factors which resulted directly from the absence of effective technology. They included:

a) The concept of the defendable bomber operating in daylight that eventually had to be modified.
b) Precision navigation and bombing at night.
c) The effectiveness of bombs.

All of these were proved to be false hopes on the part of the Air Staff. Over the four years 1936 to 1939 the level of technology rose steadily. However, the increase was greater in some areas and less in others. Some of the advances in equipment and techniques could not be applied as a standard across all first-line aircraft types; many of which were fabric-covered biplanes.

One factor in particular retarded progress with electric and electronic systems. This was the absence of or, if present, limited electrical generating capacity of the available aircraft engines. Although engine power had increased significantly from around the 500 hp of the early 1930s to 1,000 hp little had been done to provide sufficient electrical and hydraulic power. The RAF's standard engine-mounted DC generator was a 28V 500 Watt machine.

Little integration

Looking back over 60 years it is easy, as always with hindsight, to criticise. A retrospective approach is also influenced by present day technology. Today's aircraft are not, as in the past, a collection of individual, independently acting, elements. With modern aerospace technology the principal design aim, after satisfying the needs of safety and effectiveness, is integration. Each element, system, unit and 'black box' has to be part of an integrated whole. In contrast, in the mid-1930s the principal components were designed in isolation of others and were intended to work in isolation. Any necessary integration of their functions was the task of the aircraft crew. This is one reason why we cannot always make meaningful comparisons between equipment of the 1930s and that of 1990s. Had this book been written in 1950, then direct relationships, from which to make comparisons might have been made. After about 1950 aviation technology, as measured by its performance and versatility, leapt ahead. Mathematicians will readily relate the advance to an exponential curve.

Because of treasury restrictions on funds the RAF's more advanced aircraft of the first half of the 1930s decade had to operate in a 1918 environment. In other words, the service had to make do with existing maintenance equipment, transport vehicles, hangars, guns and communications.

Specific technologies

The specific technologies of the expansion programme included the following:

A new generation of automatic pilot.
Controllable-pitch, constant-speed propellers
Automatic boost and mixture controls
Eight-gun batteries for fighters
Power-operated gun turrets
New guns and new gunsights, including lead-computing sights

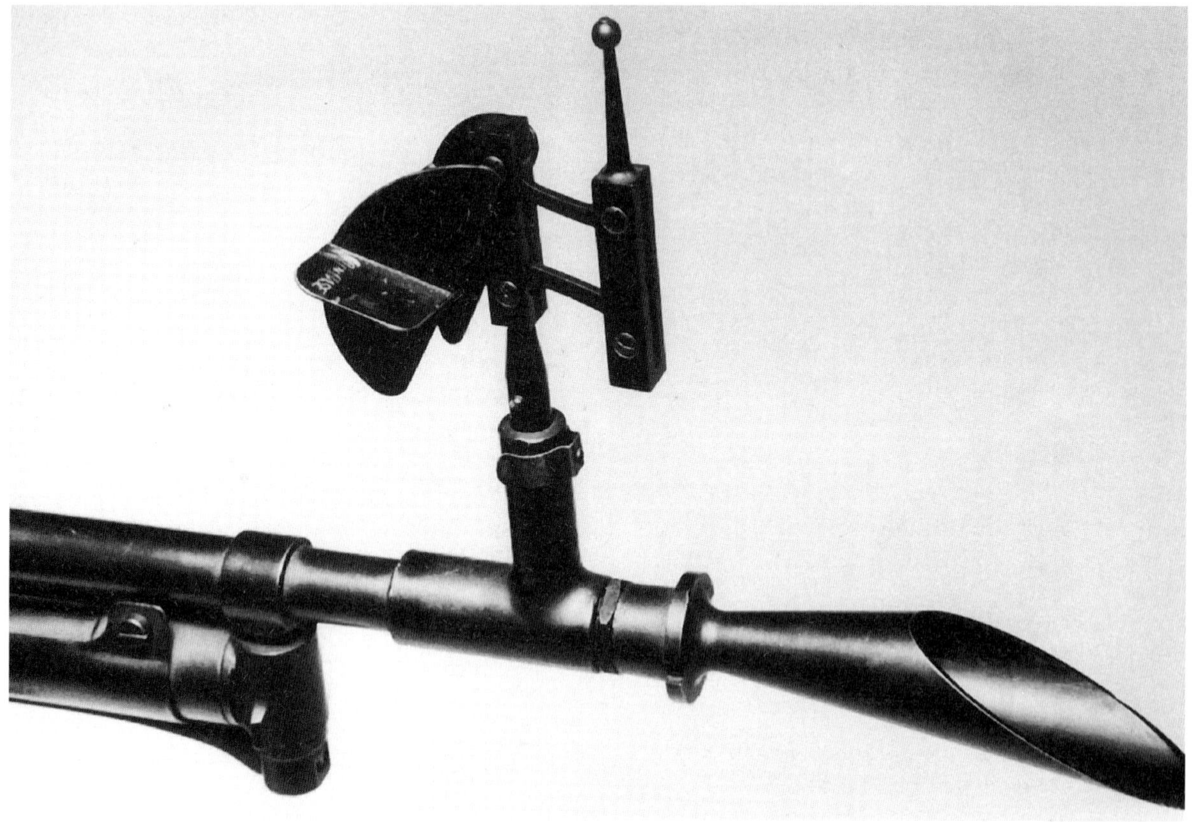

Norman-Vane compensating fore-sight on a Lewis gun. (Wallace-Clarke)

Gun heating
Armoured windscreens for fighters
Long-range auxiliary fuel tanks for Hurricanes and Spitfires
In-flight re-fuelling of bombers
Effective bombs and bomb-sights
Target illuminating flares
Flares for maritime reconnaissance
Effective and standardised airfield lighting
Secure communications network
Effective RT control of fighters
VHF RT in place of HF
A new general purpose transmitter and receiver
Effective air-to-ground radio to army units
Moisture resistant radio equipment
Complete high and low level radar coverage
Identification Friend or Foe (IFF)
Effective use of radar for early warning and fighter control
Airborne radars for navigation, interception, bomb aiming and ship detection
Cameras for recording bombing results
Cameras for reconnaissance
Electro-mechanical navigation aids
Improved integrating bubble sextant
Standard 'blind'-flying panel
Remote indicating instruments
Radio compass
Concrete or tarmacadam runways
Dispersed large-scale aircraft production
A replacement for the GR Anson
A modern torpedo bomber
Four-engine, long-range, bombers
A post-Spitfire generation of fighters

Twin-engine night fighters
A high-performance fighter trainer
A twin-engine trainer
Realistic training equipment
100 Octane fuel
Gas turbine engines
Balloon barrage
Dedicated high-speed rescue launches
Dinghies for fighter pilots

The reader will think of others. The list is not intended to be comprehensive. Its principal purpose is to emphasise the tasks facing those responsible for ensuring that the country had an airforce capable of both offence and defence. Of course, some of the items in the list were not given serious consideration until the 'shooting war' started. Some became subjects for research and development only after operational experience under war conditions had highlighted a particular need.

Some of those listed were not available by September 1939; although they may have been installed earlier as experimental equipment. For example, controllable-pitch propellers were fitted to some aircraft types but constant-speed units were not fitted to Hurricanes or Spitfires as squadron standard until mid 1940.

The radio-telephone (RT), introduced experimentally in 1918, was in general use for civil aircraft and in the airforce for fighter control but was not usually fitted to bombers. However, in the mid 1930s RT range was limited.

Important among the list of aircraft equipment and accessories is the quality and quantity of instruments afforded the pilot. As a rough guide, the number of instruments reflected the performance and versatility of a military aircraft. Similarly, the number of control levers and selector switches was an indication of the number of systems and operational equipment provided and therefore the 'lethality' of the aircraft as a weapon system.

War-winning ideas

On the subject of projects intended to improve the effectiveness of the airforce, Sir Henry Tizard emphasised that 'war-winning' ideas, of which there were many, would had to have been researched, evaluated and put into production well before the outbreak of war to have any positive influence on the effectiveness of the RAF. He also warned that even if only a few from the long list of ideas were proceeded with, the demand on manpower and production resources would be overwhelming. Sir Henry headed the Committee for the Scientific Survey of Air Defence formed on 28 January 1935.

Therefore having embarked on a policy of expanding the RAF, both in quality and quantity, those responsible for carrying out had to apply a strict order of priority among the array of potentially war winning ideas. In other words, as much as the Air Staff would have liked to have everything on the list at the same time they had to recognise the limitations of the real world. Particularly as the real world of Britain in 1935 was not at war. Furthermore it would be another three years before the Cabinet would agree that production for the armed services could take priority in resources and manpower over other industries.

The expansion programme must also be reviewed against some critically weak elements in the UK's war resources. The scientists mobilised to produce many brilliant innovations, such as radar, worked closely with the RAF but in isolation from the problems of production. The aircraft industry as a whole was made up of numerous independent companies; few of which had the ability, floor space and experience with which to go into mass production. Many of the essential precision machine tools and precision components needed for modern aircraft production had to be imported; some from the USA and many from the German sphere of influence.

Fortunately for the aircraft industry in general and the RAF in particular, the Royal Aircraft Establishment (RAE)[4] provided a sound source of scientific solutions to problems. As early as 1935 the RAE built a 24 ft diameter wind tunnel large enough to accommodate a contemporary biplane fighter. The six-bladed wooden suction propeller was driven by a 2,000 hp electric motor.

Personnel and technology

The command or executive structure of the RAF in the 1930s was made up of regular and short-service commission officer pilots. The regular officer 'corps' were mostly pilots. Aircrew positions such as observer, wireless-operator and air gunner were filled by skilled tradesman. Fitters, riggers, armourers and other technical ground staff could volunteer for flying duties. There were also a limited number of places for NCO pilots and, in 1934, for observers (navigators). However, these 'back cockpit' flyers did not necessarily get any advancement in rank or privileges. The air gunner's winged-brass-bullet arm badge, which provided a few shillings qualification pay, was difficult to earn. The time had to come when, as with pilots, flying had to be a full-time occupation without the distraction of other duties.

The personnel and their qualifications reflected the limited range of technologies of the time. As the expansion programme advanced both officers and others had to embrace more demanding skills. There had to be more specialists.

Aircrew training

The role of the RAF was definable in broad terms: bomb the enemy so as to deprive him of key industries and the morale of the people; and, at the same time, defend the realm both in the UK and abroad. However details of both the strategy and tactics needed to meet these roles were not so clearly defined. Therefore it was not always practicable to define the training programmes or the specialised training equipment needed. Even if the organisers of training exercises and the writers of training manuals tried to produce exercises related to the conditions of future wars, they had little conception of what they would be like.

They were also constrained by the limitations of the available technology. From 1936 onward plans were submitted for improving the training of aircrew: but it would be as late as 1939 before all first-line squadrons were relieved of the burden of having to train aircrew. As noted, the training of full-time NCO observers (navigators), was only started in 1934. Although the School of Air Pilotage had existed since the early 1920s, this was only for pilots.[5]

The flying hours and therefore the air experience gained by the part-time aircrew such as wireless operators and air gunners, did not always provide well-trained regular crews. The loss of six Heyfords on a cross-country exercise was contributed to by a lack of flying experience in that particular squadron.

In the mid 1930s training activities, such as navigation, air-to-air and air-to-ground firing as well as bomb dropping on ranges, tended to relate to an air war of earlier times or to punitive sorties against tribes in the remoter parts of the Empire. Such activities were also restricted in compass and effect by the need to avoid upsetting the civil population. There was little guidance from the government on the nature of any forthcoming war although admittedly the resurgence of Germany as a threatening power was a major factor in both government and service thinking.

Pageants

The RAF Pageants each year included a number of warlike items. Competitive bombing, using smoke bombs against a target, bore little relationship to real war conditions. The bombing of 'enemy' positions, such as dummy fort or harbour on the airfield at Hendon, depended for accuracy on electrically detonated charges already in position; and on someone pressing the button neither too late nor too soon. Those squadrons chosen to take part in the annual display benefited from the practice flying needed for the different events and the deployment and logistics of the whole operation; even if the warlike items were unreal.

Exuberance

In the 1930s aviation of all types was recognised as a potentially dangerous activity: even more so in service flying.

A particular hazardous peacetime exercise

The Vickers (Aviation) Ltd Type 246 private venture general-purpose bomber of June 1935. In September 1935 the Air Ministry issued Specification B.22/35 and the Type 246 was modified to comply and became the Wellesley. (Vickers Archives – Cambridge University Library)

was air-to-ground target firing. When diving towards the target panel set out on one of the coastal ranges a pilot had to make rapid assessments of height remaining, angle of dive and other factors. Visibility over a coastal range could vary suddenly from clear to a dense sea mist. In poor visibility there were a number of accidents. Added to misjudgement were engine failures and even structural collapse. On occasions a pilot would so concentrate his attention on the target, watching the effect of his guns, that he failed to pull out in time. Crashes also followed inadvertent spinning from an altitude too low in which to recover or bale out. Loss of control when flying in cloud and fog was a constant problem. Another factor that added to the annual toll of men and machines was the exuberance of a group of young men that reflected the attitude to life of the social class from which many were recruited. Fast cars and sporting activities were among the expected attributes and interests of an RAF officer. Senior officers were often reluctant to dampen enthusiasm by imposing harsh punishments on those who broke the rules or offended the civil authorities by flying under bridges or 'buzzing' the girlfriend's house.

Single-engine bombers

An interesting staff decision in 1935 was the choice of two single-engine bombers, the Wellesley and the Battle; designed to specifications issued in 1931 and 1932 respectively. One reason for the choice was based on tradition. For the 17 years of its existence the service had operated general purpose single-engine, two-seat, day bombers. These biplanes, such as the Hart and Hind, needed replacing with types having greater performance and provision for a third crew member. The important group of figures of 1000/1000/200 in the specifications for the Battle and 1000/2000/200 for the Wellesley indicated respectively range, bomb load and speed. However their specifications called for only one engine. At the time the Air Ministry was still hesitating over adopting the monoplane configuration. Only the persistence of Vickers in convincing AVM Dowding at the Air Ministry that the order against specification G4/31 should relate to a monoplane allowed them to go ahead with the Wellesley.

Both the Battle and Wellesley were long in development and would not enter squadron service until 1937. Such long gestation periods posed a particular problem for those who planned for the future. In five years the international situation and therefore potential enemies, could introduce a war scenario for which particular aircraft types were completely unsuited.

Hawker Hector

Reconnaissance and artillery 'spotting' had long been part of the RAF's work. In WWI the

Prototype of the Westland Lysander in 1936, with the distinguished test pilot Harald Penrose at the controls. (Derek James)

RFC/RAF provided a valuable service as 'eyes' for both the general staff and the guns. From the BE2c onward two-seat biplanes were used over the enemy's lines. However, none of these aircraft had been designed from scratch specifically for army co-operation tasks. A succession of aircraft types were adapted from two-seat light bombers. In 1935 the Air Ministry ordered the Hawker Hector as a quick replacement for the army co-operation Audax. This was a two-seat, biplane with two guns and 224 lb of bombs for army co-operation tasks. The first production aircraft did not fly until February 1936, thus emphasising the lingering 'biplane' image of the RAF. The Hector differed principally from the Audax in the engine. This was the 24-cylinder H-configuration 805 hp Napier Dagger. The Air Ministry wanted to avoid Major Halford and his design team at Napier dispersing should the company collapse financially. The order for 300 Dagger engines for the Hawker Hectors saved the day.

Westland Lysander

In June 1936 the Westland Lysander prototype flew. It was developed to meet specification A39/34 for army co-operation work. This single-engine gull-wing monoplane was designed to give the crew wide arcs of view. A number of interesting features were included to meet the needs of operating in and out of small fields.

Handley Page Heyford

The Heyford is chosen as an example of a 'heavy' bomber technology available in 1936. It also emphasises the need to advance the technology.

This was a metal-structured, part metal, part

Handley Page Heyford twin-engine biplane bomber. Bombs carried in and under centre section of lower mainplane. Although the type was never used in anger one is famous for participating in Watson-Watt's early radar experiment. (Smiths Industries)

fabric-covered, twin-engine biplane. It was the RAF's last biplane bomber. The all-up weight was 17,000 lb. By placing the lower wing close to the ground the loading of bombs into the lower wing centre section was simplified. The fuselage was carried close under the upper wing. The streamlined covers of the main wheels were faired into the lower centre section immediately under the engine nacelles. Incidentally, in the 1930s it was fashionable to fit streamlined fairings or 'spats' to wheels. However, as so often happened, when operating from muddy ground the fairings, and in turn the wheels, became clogged with mud.

Strange appearance

The strange appearance of the Heyford reflected both the ideas of Handley Page and the specification that it was intended to meet when design started in 1927. Specification B19/27 was drafted at a time before all-metal structures and retractable undercarriages were considered essential. Of significance was the Heyford's maximum speed of 142 mph at 13,000 feet. These figures should be compared with the top speed of WWI bombers of around 100 mph. Nevertheless and despite the Heyford, in the five years between 1930 and 1936 a revolution took place in aircraft design. This is best represented by the Boeing Flying Fortress. Although in its early versions, with its few and puny rifle-calibre guns, it was by no means a 'fortress'. However it could attain 300 mph at 20,000 feet with a bomb load of 2,500 lb. The maximum bomb load was 3,500 lb; a significant load in 1936. Therefore by comparison and from force of circumstances the Heyford was out of date when it entered squadron service in 1933. Yet it was much liked by its crews; particularly by the pilots.

In an historical context the Heyford is famous because it was the first aircraft type to be detected by Watson-Watt and his team using an early form of radar. This was on 17 February 1935. It was also one of the earliest bomber types to be equipped with a reflector sight. This replaced the Norman-Vane sight on the Lewis gun of the ventral position. In that position the mechanical compensating Norman sight was spun round and round by the slipstream.

Heyford disaster

A disaster which resulted in the loss of six Heyfords of 102 squadron highlights a number of deficiencies which had remained since the end of WWI.

A formation of Heyfords set off from Aldergrove in Ulster to fly to Finningley in Yorkshire. As the seven aircraft approached the Pennine range of hills the weather closed in and the aircraft lost sight of each other. Through a combination of circumstances, six of the seven crashed. Three crewmen were killed and two injured.

The court of inquiry established that the squadron commander failed to brief the crews adequately: particularly in view of the adverse meteorological forecast. There were inadequate means of communication between the crew positions. There was no proper navigator's station. The intercom failed; just as intercoms would continue to fail for the next six years. Many of the wireless operators, who were more used to operating ground-based radios, had insufficient air experience. Furthermore, the Heyfords did not have de-icing equipment; for that matter neither did other types of aircraft in the RAF. The accumulation of ice as they approached the rising ground of the Pennines was given as the primary cause of the disaster. The navigational techniques used relied primarily on the successful identification of successive ground features. The commander decided to 'press on' so as to reach Finningley before dusk because few of the pilots had much experience of flying at night.[6] The Heyford disaster had a number of causes. Each was an indication of the lack of progress in advancing equipment standards and flying training after 18 years of peacetime flying where the vagaries of the weather in the UK always imposed a somewhat unique set of conditions in which to fly.

On 26 November 1936 the service received its first production standard monoplane bomber. This was the Fairey Hendon, designed to meet the requirements of specification B19/27 which also applied to the Heyford. However, the two bombers were very different.

Hawker Fury II

First-line fighter technology in squadron service in 1936 was represented by the Hawker Fury II biplane with only two guns.

The concept of the Fury II spanned the years from 1918 to 1936: it combined the old with the new. The shape of the metal engine cowling and the fabric-covered rear fuselage, wings and empennage anticipated the Hurricane. This was to be expected as both aircraft came from Sydney Camm's design office at Hawkers in Kingston-on-Thames. During the 1941 siege of RAF Habbaniya in Mesopotamia by the Iraqis, unserviceable Furys had their upper wings removed so that they resembled Hurricanes.

The 'old' parts of the Fury were the open cockpit with a diminutive windscreen, descended directly from fighters of WWI. It perpetuated the twin synchronised Vickers 7.7mm gun arrangement of its predecessors; with the gun breeches accessible to the pilot. At the tip of the pointed propeller spinner there was the 1920s 'trademark'. This was the 'dog' into which engaged the driving shaft of the Hucks starter. In 1936 electric starter motors were a luxury. Either the airmen mechanics used a hand-starting crank at the side of the engine or connected the long Hucks starter drive shaft, on its venerable Ford chassis, to the propeller hub. A typical scene at a fighter station was a row of Fury fighters each being attended in turn by the Hucks starter crew. The Fury had a two-blade, fixed-pitch, wooden propeller with a spinner faired into the lines of the pointed nose. The Rolls-Royce Kestrel engine developed 575 horsepower at 13,000 feet; above which performance fell off. Significant items of equipment missing on a Fury in 1936 were navigation lights and landing lamps. Night flying was not a major part of a Fury pilot's life. When the Fury was conceived in 1929, electrical systems were limited in capacity and few single-engine aircraft had engine-driven generators.

Specification F14/32, to which the Fury was designed, demanded both speed and a good rate of climb, therefore endurance had to be sacrificed. With a range of only 300 miles from its 50 gallons of fuel the Fury had a limited radius of action. In

1936 fighter tactics were still pre-radar. The defence of London, for example, depended on the visual and aural tracking of enemy bombers. The Fury II took nearly ten minutes to reach 20,000 feet. In that time an attacker could advance 30 miles. With a speed margin over a typical bomber of about 50 mph a stern chase was unlikely to succeed. This factor and the performance and control of fighters in general during air exercises forced the development of radar.

Fighter design

Before the Hurricane and the Spitfire could emerge from the drawing boards many design conventions whose origins were in WWI had to be abandoned.

The issue of a typical Air Ministry specification for a new fighter did not constrain its designer to a particular configuration. He was free to adopt what ever shape of aircraft thought best in order to meet the specification. If a biplane with retractable skids, pusher propeller and the engine under the pilot best met the specification then that configuration would be submitted. A company might submit a new design to the Air Ministry as a private venture. If it was approved then it would be endorsed by an official specification.

Specification F7/30 issued by the Air Ministry in 1930 was for a day and night fighter having four guns and a top speed of 250 mph. Six aircraft companies built prototypes to meet the specification. In addition there were a number of projected designs that got no further than the drawing board or wooden mock-ups. Between 1930 and the emergence of the Hurricane and Spitfire there were over sixteen prototype and projected designs.

With the biplane configuration no longer acceptable the monoplane fighter with four or more guns was to be the design target. Specification F5/35 was issued from which emerged eventually the

Gloster eight-gun fighter to Specification F5/34. K5604 shown here was the prototype first flown in December 1936. It eventually lost out to the Hurricane and Spitfire and was not put into production despite some advanced features. (Derek James)

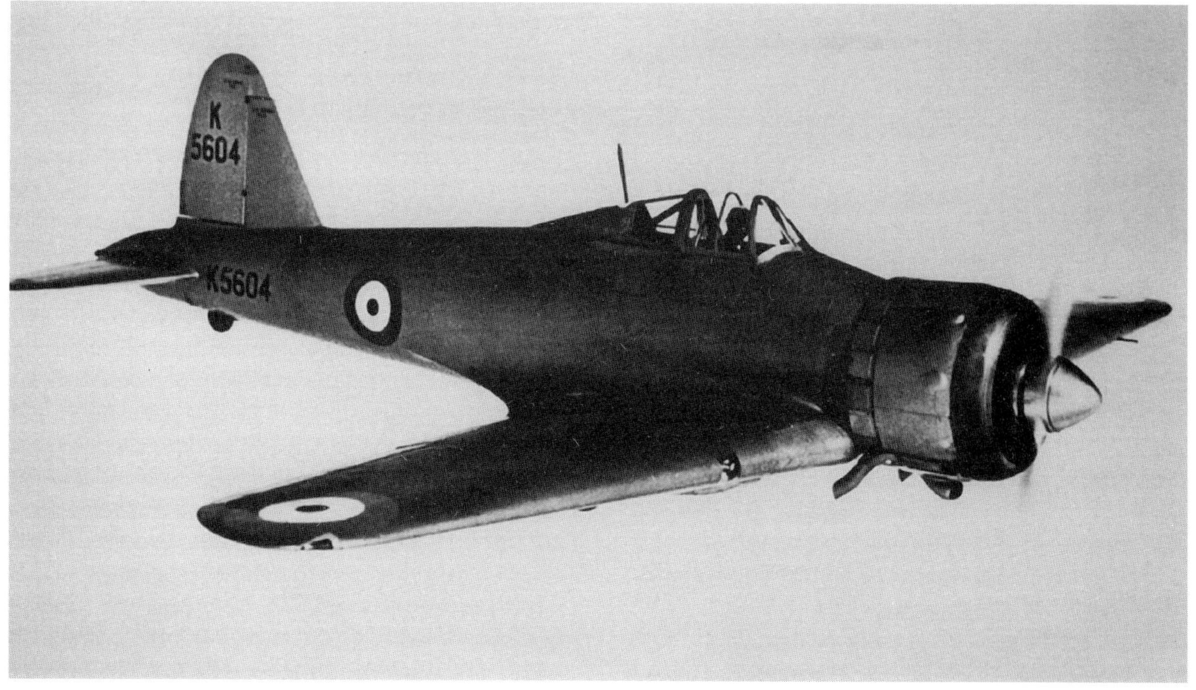

Hurricane and Spitfire. By 1936 some progress had been made towards meeting the monoplane fighter specification. Of equal importance to airframe and engine design decisions was the choice of eight guns for the new monoplane fighters. Because there was only likely to be room for eight guns in the wings then the guns had to be reasonably free from any tendency to stop firing. An equipment change that emerged with the advent of wing-mounted guns was the introduction of pneumatic firing systems in place of the Bowden cable type. With the Bowden control there was a delay between pressing the firing trigger on the control column and the guns firing.

To bring the history of fighter design up to 1936: Folland and Preston of Gloster aircraft designed an eight-gun monoplane fighter with a retractable undercarriage. This was a considerable departure from the two-gun biplane configuration. (One was flown at the RAF Pageant at Hendon in 1937.) The prototypes were well liked by the few pilots who flew them. However it was not ordered.

Fighter engines

The future of the new fighters, the Spitfire and the Hurricane depended on the successful development of the 1000 hp R-R Merlin engine. In 1936 however the Merlin, particularly in the Hurricane prototype, gave nothing but trouble. Internal glycol leaks, distorted and cracked cylinder heads were among a number of problems that had to be overcome as the new fighter and the new engine proceeded along parallel lines of development.

Looking even further ahead were those who sought an alternative to the 'prancing pistons'. In 1926 the RAE started to investigate the use of a gas turbine as a power plant for aircraft. In 1929 Frank Whittle (later Air Commodore Sir Frank) had started on a research and development career which would eventually culminate in practicable jet propulsion based on the gas turbine.[7] By 1936 the Air Ministry was backing the research programme. Throughout the years covered by this book Whittle and his team struggled to overcome formidable technical problems and even more formidable political and financial obstacles to progress. Despite some progress towards practicable gas turbine propulsion, metallurgical and other problems resulted in the jet fighter missing the first four years of WWII.

Fighter control

In the majority of airforces from 1917 onward the principle had been accepted that some degree of control needed to be exercised from the ground in order that fighters could be at the most advantageous point in three dimensional space at the right time. Both the RFC and the German air service had employed a system of ground observers linked by telephone to a central control station from which orders were passed to the operators of visual display panels set out on the ground.

In the UK the air defence system was based on visual observation by a network of observer posts supplemented by position plotting using sound locators at anti-aircraft gun and searchlight units. Because of financial limitations the system was more on paper than on actual equipment and personnel. Therefore there were few opportunities for large scale testing.

Radio telephone

The degree of interceptor fighter control, loose or tight, depended on the character of an air war. It also depended on the effectiveness of the communications link between air and ground. The link might be as simple and inflexible as the coloured ground panels used in WWI.

With the advent of the radio-telephone more precise control could be exercised from a command centre. However the information passed to the fighters was obviously progressively degraded as it passed from one element of the control system to the next. Ten years earlier when squadron-standard, as opposed to experimental, RT sets were fitted to interceptor fighters they were viewed with disfavour by pilots who commented that 'in the event of war we will throw them out'.

However RAF pilots were not alone in adopting such an attitude to 'interference' from the ground.

The German airforce, despite the availability of excellent radio equipment, made little attempt to establish a system of fighter control comparable with that of the RAF. The 'Spaniards', i.e. those pilots who had fought in Spain, such as Adolf Galland, were strongly opposed to being controlled from the ground.

HF/DF

In August 1933 Sqn Ldr L.J. Chandler, a signals technical officer, recommended that HF direction-finder stations be built for each fighter sector. Bearings obtained from three-minute interval transmissions from an aircraft would be used by a central plotting station to plot continuously the position of the aircraft. By 1935 four HF/DF stations were in operation in south-east England. The task of the HF/DF operators was simplified by the use of cathode ray tube (CRT) indicators. As will be mentioned, Chandler went on to develop 'Pip Squeak' thereby completing the essential structure of Fighter Command's reporting and control system with radar providing the final piece of the jigsaw.

Radar

The detection of aircraft other than by visual and acoustic means was always a priority for those responsible for planning the defence of the United Kingdom. The need was obvious. Also obvious were a number of well-understood scientific principles that might provide answers to the problem. Infra-red and other electromagnetic emissions and effects were alternatives to light and sound. What eventually emerged as radar was the result of applying well-understood physical phenomena. In fact had a determined effort and, of course, money, been applied in the 1920s to the detection of aircraft by observing the effect they had on electromagnetic waves, such as radio, then the RAF might have had a defence radar system in place before 1936. For example, Butement and Pollard developed a prototype pulsed radio system using, for its time, the very short wavelength of 50 centimetres. This was demonstrated in 1931 as a method of detecting ships. However, the Royal Navy was not interested.[8]

Without a belt of terrain 'illuminated' scientifically the defence of the UK was conducted along 'fire brigade' lines. If a breach in the theoretical defence line was made, fighter aircraft were rushed to the 'hole' either from readiness, quick reaction, positions on airfields or from standing patrol lines. With the visual or sound location 'horizon' little more than 30 miles away (about six minutes) a controller had a formidable task in reacting correctly and conserving his forces. The UK in those circumstances could be likened to a chicken run with a number of foxes capable of breaking through the wire at any point.

After the air exercises in 1934 Sir Arthur Longmore, the commander of one of the defence zones, concluded that:

> The successful interception by fighters of raiding bombers required more accurate information from the ground as to movements of hostile formations than was at the time available.

In exercises in 1935, when Fury fighters took off as 100 mph Heyford bombers passed overhead at 15,000 ft the 'hostiles' were 33 miles further on by the time the fighters reached them.

These facts made the Air Ministry realise that unless science came to the aid of the RAF in its task of defending Britain from air attacks then the next air war, if it were to start within ten years, would be lost. At the time experiments were continuing with large concrete sound 'mirrors' near Lydd in Kent They covered an arc of 170 degrees listening out to sea. This was one scientific approach to the problem; a possible alternative was more scientific.

Death rays

In March 1936, after eighteen months of research, Watson-Watt and his team of scientists established a set of basic principles for locating aircraft by detecting reflected radio waves. Those experiments emerged from investigation into the practicability of 'death rays' and radio waves which could interfere with the ignition systems of aircraft engines. Experiments proved that the amount of radiated power needed to raise human body temperature to 'fever' level or to interfere with ignition systems, was so great as to be impracticable. Therefore the 'death ray' scientists turned their attention to the long established principle that a metal object interfered with and reflected radio waves. In 1904 the German physicist Christian Hülsmeyer demonstrated the world's first detection system using high frequency radio waves. In 1922 Marconi conducted experiments on the detection of ships using the same principle. Claims were made for original radar development by Hülsmeyer and Marconi and many other scientists in France, USA and Japan. However, the innovation and foresight of British scientists related not just to the technique of radar but to the effective use of the information it provided.

Watson-Watt's team developed and built a radio location (radar) system on a wavelength of 26 metres at Bawdsey Manor on the East coast. Coordinates of aircraft approaching the East coast were passed to an operations room at RAF Biggin Hill. One defence exercise involved Gauntlet fighters of 32 Squadron intercepting 'hostile' Hinds. The fighter pilots were not told that the controller was using information based on radar. From then on Bawdsey and Biggin Hill became an important team in the development of effective means of using information displayed on a cathode ray tube. Scientists at Bawdsey Manor were able not only to detect an aircraft 75 miles out at sea but could determine its height and bearing. They were also developing an electro-mechanical device that converted rapidly the information displayed on the cathode ray tube of the radio location set into positional coordinates. From those experimental reporting and control systems was evolved a technique of determining the headings, heights and positions of enemy aircraft. The scientists working closely with the RAF specialists realised early on that the system had to be able to distinguish between one and many aircraft and between 'friendly' and hostile.[9]

This early example of fighter control using radar took place only twenty-two months after Watson-Watt's 'Heyford' experiment. Electronic warfare was the RAF's trump card. Not just the means to detect aircraft at great distances but the means to make the most effective use of the information. Germany developed radar at about the same time. Although its radar equipment was, in some respects, technically better than the British, in the end it was overtaken.

In parallel with the technical battle was the education of fighter pilots and their commanders in the merits of direct control from an operations room on the ground. Sir Maurice Dean provided one of the most succinct comments on the task of those responsible for finding ways to make the most effective use of radar information. He stated:

> Problem: to position fighters to intercept. Requirement: an organisation to handle large amounts of incoming information, to reject what is false, to add a little rapid trigonometry and to process the results into concise orders to fighter pilots.[10]

Typex

In 1936 the RAF's Typex encrypting communications network was established. Although similar in concept to the German Enigma machine, it was more complex and included a high-speed link. It was far more secure than Enigma and was of immense value to the RAF. Typex was developed in the RAF's own workshops under the leadership of Air Commodore O. Lywood. Twenty-nine units were supplied at the end of 1936 for secure high-speed communication between the principal RAF headquarters. At the same time orders were placed for another 238 Typex machines for use in lower echelons of command.[11]

The Task

In 1936 the re-equipment programme was starting to take effect. It would banish the RAF's WWI image and project it into the all-metal monoplane era. However, along the way there would be many setbacks and wrong decisions before the world's first independent airforce became one of the most powerful weapons of all times.

Despite financial restrictions, 'wet' politics, indifference by some and an active disarmament lobby, the RAF and the aircraft industry got on with the task. A task which built an airforce able by the next decade to reach further and further with heavier and heavier blows at the heart of an enemy.

Luftwaffe

Compared with the RAF, the training of personnel, particularly aircrew, was not given proper attention by the *Luftwaffe* general staff. The RAF gave training as much priority as first-line operations; even though there was a shortage of suitable equipment. This was emphasised in 1939 by the withdrawal of some squadrons from the order of battle to form training units.

Perhaps the most significant difference in forward planning in 1936 between the two airforces was the decision to expand the service on the basis of sound aircraft and equipment production and the realisation that any war would not be over in a summer.

The *Luftwaffe* developed and put into production its principal aircraft before 1940. German aircraft technology peaked in 1940 and there was a delay while new aircraft types were developed and tested. The lack of a long-range, heavy bomber, which might have visited great destruction on Britain's industry and population, is another example of the *Luftwaffe*'s failure to plan for a war of attrition.

At the end of 1938 and throughout 1939, the politicians and the Air Staff were faced with having to balance the needs of three different 'war' scenarios at the same time. These were: prepare for war, postpone war and avoid war. Each required a very different set of attitudes and plans.

Vickers Wellington MkI showing the casemate type forward twin-gun powered mounting for nose and tail positions; subsequently replaced by an FN turret. (Aeroplane Monthly)

CHAPTER TWO

1936

Summer in England and the annual air exercises are underway. The biplane fighters and bombers operate from large expanses of turf that provide the take-off and landing areas: landings to the right, take offs to the left. There is the ubiquitous windsock and the signal square next to the watch office.

The hangars and buildings of a typical RAF station have a Great War appearance. The building of new stations, to a standard pattern, started in 1928, is proceeding slowly and it will be another four years before the scheme is completed. After all, this year is only 18 on from the war in which the RAF had been founded as a force of nearly 300,000 men and women and 3,000 aircraft with 20,000 in reserve. From 1919 onward the service was reduced to a first-line strength of 33 squadrons: about 800 aircraft.

A leisurely pace

In 1936 the RAF exhibited a leisurely pace; both in flying and non-flying activities. Some stations closed down for an annual leave period and with few exceptions Wednesday afternoons were devoted to sport. This was not a reflection on the morale and dedication of the service. The reason: there was neither the money available nor the wish of the nation that its armed services indulge in persistent warlike activities.

The Air Staff was well aware that much still needed to be done to advance the RAF on from its 'biplane' era. The technology of the service had yet to benefit to any great extent from the 'expansion' decisions. A visitor to a typical RAF station who had served in the old RFC or RNAS found little that was unfamiliar. Aircraft were not much larger, although engines were four or five times more powerful. There was still the smell of doped fabric: still between the upper and lower wings of the biplanes were the crossed flying and landing wires. On the concrete apron in front of the hangars and on the wide expanse of airfield turf the pilots of fighter aircraft still needed the help of an airman at each wing tip when taxying.

In the early 1930s the service was a close-knit and small force whose first-line aircraft were equipped with open cockpit biplanes. The fighters had a top speed only a little faster than that of the bombers. The Hendons of 38 Squadron Marham were the only monoplane, multi-engine bombers. In 1936 the familiar aeroplane shape was about to be consigned to the drawing office wastepaper basket: but it would be a few more years before the biplane, as a first line aircraft, was phased out. For example, Swordfish and Albercores remained in service for another eight years or more.

After years of poverty the RAF began to see a glimmer of light ahead. In 1936 the light began to strengthen as the expansion programme got underway.

Eight new aircraft

In this first full year of the re-equipment programme, intended to bring the RAF fully into the monoplane all-metal era, there were still plenty of biplanes from earlier years. There were also new biplanes entering squadron service: London, Stranraer and Walrus flying boats as well as the Wallace, Hardy and Fury II landplanes. The Fury Is of 25 Squadron at Hawkinge were proving to be faster than the Gauntlet at moderate altitudes. The two Vickers 7.7mm guns of the Fury II were considered sufficient to inflict crippling damage to a similar type of aircraft. However they might be useless

Gloster SS19 'Multi-gun' fighter: the forerunner of the Gauntlet. Two fuselage-mounted Vickers 7.7mm and four wing-mounted Lewis 7.7mm guns. Presumably any aircraft in the 1930s equipped with three or more guns was a 'multi-gun' type. (Derek James)

against an all-metal bomber equipped with defensive guns. The Fury's guns would not always operate in the minus 15°C air temperature at 15,000 feet.

Although many of the new aircraft types were classified as 'all-metal', some had fabric-covered control surfaces. The Hurricane and Wellesley were completely fabric-covered apart from the engine nacelles. Eventually the Hurricane was given an all-metal wing. Therefore the 'all-metal' design target was slightly misleading because there were and would be many exceptions, particularly among training aircraft types.

In the summer of 1936, as the Fury IIs demonstrated formation low-level attacks at the RAF Pageant at Hendon, the prototype Blenheim flew in to emphasise the alternative technology. This mid-wing, twin-engine, all-metal monoplane, with a combined horsepower of over 1500 from its two engines, had a maximum speed greater than that of the Fury. Compared with the Hind, which it would replace, it was nearly 100 mph faster, carried four times the bomb load and could climb to nearly 30,000 feet. The design of the Blenheim provided the potential for adaptation to other roles; including that of a five-gun fighter. Whereas both the Fury and Hind and similar types had no 'stretch' left.

In the New Types enclosure at Hendon there were eight aircraft types: Battle, Hampden, Hurricane, Lysander, Spitfire, Vixen, Wellesley and Whitley. With the exception of the Vixen, all were to go into production.

In some respects the re-equipment policy and programme contained a significant contradiction. Although the policy was to put eight-gun 'anti-bomber' fighters into production, the RAF's bombers and general reconnaissance aircraft were expected to defend themselves with only one or two 7.7mm guns. For example, the Whitley in the New Types Park had only one tail gun on a manual mounting. If the RAF had to go to war in daylight the bombers might not have survived. As mentioned, part of the assumption being made about

Fairey Battle intended to move the RAF out of the biplane era. Unfortunately it was obsolete when it went into production in 1936 thereby depriving the RAF of the power to stem the German advance in 1940. (Derek James)

the survivability of day bombers against fighters was based on the premise that when flying in close formation each bomber helped to defend the others. Part of the bomber defence against fighter argument was also based on the small difference in speed between the two. It was argued: provided a bomber could match the speed of an attacking fighter it was necessary only to guard the bomber's tail because the fighter would have an insufficient speed margin to attack from any other direction.

Politics and expansion

When the government introduced the expansion programme in the July 1935 Air Estimates it was strongly opposed by socialists. Despite opposition to preparations to defend the United Kingdom, either for political or humanitarian reasons, the expansion and technical improvement of the service were being pushed ahead. What was happening in 1936 can be set against the thought that the RAF was only eight years away from its first jet aircraft.

Precursors

The RAF was always keen on participating in endurance, speed and high altitude flights.

The 1934 Mildenhall-Melbourne MacRobertson Race included two aircraft, the DH88 Comet and the Douglas DC-2 airliner, which influenced the Air Staff's thoughts about future aircraft design. Engine policy for the future was influenced by the Schneider Trophy racing seaplanes. The RAF High Speed Flight won the trophy outright in 1931 with the Supermarine S6 whose Rolls-Royce liquid-cooled in-line V12 engine contributed to the development of a 1000 hp engine for both bombers and fighters. Four particular technologies were advanced by the

DH Comet Grosvenor House *the winner of the Mildenhall-Melbourne MacRobertson Air Race of 1934.* (Peter Ottery)

experience gained during the flight by special versions of the Westland Wallace over the top of Mount Everest in 1933. These were:

engine supercharging
electrically heated clothing
oxygen supply
cameras

The Wallace aircraft were powered by the specially developed and supercharged Bristol Pegasus S3. A Pegasus powered the Bristol Type 138 monoplane when it achieved a record height of 48,698 feet.

Avro Anson

In 1936 the RAF re-equipped the general reconnaissance squadrons with the Avro Anson. The Hendon, introduced in 1935, and the Anson were the RAF's only first-line monoplanes. Other squadrons used Overstrands, Vincents, Harts, Hinds, Furys, Gauntlets, Valentias, Perths, Stranraers, Scapas, Singapores, Londons, Walrus, Wallace, Wapiti and Virginias. This diverse collection of biplane types was the result of years of financial restriction. New aircraft were supplied in penny numbers so that the airforce had to operate the new alongside the old. Sometimes the contrast was marked; for example, the Anson and the Valentia.

The Anson represented a new start. A distinguishing feature was the enclosed crew space with extensive window area for pilot and crew and with unrestricted access to all positions. The retractable undercarriage, albeit manually wound up and down, was a novelty to many pilots. Despite its docile handling characteristics the peacetime accident rate continued to be significant: for example, 48 Squadron soon lost an Anson when it crashed into the sea. The Anson had a flat approach to land and a wing that produced considerable ground effect or 'float'. There was a tendency to overshoot on

Rolls-Royce R Type engine that powered the Supermarine S.6B when it won the Schneider Trophy outright for Britain in 1931. Indirectly the technology applied benefited the subsequent development of the Merlin. (Rolls-Royce)

landing. During circuit and landing exercises the undercarriage, as squadron records show, was not always wound up; particularly if the pilot was flying solo. In consequence on longer flights, when the undercarriage was retracted, it might be forgotten on the final approach at the destination.

Although the Anson was one of the RAF's new types its technology was not very different from the tubular-framed and fabric-covered construction of older aircraft. Therefore it did not impose too great a strain on the training, servicing and maintenance facilities. Squadron establishments were small compared with what they would need to be when more complicated aircraft entered service. If, for example, the Anson had been equipped with a power-operated gun mounting or turret, hydraulically-operated undercarriage, power-operated bomb doors and other 'modern' systems then additional men and skills would have been needed.

Aircraft development

The success of an aircraft type did not always depend just on good design, materials and equip-

Cockpit of an Anson aircraft for maritime reconnaissance. This shows the pilot-on-left with gangway to the right layout used for the majority of RAF multi-engine aircraft from 1930 onward; having abandoned the WWI pilot-on-the right type cockpits for new aircraft. (Aeroplane Monthly)

ment. A good design and development programme from inception to entering squadron service was most important. Many a good design was either delayed in development or abandoned because of a badly organised programme. An essential requirement throughout an aircraft's life was that of direction. Those concerned with development, production and, particularly, the user needed to know what was wanted and when it was wanted. Too many aircraft designs were compromised because of uncertain specification writing and because of subsequent changes in operational requirements; both of which were symptoms of a lack of direction. Above all, there was little point in having an aircraft that was faster, flew higher and further than others if it could not find or hit the target, be it enemy bomber, factory or ship.

Testing new designs

It was generally accepted that it would take at least six years, the lead time, in which to get a new bomber ready for operational service. Aircraft designs that embraced novel ideas were not ordered for the RAF until they had been thoroughly tested; by then they were no longer novel. Indicative of the results of this policy was the fact that the majority of new aircraft designed in the early 1930s were outclassed in speed, range and load-carrying potential by the all-metal monoplanes being produced in Germany and the United States.

The lead time for any new aircraft depended on a number of factors. Two of these were size and complexity. The Anson, for example, had gone from drawing board to squadron in under two years. However it was derived from the civil airliner the Avro 625; thus speeding up design and development. The Blenheim, which first flew on 25 June, 1936 took a little longer. Therefore when a design team started on one of the next generation of large, long-range bombers specified by the Air Staff, progress from drawing board, through development, testing, prototype and production and working up to squadron standard could take up to five years in which to complete the programme and eliminate all snags. Even on paper the bombers-to-be represented a massive upward step in technology which was much greater than that between the Anson and the Blenheim.

The new bombers would eventually become the 'sharp end ' of the RAF. Fighters were viewed with some disfavour by the Air Staff because they diverted financial resources away from the bomber force. The Trenchard doctrine of a strong bomber fleet exercising the maxim that the best form of defence was offence, dominated RAF thinking. Lord Trenchard, 'Father of the RAF', persisted in advocating pre-emptive bombing of a potential enemy and freeing the RAF of any political constraints over area bombing. In 1916 Trenchard, when considering that the Germans might adopt an offensive air campaign, argued against the RFC allocating squadrons to a defence role so as to protect important targets. He firmly believed that the best form of defence was attack.

Hughes H-1

The Air Staff and the intelligence service endeavoured to keep up-to-date with information about the aircraft of other nations. In 1936 they tried to find out what was happening in Germany. In this they were not very successful; despite Germany's deliberate policy of opening development and production facilities to inspection so as to impress others. Intelligence gathering for the Air Staff tended to concentrate on the USA. The results were treated in an ambivalent manner. On the one hand the Air Staff were often impressed by aspects of American technology. On the other, as mentioned in Chapter One, there were some in high places who refused to acknowledge obvious advances made in the USA.

An example of an aircraft that advanced technology to its limits, and was therefore of interest to other nations, including Britain, was the Hughes H-1. It first flew in 1934 and was powered by a Pratt & Whitney 14-cylinder Twin Wasp Junior tuned to develop up to 1,000 horsepower. It had a 25-foot wing span and 138 square feet of wing area giving a wing loading of just under 40 lb per square foot for an all-up weight of 5,500 lb. The power loading was 5 lb per horsepower. At sea level it attained 360 mph and after further development it was capable of flying from California to New Jersey at an average speed of over 300 mph.

The H-1 had a close-cowled engine, constant-speed propeller, retractable undercarriage powered by a hydraulic engine-driven pump and a steerable tailskid. These features plus its performance had a significant impact on design offices throughout the world; particularly in Japan and Germany. It has been suggested that many of its details influenced the design of the Zero and the FW190. However, although the fuselage and empennage were of flush-riveted duralumin with fabric-covered control surfaces, the wings were wood, plywood and fabric construction. The H-1 was used by some as a yardstick against which to compare current British designs. However, what of its performance had it been equipped with eight guns, radio, armour plate and other 'fighter' items? The Vickers Venom was flying armed with eight guns and was a true 'fighter'. It might have paid in the long run to have concentrated more on developments in Germany.

Large bombers

Specification B13/36, to which Avro and Handley Page were working, suggested a large twin-engine, long-range, bomber for use throughout the RAF's far flung 'empire'. It was proposed, in the small print of an appendix to the specification, that a catapult-assisted take-off would be acceptable for operations at maximum range and bomb load. The cruising speed had to be 250 mph carrying a bomb load of 4,000 lb. Both aircraft were to be designed to take two Rolls-Royce Vulture, 24-cylinder engines. The other bomber specification, B12/36, predicated the use of Bristol sleeve-valve engines mounted on a Sunderland type wing.

There was a considerable difference between the 'large' generation bombers and the Wellington, Whitley and Hampden. The future bombers would be not just twice as large; they would be more than twice as complex. The bombers on the drawing board in 1936 were to be capable of reaching far into Europe: each would be defended by guns in power-operated turrets: each would be all-metal,

Bristol Mercury 9-cylinder engine used in the: Blenheim, Gladiator, Lysander, Short-Mayo S.21, Sidestrand and Sunderland. (John Heaven)

have retractable undercarriages, flaps and engines equipped with constant-speed propellers as well as automatic boost and mixture controls. Structurally they were designs that took the key items of crew positions, turrets, bomb stowage and fuel tanks and selected them in accordance with the power available either from two Rolls-Royce Vultures or four Bristol Hercules engines.

Conservative shapes

Although each of the three bomber designs accepted by the Air Ministry differed from the others in detail and arrangement of equipment none was an innovative departure from the classic aircraft shape: there were no tail-first 'canards' and no pusher propellers. Above all they followed the Air Staff's concept of the defendable bomber. Therefore powered turrets, each with at least two 7.7mm guns, in nose, tail and dorsal amidships positions were required.

A price or penalty had to be paid for a reasonable degree of defensive armament. For example: three turrets, their hydraulic or electrical system, ammunition and the gunners added considerably to aircraft weight and complexity; more complexity meant more maintenance. Turrets also demanded space and added to drag. 1.5 tons of a Halifax's loaded weight was debited to the armament of three turrets. The ventral turret of the Stirling was found to add too much drag and therefore it was removed. In 1936 the Air Staff was still thinking along 'general purpose' lines. They wanted the next generation of bombers to continue the service's traditional role of Jack-of-all trades; even if that meant in practice he became master of none. The four-engine specification B12/36 even mentioned the provision of carriers for two 18-inch torpedoes. However, initially none of the three was to be other than a carrier of bombs.

Simple and wooden

As the designers, stressmen and draughtsmen laid clean sheets of paper on their boards and began the fascinating task of reconciling numerous conflicting requirements to meet Specification B12/36 de Havilland (DH) had other ideas.

The bomber policy at the time was not necessarily the only one. There was an alternative to large, four-engine, complicated, expensive and 'crew hungry' aircraft. This was the un-armed, high-speed, twin-engine bomber carrying a 2,000 lb bomb load and needing a crew of only two; and without

Frise-Bristol hydraulic-powered gun turret for the Blenheim under test in a Battle. (Derek James)

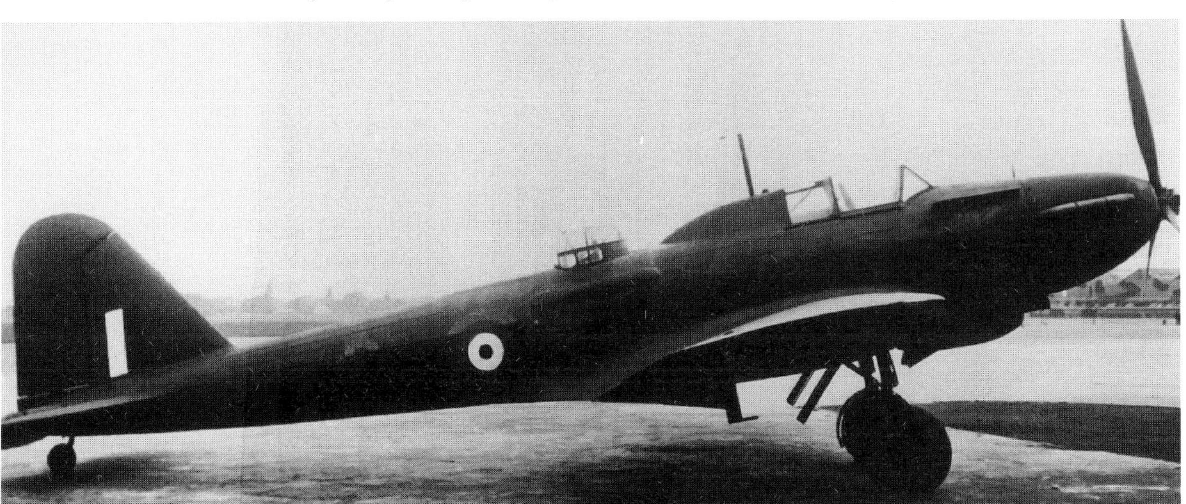

Hessel Tiltman and Nevil Shute Norway of Airspeed's AS29 proposed four Aquila-engined bomber. The fuselage lines were far from elegant: the top was humped and the nose fenestration tilted forward. (Author)

the weight and drag penalties of guns and turrets. Not only would such an aircraft reduce aircrew training requirements by about half, it would halve the number of engines needed and therefore reduce the servicing requirements in proportion. It might have been argued that the 2,000 lb bomb load of the 'simple' bomber would not be as effective per sortie as the 'on paper' 4,000 lb plus load of the new 'heavy' bombers about to enter production, the Wellington and Whitley.

The DH88 Comet and the DH91 Albatross were mostly of all wood construction. DH believed that an all-wood design for a twin-engine bomber was not only good sense but its production would be independent of strategic metals in the event of war. In 1934, DH tried to gain the interest of the Air Staff in a bomber version of the DH88 that could carry 1,000lb of bombs. After a number of 'delaying' letters interest in the proposal faded. Although a compact bomber relying on speed for defence, rather than on guns, was an attractive idea there were drawbacks. One was the low standard of navigational skills at the time. Another, the absence of navigational aids in the form of beacons and beams that would provide at least a 75 per cent certainty that a target could be reached and a return made to base after flying at night, through cloud and in unknown and varying winds. A '1000 mile' penetration bomber still needed a navigator at a chart table and a wireless operator with a direction-finding radio. The addition of two extra crew members and the space needed for navigation and radio equipment weighed against keeping the undefended bomber to a size for which two 1,000 hp engines would be sufficient to give the required speed to avoid being intercepted.

Airspeed's ideas

Many of the companies competing for ministry contracts spent some of their meager resources on scheming innovative designs for all types of aircraft. Airspeed, under the leadership of A. Hessell Tiltman and Nevil Shute Norway, schemed aircraft of many different shapes. These included a twin-tandem-engined fighter, transports and bombers. Tiltman tried to gain the approval of Dowding at the Air Ministry for the AS29 bomber concept He wanted to tender to the Wellington replacement Specification B1/35. Dowding agreed to consider the design on the understanding that it was submitted as a private venture. According to Middleton, the Air Ministry staff never bothered to look at it.[1]

The AS29 projected four-engine bomber provides an example of mid-1930's thinking. It would have been powered by Bristol Aquila engines each of 650 hp. The leading edge of the wing would be swept back some 20 degrees and the wing roots merged into the egg-shaped cross section of the fuselage. The outer engines were to be set back by six feet from the inners. In plan view the AS29 exhibited a blended wing and tailplane and was in general a graceful looking aircraft. However, in side elevation Tiltman had to let aerodynamic and structural factors dictate the lines. The top line of the fuselage was hump backed and the nose section tilted downward. The edges of the fin and rudder were made up of curves. The leading edge of the rudder was swept forward. This was one of Tiltman's trade marks. Much thought went into the selection and layout of equipment, as described in the 113 pages of technical descriptions and drawings submitted to the Air Ministry. However, in the absence of guidance from the Air Staff the proposed defensive armament was not comparable with the overall standard of technology applied. Drawings indicate that there would have been only three Lewis guns. One gun would have been in a retractable dorsal turret that might have been powered. The gun in the nose may have required a complicated mounting and cupola to make it effective. As drawn, the gun position in the tail cone would have been cramped for the gunner and have restricted arcs of fire. The design also provided for a retractable ventral gun-position or turret.

The AS29 is an example of a design philosophy that resulted in an aircraft which needed a crew of six men and a lot of structure as well as four engines to carry a small bomb load for an ineffective distance. One pilot, one navigator and one wireless operator would have sufficed for night attack at a time when there were no radar equipped night fighters. Of course Airspeed may have envisaged the AS29 as a high-speed, high-altitude day bomber and therefore defensive guns and their gunners were necessary. Unfortunately the three or four 7.7mm guns would not have detered the average fighter pilot.

A conclusion that is often reached when studying the records of the different 'paper' aircraft of the mid-1930s is a designer's decision to provide more gun positions or turrets than the number of gunners. The idea being, apparently, that they could move from one position to another depending on the direction from which a fighter was attacking.

Two significant features of the AS29 project were the 'wet' wing, in place of individual fuel tanks, and the provision for in-flight refuelling. But what the drawings do not show is a tricycle undercarriage. The AS29 would have been a 'tail-dragger' like all the next generation of bombers for the RAF. It would also have had a radius of operation of only 800 miles when carrying 2,000 lb of bombs.

Most of these comments on the AS29 are based on conjecture and hindsight but they do serve to indicate the general thinking of bomber designers in the mid 1930s.

Dive-bomber

One aircraft type that rarely appeared in Air Ministry plans was the dive-bomber. An exception was the Blackburn Skua for the Fleet Air Arm and, as will be mentioned, the Fairey Battle. All things being equal, the dive-bomber could achieve a significantly higher percentage of hits on a target than a 'straight and level' bomber. That is, provided it was unaffected by anti-aircraft fire or fighters. Fortunately, with hindsight, the Air Ministry resisted the temptation to divert valuable resources to the large-scale production of dive-bombers for the RAF.[2]

As an aircraft dived close to the vertical and approached its terminal velocity the control characteristics changed. This could make the pilot's task of holding the aircraft to the optimum diving line difficult. Therefore a dive-bomber usually had some form of speed limiting device, such as dive-brakes. It also had a stronger than normal structure to cope with the loads applied during the pull-out above the target. Those requirements conflicted with the specifications for general-purpose medium bombers. The *Luftwaffe* at the time was specifying that some of its new multi-engine bombers be capable of making steep dive attacks. However, with hindsight this was a decision that subsequently handicapped German aircraft development.

Battle

The prototype Fairey Battle arrived at Martlesham Heath in 1936 for approval testing. As a replacement for the Hart it had to carry a 1,000 lb bomb load for not less than 1,000 miles at 200 mph or faster.

The '1,000 lb of bombs for 1,000 miles' part of the specification should have read '1,000 lb for an operational range of 500 miles' because it was usually expected that a sortie would consist of both an outward and a return flight. An operational radius of action of 500 miles from an East Anglian or Kentish airfield could only reach such potential targets in Germany as Düsseldorf, Bremen and Wilhelmshaven. Although not a biplane the Battle was reasonably docile for an all-metal 1,000 horse-power monoplane. For example the speed over the airfield boundary, wheels down and full flap, was about 58 mph and therefore not too demanding on landing area length. Harald Penrose found the Battle easy to handle though the controls were heavy. The stall was gentle and the cushioning effect of the low-set wing made it simpler to land than the Tiger Moth.

Structurally the Battle was of sturdy build and did not suffer to the same extent as other types from 'ploughed field' operations. The R-R Merlin engine drove a two-position three-blade propeller. There was an engine-driven generator for the electrical system and a hydraulic pump for the undercarriage and flap systems. A fully enclosable, sliding hood, cockpit and hot air supply for the pilot and the observer/navigator positions gave reasonably comfortable working conditions. However the gunner's position at the aft end of the long 'greenhouse' could be freezing cold at high altitude and in winter. With the canopy hinged up, when using the single Lewis or Vickers K gun, the air gunner could easily be frozen into immobility.

The cockpit of the Battle was little better or worse than that of other aircraft. Levers, wheels, switches and knobs were positioned to suit the convenience of their associated rods, wires, pipes and wiring and not necessarily to suit the pilot's hands. The undercarriage, flap and bomb-bay door levers were grouped low down to the left of the pilot's seat. As was customary, the undercarriage selector lever was protected by a fiendishly clever guard. The designer of this did not take into account the various things the pilot had to do during take off when there was little time in which to fiddle with an awkward, finger-cutting, control. Just to make the pilot's life even more difficult, the elevator and rudder trim wheels were on a common axis and located behind the pilot's left elbow. The rudder trim wheel worked in the same plane as that of the elevator wheel and therefore, without being able to read the direction arrows, the pilot had to remember which wheel did what and which way to move it to effect a trim change.

The description issued by the Fairey company of the bomb carriers in the wing bomb-cells suggested a dive-bombing role for the Battle: 'The hydraulic jacks mentioned in connection with the internally stowed bombs are used not only for loading of the bombs but for their transferring into free air for diving bombing'.

The Air Ministry specification, to which the Battle conformed, was also answered by Armstrong Whitworth with its AW29. Like the Battle, this was a single-engine monoplane. However the 870 hp Siddeley Tiger did not match the power of the Battle's Merlin engine. Fairey received an order for 155 Battles and therefore the future of the AW29 became uncertain; particularly as its performance did not match that of the former. Once again the RAF was having to make do with a single-engine bomber, the Battle, in the face of a world-wide move towards multi-engine bombers with room for a navigator and wireless operator, as well as for a gunner or gunners to man the defensive armament.

Bent aircraft

The number of aircraft damaged or written-off continued to be significant. Contributing to the toll was the time honoured approach to a landing with the engine ticking over. This required a carefully judged approach with the speed only just above the stall. Sudden engine failure, an adverse gust, or pilot error, would result in a stall and a spin with insufficient height in which to recover. Should a pilot have to 'open-up' the engine, to stretch the approach, the sound might be heard by his fellow officers who would then impose a 'drinks all round' penalty. Other airforces commented adversely on the RAF's engine-off approach. They argued that, whereas it might train pilots to make successful forced landings away from an airfield, the incidence of engine failures did not warrant the deaths and injuries. However, times were changing, aircraft such as the Blenheim, Hurricane and Whitley with flaps would be 'motored' in.

There was also the annual loss and damage to Fleet Air Arm aircraft. In November 1936 a cyclone swept across RAF Hal Far, Malta. Hangars and the Baffins of 812 and the Nimrods of 802 Squadrons were wrecked. On another occasion two of 802's Nimrods collided during formation flying. As they fell they hit a third that also crashed.

Signal square

Without any form of direct aircraft control in the airfield circuit or when taxying, other than the basic rules indicated by the signal square, collisions also contributed to aircraft damage and write-offs. The restricted view in some directions from the 'wooded' cockpits of the biplanes also added to the risk of collisions.

Few RAF aircraft were fitted with radio-telephones and therefore control of aircraft on and in the vicinity of an airfield depended on visual observation and signals. Alongside the Watch Office, from which the Duty Pilot controlled the movement of aircraft in the circuit and about to take off, there was a large white-bordered signal square. Different symbols were placed in the square, such as the 'landing T' to indicate the direction of take-offs and landings and to convey other information to pilots. A red right-angle symbol was used to indicate that a right-handed, i.e. clockwise, circuit was in use instead of the normal left-hand circuit. If there was a significant change in wind direction then the Airman of the Watch would be ordered to hoist a large black ball to the yardarm outside the watch office.

Other than prohibitive signals, such as a red light or coloured signal flare or semi-permanent symbols in the signal square, pilots could take off and land without any form of permission. The usual wide expanse of grass gave room, when facing into wind, for take-offs along the left side of the field and landings on the right. An essential part of airmanship training was learning the rules of the air and of landing grounds. Provided all pilots kept a careful watch out for other aircraft when flying in the circuit and when taxying, and obeyed the rules, accidents could be avoided. Despite, however, the generally low level of traffic there were many collisions.[3] In the coming year a course would be started for the training of Flying Control Officers.[4]

North West Frontier

In 1936 the RAF continued to exhibit two contrasting images: one in the UK as an 'exclusive flying club' where life was only interrupted by the annual air-firing and bombing exercises: the other image, the harsh 'war' life on the stations of the North West Frontier of India. As the plans were being prepared for a new airforce, life in the squadrons stationed on the border between India and Afghanistan had changed little over the service's eighteen years. In extremes of heat and cold the squadrons patrolled and scouted and kept the isolated army posts in contact with civilisation.

In 1936 the annual November move of units to the air-firing and bombing practice camps were interrupted by the Faqir of Ipi's full scale uprising. The frontier airforce went into action with its customary skill and determination to restore order. It had as its principal weapons the Wapiti and the Valentia. Rarely seen in the UK, these two biplane types epitomised an airforce that operated from sunbaked and rock-strewn landing grounds. In some respects the very age of these two aircraft types was an advantage: short take offs and slow approaches to land were less demanding on machines and men than high performance monoplanes operating in and out of the euphemistically called 'landing grounds'. To quote Sir Maurice Dean: 'It was always a firmly held logistic rule of the RAF that the further the squadron was away from home the older must be its aircraft'.

When the 'revolting' tribes along the frontier were finally subdued in 1937 the RAF had completed 11,000 flying hours during which only three men were killed and three injured in operational flying. In contrast and to emphasise the economy in human and material resources of air operations, the army lost over 1,000 men killed or wounded during the campaign.

Barrage balloons

Although gas-filled kite balloons had been a familiar sight over the Western Front, when they were used as observation posts in the sky, their use was discontinued in 1918. The Air Ministry investigated the potential of the balloon and its tethering cable as a defence against attacking aircraft. The members of the research team included Lockspeiser and Roxbee Cox. The test aircraft was a Miles Hawk that was flown into a length of cord depending from a parachute. The cord cut deeply in to the wing. From these experiments evolved plans for a massive barrage of balloons to defend major targets in the UK.

Guns

The British preference for avoiding the pragmatic approach to a problem handicapped the Gun

* later Sir Ben

** later Lord Kings Norton

Department of the Air Ministry. This department was dependent on the Ordnance Board of the War Office. The Air Ministry representative on the Board, Air Commodore A.W. Tedder, found it hard to believe that in the 20th century there still existed such an organisation with traditions and methods so utterly unsuited to meet the need for rapid decisions essential in coping with the changing conditions of air warfare. The meetings of the Board reminded him of nothing so much as the tea party in *Alice in Wonderland* – except that there was certainly more than one dormouse.[5]

The two men on whose shoulders rested much of the day-to-day practical improvement of gun technology for the RAF, Thomson and Adams, strove to wrest control of gun development away from the War Office. Tedder acknowledged that great credit was due to them that so much had been achieved under their leadership by the Gun Department of the Air Ministry; despite the dead hand of the Ordnance Board.[6]

Often when the vital performance figures of a new aircraft were printed in the press there was little detailed comment on its guns. Their calibre and number were listed. If there were more than two machine-guns then the armament was often described as being 'formidable' or capable of delivering a devastating burst of fire which would bring down any aircraft. But little was written about the guns as pieces of intricate machinery which had to be reliable and therefore not adversely affected by extremes of temperature or ammunition which was below standard .

Since WWI the guns of the RAF had usually been mounted within reach of the pilot or gunner. The remote location of guns was not favoured because neither the Vickers nor the Lewis 7.7mm types was developed to a sufficient degree of reliability. They had to be close to hand in order that the various types of stoppage, to which they were prone, could be dealt with using probing and persuading tools, such as a leather-headed mallet. There was also the difficulty of arranging Bowden firing control cables from the cockpit out to guns mounted far away from the cockpit. As mentioned, pneumatic control was introduced earlier to overcome this problem.

Guns of expansion

The aircraft types specified for the Expansion Scheme would be fitted with 7.7mm or 20mm guns. The popular press usually described an aerial duel as being made up of a stalking phase followed by a long drawn out bursts of fire at the target; despite the fact that an unbroken burst of fire exceeding 15 seconds would ruin a gun barrel. Sqn Ldr Sorley and his team at the Air Ministry studying fighter armament, realised that, as in the WWI, fighter against fighter actions afforded a pilot only fleeting opportunities to hold an enemy in his sights. It was expected that an engagement between aircraft, which were approximately equal in performance, would consist of a period of manoeuvring to gain an advantageous position followed by only a few seconds in which the enemy was held in the gunsight; during which a three second burst of fire might be got in before the image in the sight was lost as the enemy attempted to escape.

Eight-gun fighter

The choice of eight guns for fighters was anticipated by the Folland/Gloster prototype fighter of 1930. This had twoVickers and four Lewis 7.7mm guns: at that time few other aircraft had such a 'formidable' array of guns. Although the Folland fighter was undoubtedly ahead of its time, the Air Ministry was mindful of the fact that neither of the two gun types was reliable enough to be remotely mounted. The Gloster developments led to the 'eight-gun' specification F5/34 of 1934. Eight Colt-Browning 7.7mm guns in a fighter, as in the Venom, each firing at over 1,000 rounds per minute, would deliver a greater weight of projectiles than the combination of 7.9mm and 20mm guns being considered for the Bf109 fighter of the *Luftwaffe*. A three second burst from an eight-gun battery delivered 30 lb of bullets.

The Gloster fighter biplane of 1935, from which the Gauntlet was derived, had, as an experiment, four wing-mounted Lewis guns, remote from the pilot, in addition to the 'traditional ' synchronised Vickers 7.7mm guns in the fuselage.

Vickers K Type, gas-operated, 7.7mm gun which replaced the Lewis gun. It was primarily intended for use on a flexible mounting although it was also fitted to the nose turrets of Whitley Vs and Bombays. The ammunition drum on a Lewis gun rotated but on the K gun the drum was stationary, the rounds being forced into the feed opening by a powerful wound-up spring. (MoD Pattern Room)

Colt-Browning 7.7mm, British MkII version, 1200 rpm gun, primarily for fixed mountings or in turrets. Unlike the Vickers K and the Lewis, the Browning operated by recoil. As with the Vickers Mk II, which it replaced, the Browning was fed by rounds held in belts of disintegrating metal links.* (MoD Pattern Room)

The 20mm gun

There were a number of 20mm aircraft gun makers in the 1930s. They formed the 'big' gun lobby. The claims of the 20mm gun designers that their explosive shells were necessary to cause sufficient damage to modern all-metal aircraft were not immediately accepted by the Air Ministry. The merits of the different 20mm guns available for mounting in an aircraft were compared. The short-barrel 20mm Oerlikon, with its comparatively short range and oversensitive shell fuses, might not be as effective as three 7.7mm Colt-Brownings specified for the RAF's next generation of fighters. The Air Ministry also studied the potential of the 20mm Hispano Suiza gun.[7]

The 20mm gun-makers argued that such was the power of their calibre that only one gun would be sufficient to bring down another aircraft. This idea was tempting to fighter designers; particularly if they adopted an engine-mounted gun; such as the French moteur-cannon, lying between the cylinder banks of a V engine and firing out through the propeller hub. Both Hispano Suiza and Daimler-Benz were designing engines into which a 20mm gun could be integrated. Ministry officials examined the 20mm Oerlikon gun mounted in the cylinder 'V ' of the Hispano Suiza engine of the Fairey biplane entered for the Belgian fighter competition. However, although for the time being the standard gun for the RAF was to be 7.7mm, the 20mm was 'pencilled into' the specifications of the next generation of fighters. Both the Spitfire and the Hurricane, being developed to meet specification F5/34 by Supermarine and Hawker respectively, were being considered as suitable, with modifications, for arming with 20mm guns. Specification F37/35 for a four 20mm gun fighter indicated that, although there might be uncertainty over which of the competing gun makers would be favoured, there was no doubt in the mind of the Air Staff that 20mm was what they wanted.

Power for guns

The development of powered mountings and turrets for guns, the two were not necessarily the same thing, was another important programme in 1936. An early example of a powered mounting was the Barnes-Wallis windmill-operated development of an idea proposed by F. W. Scarff during the Great War. This was installed in the Vickers 6/41 prototype biplane of 1934.

There were four companies taking an interest in solving the problems of protecting the air gunner from the slipstream and relieving him of the physical effort of training and elevating a gun or guns. They were: Nash and Thompson (NT), Boulton Paul (BP), Vickers Armstrongs (VA) and Bristol. Two names are important in the history of the development of powered mountings and gun turrets. They are: John D. North of Boulton Paul and Frazer-Nash of Nash and Thompson. Boulton Paul already had a turret in production. This was John North's compressed-air powered design installed in the nose of the BP Sidestrand, a biplane, twin-engine bomber. In 1935 Boulton Paul reached agreement with Machine Motrice SA of France. This covered the development and production of an electro-hydraulic four-gun turret. The company also started on the design of a two-seat fighter to be armed with the new turret but, as already noted, without any forward-firing guns for the pilot. This became the Defiant.

Archibald Frazer-Nash, of sports car fame, was a prolific inventor and solver of difficult engineering problems. In 1932 he and his partner, Grattan Thompson, demonstrated their hydraulic-powered and controlled mounting for aircraft guns. The favourable report by the then Group Captain Tedder and Squadron Leader Davis to the Air Staff was the start of a succession of powered gun turrets for many different types of RAF aircraft.

The first application of the Nash and Thompson system was to the Hawker Demon. In 1935 one of these powered mountings for a Lewis gun was fitted by Parnall Aircraft Ltd . The 'turret' was referred to as of 'lobster back' appearance. The parts above the gun mounting ring were in four sections, three of which folded in or opened out in synchronism with the elevation of the gun. This arrangement provided protection for the gunner from the effects of the airstream. Parnall claimed that the 'lobster back' cupola: 'gives the gunner personal protection against hostile fire'. However, considerations of weight limited the gauge of aluminium employed and therefore the 'protection' may have been more psychological than real. As it was, the 169 lb weight of the gun mounting, plus 200 lb of gunner and his equipment, moved the aircraft's centre of gravity too far aft. The Demon installation demonstrated, according to those who operated the system, how smoothly and accurately its action responded to the gunner's commands.

Nash and Thompson started on the development of types FN4, FN5 and FN20 turrets for use in medium and large bombers. Development was encouraged by the close co-operation that existed between Captain Frazer-Nash of NT and the squadrons and by Sq Ldr Davis of the Air Ministry. Nash and Thompson also provided power and control units to Vickers for the Barnes-Wallis casemate mountings in the early version of the Wellington and to Handley Page for the twin-Lewis Hubbard gun turrets of the Harrow.

It says much for the hard work and dedication of the turret companies that the RAF was able to enter WWII armed with defensive equipment that was technically well ahead of other countries and particularly of Germany. In this respect not only was it absolutely essential to avoid advertising the production plans for long-range heavy bombers but to keep secret the advances made by Nash and Thompson and by North. This was one area of technology that was not only right, it was one that emerged right on time. Incidentally, although all Nash and Thompson turret patents were put on the secret list, the Bristol Frise mounting for the Blenheim and the Barnes-Wallis 'windscreen' for the Wellington patents were published.[9]

Remotely-controlled guns

Throughout the 1920s and in the early years of 1930s inventors and designers looked for ways of installing remotely-controlled guns in inaccessible locations. Patent application files contained numerous schemes for controlling guns remotely. Remotely located, powered gun mountings were proposed for a Fleet Air Arm aircraft designed to meet specification S 9/36.

New commands

Fighter and bomber squadrons were part of one command; Air Defence of Great Britain (ADGB). On 14 July 1936 they were split into Fighter and Bomber Commands. In contrast, the German airforce was being organised into multi-function air fleets. The new one-function commands of the RAF were considered better than the multi-function ADGB. However, only time and in particular war, would prove the effectiveness of separating defensive and offensive functions. Would each be able to learn from the other and to share innovations?

Fighter Command was building up a large and expensive control and communications network for linking the radar stations, observer posts, group and sector operations rooms with the fighters.

Bomber Command

Any improvements in the aircraft of Bomber Command were not necessarily being matched either by crew training facilities or by radio and navigational equipment needed to find a target 500 miles away. Navigational accuracy, when flying out of sight of land and brightly lit towns, was not high enough to carry an air war into the heart of Europe in all weather conditions by day or night. Should a target be found, the aircraft were not equipped with a bombsight which would give a reasonable chance of hitting the target. Bombing accuracy predictions were based on the results of exercises with small smoke bombs and without the distraction to the bomb-aimer of anti-aircraft fire and searchlights and without manoeuvres needed to avoid the fire of an attacking fighter.

In 1936 the RAE was charged with developing an improved bomb sight in which the target could be held in the aiming graticule irrespective of the movement of the aircraft. Once again the gyroscope provided the basic solution. Unfortunately development, as usual, took longer than expected and the Stabilised Automatic Bomb Sight (SABS) was not ready for Bomber Command until the middle of WWII.

All this may suggest an ill-equipped and poorly

trained bomber force. In some respects this is true, but there were wide variations among the major elements of Bomber Command. As an example, engines and airframes were much improved over those of the first five years of the decade. The modern aircraft types about to enter service were significantly in advance of the earlier types. The majority were monoplanes and they had retractable undercarriages. However the specialised equipment needed to make the most effective use of their speed, load carrying capacity, range and operating height lagged about four years behind.

It appears that Bomber Command looked at the results of its exercises and decided that 'It will be all right on the night, or on the day'. However, it was unlikely that the airforce of any other country could perform any better. The infant *Luftwaffe* in Germany looked most impressive at air shows and during exercises with the army. However what little was known at the time about its command structure, communications and administration suggested that its 'tail' was far from complete. In contrast, the expanding RAF was paying great attention to second echelon services; such as aircraft maintenance and well-equipped air stations.

Bombs and bomb-aiming

The offensive aspects of the expansion programme were encouraged by the results of the raids by bombers of Trenchard's Independent Air Force in 1918. The Air Ministry placed great reliance on the material effect of bombing. It was believed that if a formation of bombers appeared over an enemy target in daylight and released 50 tons or more of bombs then a claim could be made that:

> Our bombers have struck a devastating blow at X. The enemy's industrial capacity will take months in which to recover.

The Air Ministry, with the backing of its political masters, also placed much faith in the psychological effect of bombing. In that respect, the ministry was mindful of Trenchard's dictum that the morale effect of bombing was twenty times greater than the destructive effect.

In 1934 there were five classifications of bombing techniques: pattern, diving, gliding, 'B' and precision. The classification 'B' referred to a method of pressure-wave bombing which affected the underside of a ship. However, irrespective of the technique used and whether from high altitude or low, the reports from the bombing ranges, following each squadron's annual bombing 'camp', listed results that were unacceptable.

Concern was expressed that the production of bombs might not be adequate in the event of war. Thin-cased bombs in the form of a metal cylinder had to be replaced by thick-cased bombs. The cases had to be forged. Forging capacity was limited in peace-time. The Air Ministry had to make great efforts to persuade the steel forging industry to plan for the production of cases at least at the rate of 1,000 every day. This was another area in which the Air Ministry found itself in competition with the Navy and the Army. In war, both would need gun barrels and shells in enormous quantities and place great demands on forging capacity in the steel industry.

Bombing errors

In 1935 it was deduced that aiming errors were the result of aircrew fatigue during operations above 10,000 feet. However, that did not equate with the fact that the aiming errors recorded during the first of a series of sorties, each lasting about two and a half hours, were as great as those recorded for the later sorties by the same crews. Therefore fatigue was not necessarily the principal problem. The results also indicated that bombing from 12,000 feet, for example, was no less accurate than from a lower height.[10] Many of the bombers used during the 1935 exercises were single-engine Hawker Harts, whose steadiness as an aiming platform left much to be desired. The new twin-engine bombers, therefore, were anxiously awaited if only for the reason that they were expected to provide a steadier flight and better working conditions for bomb aimers.

Attention was paid to the particular bombing problem of locating targets; both at night and in daylight. Crews even failed to locate the group of

The Guinness Brewery at Park Royal London NW 10 used as a 'target' during air exercises. (Arthur Guinness Son & Co Ltd)

large buildings of the Guinness Brewery at Park Royal in West London used as a 'target'

In addition to the targets set on the coastal bombing-ranges, on which practice bombs were dropped, the RAF used a simulated bombing technique. This was the Hill's Mirror on the ground and Sashalite lamps on the aircraft. The umpires and recorders looked down at the reflected image of the aircraft. When the bomb-aimer pressed the bomb-release button this switched on the Sashalite lamps to indicate the simulated release point. The aircraft sometimes emitted a trail of smoke to aid the observers who recorded the track of the aircraft towards the target. However, on too many occasions aircraft were observed to be flying on the wrong track and 'releasing their bombs' at the wrong target. Even when the correct track was made towards the correct target, real bombs would have landed far away because the bomb-aimer had not made the correct allowances for the effect of the wind. Those who studied the problems of locating targets and accurately aiming bombs recommended both improved bomb-sights and drift-sights from which a bomb-aimer could determine wind direction. In addition there was an urgent need for better communication between crew members. The Gosport speaking tube and the telephonic intercommunication systems were often ineffective; the latter suffering from the ingress of moisture. A visual telegraphic system was proposed as a stand-by intercommunication method.

In November 1936, trials of parachute flares took place over Lough Neagh. The flares were timed to ignite after falling 900 feet after release.[11]

Despite the urgent need to do something about the ineffectiveness of high-level bombing, the Air Ministry committee studying bombing tactics spent much of its time discussing who should form the committee and when it should meet. The minutes of meetings included the revealing comment: 'Too many people are attending meetings.'

More complexity

The Bristol Type 130, seen for the first time in public in the New Types Park at Hendon in 1935, was delayed in production because of the urgent need to speed up production of Blenheims. Therefore the 130 production line was transferred to Short and Harland in Belfast. Much of the 130's equipment was in advance of that in other aircraft. For example, the production version had variable pitch propellers and flaps. For many airmen, the 130's 'plumbing' was an introduction to elaborate hydraulic systems. However with a bomb load of only 2,000 lb, on external racks, and a range of only 800 miles it did not compare with the nominal 1,200 mile range and much greater bomb load expected from the Wellington and Whitley.

Plan F

From where were all the new bombers and fighters coming? Successive economies and the disarmament policies of the 1920s and those of the early 1930s, had left the aircraft industry weak and disillusioned. Already mentioned was the slow progress made by the British aircraft industry toward the modern aeroplane. Much of this could be attributed to the lack of financial and moral support from the government during the previous eighteen years. Fortunately under the leadership of Lord Swinton (Sir Philip Cunliffe Lister) and Lord Weir, two of the architects of the expansion programme, the industry was revived and put to work. In 1936 the aircraft industry started to work towards Plan F whose target was 160 squadrons, about 2,000 aircraft, for home defence within three years. An important decision was taken by the Air Ministry, in consultation with the research departments of the universities, to attach civilian scientists to the RAF in order to study and find solutions to various technical and operational problems.

Swinton relied on Weir for expert advice. Weir was a demanding 'trouble shooter'. When he studied Spitfire production, with the object of arranging the sub-contracting of components, he asked Supermarine to display for his inspection every detachable part. He wanted to see if there were any that might be eliminated. Weir believed that there were no short cuts to high quality quantity production. He commented that: 'it [the Spitfire] was an engineer's nightmare to build. It's small wonder the Hurricane came into the line long before the Spitfire'.[12]

New stations and airfields

In 1936, the Air Ministry's 'Works and Bricks' department accelerated its building programme for new stations which had started in 1928. Most of the new stations were to be in eastern England. As mentioned, in the decade after WWI the majority of new airfields were located in the southernmost counties of England; but now the most likely enemy was Germany and not France. The new stations were being built to a standard pattern of hangars and buildings. Their specification required them to be blended into the landscape and the Air Ministry commissioned Sir Patrick Abercrombie to apply his experience of civic design to their appearance. The standard pattern and the many trees made one station look like another; much to the confusion of pilots who were lost.

Pilot training

There were few if any Pilot's Notes for each type of aircraft. The aircraft type manual might include a chapter addressed to the pilot, but it only gave a description of which lever or switch operated what. The information was not as comprehensive as that of the Pilots' Notes which came later. All that was usually provided were the Handling Notes prepared by the test pilots of the Aeroplane and Armament Experimental Establishment at Martlesham Heath.

Pilots rarely received special training on a new aircraft type. Although all pilots were capable of flying an unfamiliar aircraft, nevertheless they needed expert advice on how to fly the aircraft so as to make the most efficient use of its performance. Most importantly they had to learn what to do in the event of an emergency; such as engine failure. Most engines and aircraft systems were easily understood after a familiarisation flight and some expert advice. But from 1936 on, the more complex aircraft required a more rigorous and systematic approach to pilot training.

Research

Behind the scenes and at the shoulder of the RAF at all times was the Royal Aircraft Establishment. The establishment was also turned to by the aircraft industry whenever a problem needed solving for which there was neither sufficient funds for research nor facilities. In 1936 the RAE was involved in numerous research and development programmes; the majority of which resulted from the increase in aircraft performance and versatility. All-metal structures had been around some years but not enough was known about effective design and the mathematics involved in calculating stresses and safe working loads. The RAE provided industry with guides to good design, stressing, structural analysis and alternative forms of structures and materials.

The 24 ft diameter wind-tunnel was used both for full-scale investigation of airflow over airframes and wings and the cooling of radial engines as well as heat exchangers (radiators) for liquid-cooled engines. No part of the aircraft was left off the list of projects and the research included radio equipment, automatic pilots, armament and even a hydro-pneumatic catapult for launching bombers with a take-off weight of 32 tons. The establishment investigated bombs, incendiary devices, parachute-and-cable defence system and rockets.

Rockets

In July 1936, the Sub-Committee on Air Defence Research of the Committee of Imperial Defence decided that the study of rockets, started in 1934, and encouraged by Professor Lindemann, should continue.

The following order of priority was agreed:

a. Anti-aircraft rockets.
b. Long-range attack rockets.
c. Air-to-air aircraft rockets.
d. Rockets for assisted take-off.

Only the anti-aircraft rockets were developed by the start of WWII. The others were held back by the need to develop other weapons. The air-to-air rocket evolved into the air-to-ground rockets used with effect by the RAF in the last two years of the war.[13]

Perhaps to raise public awareness of the importance of air power, King Edward VIII on his accession started to use an aircraft regularly; this was an Airspeed Envoy of the newly-formed King's Flight.

Hendon Air Display 1936: left to right, prototypes of Hurricane and Spitfire and the Vickers Venom. The last equipped with eight guns and with a Bristol Aquila engine of only 625 horsepower but a top speed of over 300 mph. (Aeroplane Monthly)

Chapter Three
1937

By now the RAF felt reasonably free of threats from the other two services who had wanted to 'kill' it or absorb it. During the preceding years the RAF had suffered restriction after restriction as successive expansion schemes were cancelled or deferred. Now the service was less subject to the pecuniary attitude of the nation engendered by the policy expressed by so many political lobbies of: 'Peace at any price as long as we do not have to go to war'.

Expanding the whole

The expansion programme which had started in 1936 was not just a matter of new aircraft of more advanced design; the programme had to include the expansion of the RAF as a whole. After the Great War Trenchard ensured the survival of the RAF as an independent force by keeping it small so that it did not require large sums of public money. This fragile, in the political sense, force had to maintain high standards of performance and training, despite limited funds, in order to avoid criticism that might provide ammunition for its enemies.

Output of aircraft and equipment

In 1937 the shadow factory organisation for aircraft production was asked to double its output. However if that was to be achieved it would have meant double shift working. Finding the necessary skilled hands was another matter. Without the control and direction, as might happen in a war, it took some time before production increased. It took over a year before output rose to 200 aircraft each month.

More and more new aircraft types were entering the squadrons. Those squadrons re-equipped in 1936 had mostly got over teething problems. However, although a squadron might have its full establishment of aircraft it did not necessarily mean that each aircraft was fully equipped for its intended operational standard. The Ansons of 224 (GR) Squadron, for example, took part in simulated attacks against the battleships *Nelson* and *Rodney*. But no more than five aircraft were serviceable at any one time because of shortages of vital components. In another exercise with the Royal Navy, only two Ansons out of the eleven took part; the others had no wireless sets.

Already mentioned was the low standard of bombing and the expectation that it would be more accurate 'on the night'. Bombing records of 224 Sqn listed average errors of 138 yards from 10,000 ft, 28 yards from 500 ft and 19 yards from 250 ft. Those results were considered acceptable by Coastal Command. This raises the question: were the optimists right? Particularly as similar results may not have been attainable in a real war attack with the aircraft subjected to intense anti-aircraft fire. Four years later the average bombing error when attacking ships and submarines would be 600 yards.

Coastal Command had no effective method for attacking submarines even if they could be located. Despite the experience of WWI the Admiralty and the Air Ministry in the 1930s greatly underestimated the importance of deploying aircraft for the protection of convoys of ships. They also failed to appreciate the potential of the aircraft as a means of attacking merchant ships. Therefore they were tardy in developing aircraft suitable for both offensive and defensive tasks.

Handley Page Harrow

In 1937 four squadrons were equipped with the Handley Page Harrow. This was a high-wing, twin-engine, bomber-transport. Its dual-role title reflected the continuing parsimony displayed towards the service by those who held the purse strings.

The Handley Page Harrow was designed to meet specification 29/35. As mentioned, it incorporated FN powered gun mountings. It has been suggested that the dorsal gun position may also have been powered. One historian suggests that the Harrow II was ordered for the Fleet Air Arm but that the order for 100 aircraft was cancelled because of the lack of production capacity. The possible role of the Harrow II with the FAA, other than as a transport, is hard to visualise.[1]

The Deputy Director of Plans on the Air Staff, Slessor (later MRAF Sir John), and the other deputy directors submitted a paper to the Chief of the Air Staff (CAS) on the 3 September. This summed up the weakness of Bomber Command. The paper argued that the command was almost totally unfitted for war; that, unless the production of new and up-to-date aircraft could be expedited the command would not be fit for war for at least two and half years.[2]

Vickers Wellesley

In 1935 Vickers had offered a private-venture, general-purpose bomber to the Air Ministry. This was the Wellesley now entering squadron service.

This single-engine monoplane was of metal geodetic construction with fabric covering. The wingspan was 74 ft and the loaded weight was six tons. The method of construction devised by the designer Barnes Wallis was anticipated by the designer of the German Schutte-Lanz military airships of 1911. It had a retractable undercarriage and a two-position variable-pitch propeller. Those features gave it distinct advantages over the Harts and Hinds which it replaced. Their 186 mph, 430 mile range and 26,000 ft ceiling were bettered by the Wellesley's 228 mph, 1,100 mile range and 33,000 ft ceiling. However despite its performance advantage over its contemporaries, the Wellesley did not give the RAF a sufficiently upward step in striking power; even though it could carry a bomb load of 2,000 lb compared with the 500 lb of the Hind.

The novelty of the geodetic structure and the reluctance to interrupt the continuity of the geodetic members weighed against having a large cut-out section to form an integral fuselage bomb compartment. Therefore, the offensive load was carried in under-wing containers. These facilitated loading the bombs and, at the same time, helped to reduce the bending loads at the wing roots during flight.

When the new bombers arrived at the squadrons of Bomber Command, many of the riggers and fitters had to extend their skills to cover retractable undercarriage gear, flaps and variable-pitch propellers. Few aircraft histories mention the need to train a special group of maintenance personnel for each new aircraft type about to enter squadron service. With the RAF acquiring a diverse range of types there had to be a corresponding expansion in training.

By 12 April 1937, 76(B) Squadron had acquired enough experience and sufficient number of Wellesleys to take part in a formation fly-past at RAF Mildenhall on the occasion of the visit by generals of the *Luftwaffe*. However, England's special weather closed in and 76 Squadron stood down because of the risk of collisions.[3] No 35 Squadron suffered persistent undercarriage troubles with its Wellesleys. Of three aircraft only one completed the required 500 hour programme of operational development flying.

During the annual air exercises the Wellesley and other squadrons operated in accordance with the current Manual of Air Tactics. This stated that: 'Most attacks will take place by day.' Should bomber squadrons indulge in night attacks, few could guarantee with any certainty to find their targets and aim their bombs accurately. Already mentioned was the lack of suitable aids to navigation and bomb-aiming. In that connection Group Captain Arthur Harris was having great difficulty in convincing the Air Staff of the need for target-illuminating and target-marking flares. Eventually,

Vickers prototype bomber intended to meet specification B.9/32. There had to be many changes, both large and small, before it metamorphosed into the Wellington.

when flares were provided, their use in exercises was limited by a set of rules which prohibited the dropping of flares onto the sea if there was an onshore wind.

In some respects the Wellesley was, like the Battle, a good idea but it was not really in step with the needs of fighting in a full scale war against a determined opponent. If a Wellesley had to defend itself against a fast, multi-gun fighter, its chance of survival was slim. At least, as Gunston points out, the Wellesley convinced the Air Ministry of the advantages of the monoplane bomber over the biplane.[4]

Wellington prototype

In the meantime Handley Page and Vickers had been progressing with their answers to Specification B9/32. The Air Ministry had issued an invitation to the aircraft industry in 1932 for the design of a fast day bomber. A twin-engine monoplane was preferred having a landing speed of 60 mph and a span of only 70 feet. These and other qualities reflected the fact that RAF airfields in general were limited in size and there were no hard runways. Britain's adherence to the Geneva Disarmament Conference meant that bombers must not exceed a tare weight of three tons. The conflict between a low structural weight and high engine power to meet the weight limitation and the required cruising speed could not be resolved by Handley Page and Vickers. Within two years the Air Ministry was turning a blind eye to the three ton limitation.

Eventually Vickers received a contract to build a B9/32 prototype. In the meantime the Air Ministry increased the required range from the original 600 miles to 1500 miles and the original span limitation was relaxed to allow one of 86 feet. The geodetic form of construction adopted for the Wellesley was applied to the B9/32 bomber because it gave great strength with low structural weight even though it would complicate production and require a higher than usual level of skill in component manufacture.

In view of the original three ton limit it is interesting to note that during the first trial flights of the prototype the take-off weight went up to over ten tons. As with all new types there were handling problems with the B9/32. Apart from limited wind tunnel research, using models, there were none of today's computer simulations. Both the aerodynamicists and the test pilot ventured into unknown territory with every new design.

The Vickers B9/32 is yet one more example from the 1930s of the lack of attention given to the design and position of the controls in the cockpit. When the aircraft was tested at RAF Martlesham Heath the two-position propeller controls could be confused with those for the main fuel cocks: both pairs were identical and operated in the same way. The carburettor cut-out and the air intake controls were poorly positioned and difficult to operate. Even though the cooling gills for each engine could not be seen by the pilot no indicators were provided in the cockpit. Despite the preference for rudder pedals in other aircraft types, Vickers equipped the B9/32 with a simple and short span rudder bar.

In 1936 many aircraft had Rhodoid transparencies for windscreens and other fenestration. Rhodoid panels were used for the B9/32 but had to be replaced by Perspex units which were less likely to become opaque or crack in temperatures below minus 30 degrees Celsius.

Martin's bomber

The American bomber designer Glenn Martin discussed with the British Air Attaché in Washington DC a design which he suggested would meet the RAF's needs for a fast medium bomber.

The Martin design featured a mid-wing monoplane layout with two radial engines, twin fins and a tricycle undercarriage. Although nothing came of this, an appreciation of Glenn Martin's design, written by an Air Ministry staff officer in March 1937, contained some interesting observations on British and American aircraft design.

> There is no doubt that the latest American bomber aircraft features characteristics which are well ahead of general European standards. You will remember that one of the biggest steps forward in British service aircraft occurred when Fairey produced the Fox with an American engine. . . . I suggest the importation of American design bombers and fighters into our own service might have similarly favourable effects, not because they are generally superior, but because they have certain superiorities which ours may lack.

Had the suggestion been adopted there could have been opposition from British aircraft manufacturers; not all of whom were inclined to learn from foreign experience. The discussions with Martin included a proposal to produce his medium bomber in the UK.[5]

Blackburn Skua

Comment has already been made on the lack of interest in the dive bomber. However, a two-seat, carrier-based, fighter/dive-bomber was designed by Blackburn for the Fleet Air Arm. It was the first British specialised dive-bomber. During the evaluation flying the test pilots found the dive-brakes most effective. The dive-brakes, which limited the speed to 220 knots, also had take-off and landing settings. During tests, the Skua was dived at angles of 80 and 90 degrees to the horizontal. There were four fixed forward-firing 7.7mm guns and one 7.7mm on a flexible mounting in the rear cockpit. Provision was made for carrying a 500 lb bomb in a recess under the fuselage, with hinged arms to swing it clear of the propeller on release.

The Skua provides an example of the 'step into the unknown' that still characterised much aircraft development progress. The early flights showed that its longitudinal stability was marginal because the centre of gravity was too far aft. Therefore the engine had to be positioned two feet further forward. This required a major re-design of the forward part of the fuselage. Adjusting major wing, empennage and fuselage dimensions following the first flight had to be resorted to with a number of new aircraft designs.

Battle squadron

To meet the expansion programme a number of dormant squadrons were reformed. Among them

Blackburn Roc: the four-gun turret version of the Skua intended as a fleet defence fighter operating from aircraft carriers. In the event the Roc never went to sea. (Derek James)

63(B) at RAF Andover with seven Hinds as an interim allocation pending the arrival of its Fairey Battle light bombers. The Battles were delayed in production and 63 had to make do with some Audax; the army co-operation version of the Hart.

Sixty-three Squadron moved to RAF Upwood, still awaiting its Battles, and one of its first tasks was to search for the Gipsy Moth flown by the Duchess of Bedford which was thought to have crashed nearby. Eventually 63 received some Battles and was able to join in bombing exercises by No 2 Group. It also featured in a Gaumont British film *Under The Shadow Of The Wing* intended to impress possible enemies with the strength of the RAF. Although the Battle was more complex than its predecessors, the ground staff appreciated the good accessibility for maintenance and servicing and the rodded control lines in place of the difficult-to-adjust cable systems of other aircraft.

No more silver dope

Indicative of the deteriorating international relationships among European nations was the decision to abandon the silver dope finish for fighters, light and medium day bombers and torpedo-bombers. The dark matt green used for night bombers was also given up. The new finish for the majority of aircraft was a camouflage scheme of dark green and dark brown for the upper surfaces and black for the underside. In order to avoid negating the desired visual effect there were two standard patterns of green and brown, each the mirror image of the other. Scheme A was used on aircraft having even serial numbers and Scheme B for the odd numbers. The new finish was applied from January 1937 to all new aircraft on the production lines. Aircraft already in service were re-painted at the first available opportunity.[5]

One technical problem with new colour schemes was the adverse effect layers of paint had on the balance of control surfaces. This effect first became serious when Fury fighters experienced control surface flutter. Successive re-painting and re-touching affected the balance of the control surfaces. In autumn 1934 Fury squadrons had been instructed to limit the diameter of wing roundels so that they did not overlap onto the ailerons and to discontinue the painting of red, white and blue stripes on rudders.[6]

During the summer air exercises the Observer Corps posts were finding the task of distinguishing between 'friendly' and 'enemy' aircraft made more difficult by the standard green and brown schemes: particularly between Fury and Hart and between 'friendly' and 'hostile' Blenheims . Therefore it was decided that 'friendly' aircraft would have an all-white under surface on the starboard wing. Later on the white undersurface for the starboard wing was complemented by a black underside for the port wing.

Incidents and accidents

Any study such as this cannot ignore the continuing annual aircraft damage and losses arising from incidents and accidents. Each incident or accident provided an insight into either inadequate training standards or inadequate aircraft design. Both around the UK and overseas the RAF operated a number of flying boat squadrons. Their dual element of land and water added to their problems. Indicative of this was the loss of three Singapores during the year. First K4582 sank at Paola. Then K4582 hit the sea-wall at Aboukir attempting to take off and K8858 ran onto a hidden reef off Hurghada in the Red Sea.

Concern was still being expressed in Parliament, at the Air Staff and at the different operational commands of the RAF over the number of incidents and accidents resulting from the mis-

Gloster Gladiator, showing the white and black underwing paint scheme introduced to enable the observer corps (later the Royal Observer Corps) to distinguish more easily between 'friendly ' and 'enemy' aircraft during air exercises. (Peter Ottery)

handling of engine and fuel systems. Included in this number were examples of failures on the part of ground crews to fill fuel tanks properly and on the part of pilots to check the contents of tanks before taking off. In the 1930s, fuel tank contents indicators were either rudimentary and difficult to read or inaccurate and unreliable; an example of equipment whose design could induce errors.[7] Mishandling of the throttle when opening up the engine after a glide could cause the engine to stop. Gliding for too long, thereby letting the engine become too cold, was another cause of engine failure. In addition spark plugs were prone to oil up unless the pilot remembered to give bursts of throttle at intervals when gliding and taxying. Typical of the pilot's task being made more difficult by poor design of cockpit controls was the crash of a Battle in which the pilot operated the fuel tank selector valves incorrectly. As the engine stopped the pilot tried to restart it. He pulled the throttle back to the 'start' position. This, in turn, activated the undercarriage warning horn. To stop the noise, the pilot switched off the horn circuit, but as this was interconnected with the ignition system the engine could not be restarted. In poor visibility the pilot of a Hart began to search for landmarks in order to check his position. As he reached down for a map he accidentally knocked the ignition switches down to the 'off' position. Before he could re-start the engine, the aircraft hit the ground.

Harrow K6940 had a shorter life than some. On 25 March, Sgt Morton flew this 214 Squadron Harrow from Scampton to Radlett. During the approach to land the engines began to falter. Sergeant Morton continued with the approach over the twenty-foot high railway embankment forming the eastern boundary of the airfield. Unfortunately the 10.25 am train out of St Pancras London steamed across the aircraft's bows. The roof of the kitchen car was ripped off by the aircraft's undercarriage. The Harrow crashed on the edge of the airfield. The pilot and his seven passengers escaped with minor injuries. With only thirteen hours logged, K6940 was 'reduced to produce', having been damaged beyond economical repair.

An analysis of causes of accidents by the Air Staff, which occurred over six months of flying, showed that one in four of the engine failure cases were due to pilot error. The report listed 67 accidents and incidents attributable to pilot error. However, the analysis did not identify those 'pilot error' accidents in which ' poor cockpit design' was a contributory cause. At one time serious consideration was being given by the Air Ministry to the subject of fines for the mishandling of engines and aircraft.

Take aim

Since the end of the WWI the RAF had only two standard types of gunsights: the Aldis and the ring and bead; the latter sometimes with a Norman vane type foresight. However, neither was suitable for modern air fighting. A better form of sight was available. This was the collimated optical reflector sight which did away with the need to align the fore and back sights of a ring and bead sight and did not restrict the pilot's or gunner's field of view, as with the Aldis. Patent drawings were published during WWI. In 1918 the details of Sir Howard Grubb's patent of 1900 for a collimated, i.e. focused at infinity, gunsight were used by Oigee of Berlin to develop a reflector sight for aircraft use. After WWI, Barr & Stroud of Glasgow developed the GD1 reflector sight. This was tested at Martlesham Heath on an Avro 504K. An improved version, the GD2B, followed. Reflector sight development continued throughout the 1920s culminating in the GD5 of 1934, designed specifically for the Hawker Demon fighter. This and other reflector sights used the sloping Triplex glass of the windscreen as the reflecting surface. This arrangement was not satisfactory. Eventually the GM2 reflector sight with an integral reflector was adopted for the RAF as the MkII. An initial order for 1,600 was placed on Barr & Stroud and the first units were delivered in 1937.

Throughout the development years of the reflector sight it was subjected to high levels of secrecy. Rarely were printed descriptions and illustrations released outside the RAF. Secrecy was helped by the

The Barr & Stroud GM 2 reflector sight (RAF Fixed Gun Reflector Sight MkII) adopted in 1938 as the standard sight for fighter aircraft. (R. Wallace Clarke)

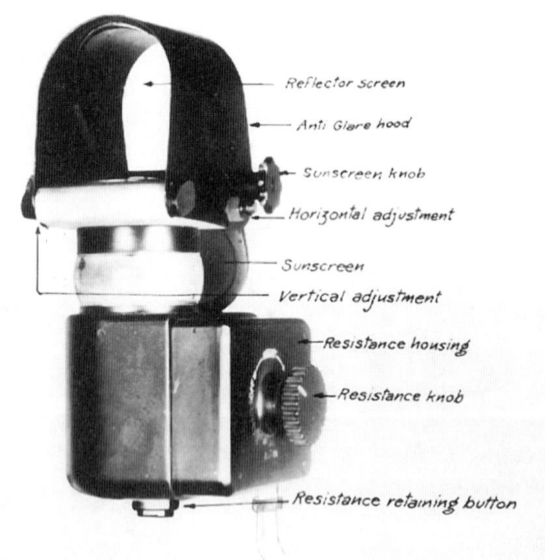

Optical reflector sight for turret and manually-aimed guns. (R.Wallace Clarke)

financial restrictions of the 1920s and 30s resulting in few aircraft equipped with the new sights. The early models had no reflector glass, so there was little to be seen above the top of the instrument panel in the cockpit. This helped to conceal the presence of the new method of aiming a fighter's guns.

The first squadron to be equipped with production standard reflector sights was 65 with its Gladiator fighters at RAF Hornchurch. General Milch of the *Luftwaffe* visited Hornchurch and the station commander ordered the Gladiator pilots to avoid drawing attention to the new gunsight and not to discuss its use. However the Air Vice-Marshal accompanying the German visitor did discuss the sight. It is likely that the 'sensitive' part of the reflector sight was the knurled range setting wheel at the base of the sight. Although the MkII sight was to be standard on all fighters few were equipped with it until the supply problems were sorted out. Many Hurricane and Spitfire pilots had to make do with the traditional ring and bead sight. No provision appears to have been made to install an Aldis sight. In 1926, Barr & Stroud designed a reflector sight for 'free' mounted guns. This went through a number of tests and subsequent improvements until the standard MkII (for fixed guns) and MkIII (for turret and flexible guns), used throughout WWII, went into production in 1937.

First Hurricanes

The delivery of No 111 Squadron's first Hurricanes introduced pilots not only to an entirely new type of aircraft but to one whose handling characteristics were very different from those of the Fury and Gladiator.

No longer was the 'engine ticking over' approach to land being used. A characteristic of many high-powered engines, such as the R-R Merlin of the Hurricane, was the dazzling exhaust flames at night. With the engine throttled back during a night landing the pilot was presented with a display of flames from the short exhaust pipes. Both the Fury and the Gladiator had long 'racing car' type exhaust pipes. A number of night landing accidents were being attributed to the pilot's difficulty of seeing ahead because of the glare from the exhaust flames.[8]

With its metal-tube structure and fabric-covering abaft the engine, the construction of the Hurricane was similar to that of the Fury. Access to the structure and equipment following damage was facilitated by the ability to remove the fabric easily. However, compared with the Fury, the Hurricane had the complexities of a retractable undercarriage, eight remotely-operated guns, flaps and a more comprehensive electrical system. Pilots had to go straight from the biplane fighters to the Hurricane which was far less forgiving of mistakes. An advanced two-seat monoplane fighter-trainer was needed urgently: one whose performance was close to that of the Hurricane and the Spitfire. Waiting in the wings, the Miles Master.

Bristol 146

One of the 'might have beens' was the Bristol 146. This radial-engine monoplane was designed to reach 10,000 ft in under five minutes and attain 38,000 ft. However its top speed of only 287 mph at 15,000 ft was not as good as the Hurricane's performance. In addition Bristol was committed to the Blenheim, so the 146 gave way to the Hurricane and Spitfire. Hawker already had an order for 600 of the former and Supermarine for 310 of the latter. Any hopes that Bristols had that the 146 might be reprieved were to vanish at the 1938 Empire Air Day when it collided on landing with some set-piece scenery at Filton and had to be written-off.

Army Co-operation – Henley and Hotspur

The Hawker Henley caused a 'stir' in the New Types Park at the 1937 Hendon Pageant. Here was an aircraft with a top speed close to 300 mph able to carry 1,000 lb of bombs. Many of its components, such as the wings, were interchangable with the Hurricane. It appeared to be a better proposition than the Battle as a light bomber. However the Shadow Factories were committed to Battle production and for political reasons production could not be stopped; even though the Air Ministry appeared to have second thoughts about light bombers. Hawker also developed a variant of the Henley to meet Specification F9/35 for a turret-armed two-seat fighter. This was the Hotspur, but it did not go into production and the Henley was modified to become a target-tug. Whether or not the Henley was a good light bomber is not the question. The question that needed answering at the time related to lessons being learnt from the use of aircraft in close support of troops in the Spanish Civil War. The concept was not fully understood; despite strong representations from some generals that the British Army should have aircraft for close-support attack. In WWI fighters were used, at great cost, to attack enemy trenches from low level; using machine-guns and bombs. Although the 'cavalry' generals in the army were fighting a paper battle to prevent the armoured vehicle, such as the tank, from superseding the horse in battle; nevertheless the War Office was slowly coming round to the potential of the tank. Military writers, such as Liddell Hart, kept hammering away in the press at the need for tanks. At the same time they warned of the need for means, such as aircraft, to defeat the tank. The existing army co-operation aircraft were only lightly armed with guns and bombs. Also, in the event of war, it was envisaged the co-operation aircraft would be used in 'penny numbers'.

RAF aircraft types allocated to army co-operation had mostly been used against lightly armed tribesmen on the fringes of the Empire. Where was the flying 'tank destroyer'? Indeed, where?

Radar information

Throughout the year the RAF and its dedicated group of scientists concerned with the effective use of radar information, continued to work round the clock in what was clearly 'a race against time'. The co-operation between the service and the scientists was the start of Operational Research. Among the highlights of the visit of *Luftwaffe* generals to RAF Hornchurch was General Milch's exclamation: 'Now, gentlemen, how are you getting on with the detection of aircraft approaching your shores using radio location'.

To see in the dark

From the start of the research into radar Sir Henry Tizard had been arguing that an enemy denied the freedom to bomb Britain by day would turn to bombing by night.

The technical problems of detecting the approach of enemy aircraft and the methods for directing the defending fighters were being solved one by one. The RAF was relying on the CH stations to give sufficient warning and details of attack so that it was not necessary to use standing patrols of fighters. The defence system enabled the controllers to position fighters within three or four miles of enemy formations. From that distance the fighter pilots had a reasonable chance of achieving visual contact. However, if the enemy chose to attack at night the defending fighters had to be positioned to within 500 to 1,000 feet to ensure visual contact. Therefore the development of radar sets small enough to be carried in an aircraft was an urgent need. Once again the Heyford found a place in scientific history as an experimental vehicle. An Anson was also used and on one occasion at least, despite the crude equipment, the crew were able, by following the indications displayed on the small CRT, to 'feel' their way back to Martlesham Heath, through low cloud and in poor visibility. At the time, Sqn Ldr de Haga Haig was developing his Radiaura electronic system for what we now call collision-avoidance.

The Anson experiments proved to be seminal to two main branches of radar development: airborne interception (code name AI) and air-to-surface vessel (code name ASV). On 3 September, Anson K6260, equipped with a very prototypical set, detected HMS *Rodney* and HMS *Courageous* passing through the Straits of Dover. The ships were detected again the next day.

Where are our fighters?

The development and building of the chain of radio location stations around the coast (the Chain Home) was not enough in itself. The fighter controllers using information from the CH stations had to be able to communicate at all ranges and heights with the fighter pilots. Therefore there had to be an effective radio-telephone system and equipment for Fighter Command. Furthermore although controllers were made aware of the positions of enemy aircraft this in itself was of little value if they were unaware of the positions of the fighters they were controlling. Therefore the scientists had to concentrate on establishing both good communications between ground and air and on the HF system which continuously tracked the position of defending fighters.

Pip Squeak

The versatile Chandler, who developed the RAF's fighter HF/DF position finding system, was also working on an adjunct to HF/DF. This was a system whereby the RT set of a fighter was automatically switched on for fourteen seconds in every minute. During this period the HF/DF stations determined its position. For the reminder of each minute the RT was available for controller-pilot communication. With hindsight we can understand how important HF/DF and Pip Squeak were to the eventual complete defence system based on radar. These three important technologies merged in 1937 to give Fighter Command its basic detection and control system.

Transmitters and receivers

It was not only the aircraft of Fighter Command which needed effective and reliable means of communication with ground stations. Other Commands, such as Bomber and Coastal, were still using radio transmitters and receivers whose designs were not much in advance of those of 1918. For example, the tuning of both transmitter and receiver within different frequency bands

Bristol Pegasus 9-cylinder engine. Among the many applications were: Bombay, Bristol 138A, London, Stranraer, Sunderland, Swordfish, Valentia, Vildebeest, Walrus, Wellesley and Wellington. (John Heaven)

required the use of plug-in coils. Changing to another band of frequencies took time. Even longer if the tuning coils of the 1082/1083 sets were jammed in position by expansion or frozen in their sockets.

Engines

By 1937 the RAF was looking forward to two powerful new engines for the future, the Merlin and the Pegasus, to replace the Kestrel and other older types. From now on a succession of aircraft types would have the Merlin. This nominally 1,000 hp engine had the design potential, when a number of serious problems had been overcome, including reverting to the integral cylinder head design of the Kestrel, to deliver even more power. The Bristol Pegasus which powered the Bombay, Harrow, Wellington and the Mercury in the Blenheim did not have the potential for developing significantly more power. Fortunately the Bristol engine company had sleeve-valve designs on the test-beds, including the Hercules and the Centaurus, which eventually would provide more power for both bombers and fighters.

Variable-pitch

As well as new all-purpose engines, the RAF was becoming used to variable-pitch propellers: in, for example, the Blenheim, Wellington, Wellesley and Whitley. However, the two fighters on which the defence of the kingdom depended in the event of war, the Hurricane and the Spitfire, were fitted with two-blade, fixed-pitch propellers. As will be discussed, variable-pitch propellers had been around for over fifteen years. Despite developments in Britain, which demonstrated the benefits of variable-pitch, the anti-variable lobby exerted great influence for many years.

Bristol Blenheim

The Blenheim represented a significant advance in technology. It was the RAF's first high-performance, twin-engine, monoplane light bomber. The design team at Bristol Aircraft, ever mindful of the Air Ministry's predilection for general-purpose aircraft, envisaged a number of different versions.

The designers at the Bristol Aeroplane Company developed a bomber that incorporated a number of technical innovations including a power-operated dorsal gun turret. This was a unique approach to solving the dual problem of protecting the air gunner from the harsh environment of high-speed flight and of relieving him of the considerable manual effort needed to move a machine-gun against a combination of air and G loads. The Bristol turret designed by L.G. Frise was of particular interest because the gun could be trained independently of the turret's rotation, thereby enabling the gun to be aligned tangentially to the turret's circumference as with the earlier 'flexible' gun mountings, such as the Scarff. When the Frise turret was being designed and developed, the optical reflector sight had not superseded the ring and bead type. Therefore a fundamental feature of the design was the method by which the gunner's head was kept in alignment with the gun as it is elevated. A system of hydraulic jacks raised or lowered the gunner's seat in step with the elevation of the gun. Unlike the Frazer-Nash mountings, the Bristol turret was trained by a hydraulic jack rather than a rotary hydraulic motor. To reduce drag when not in use, the cupola of the Blenheim's turret could be retracted. However, the Frise turret was an awkward location for the wireless-operator/gunner whose radio equipment has to be shared with the pillars, jacks, lever arms and other mechanism of the turret. The operator had to reach round the central pillar in order to adjust the controls, including changing coils, of the 1082–83 radio sets.

Although the Blenheim had two engines there was only one electric generator and one hydraulic pump. In the MkI aircraft both were driven by the port engine. This was not an ideal arrangement and was in contrast to twin-engine aircraft of other countries which had adopted a more generous provision of generators and pumps. Should the port engine fail the pilot found that he was deprived of electric and hydraulic power. The gun turret was deprived of power whenever the pilot selected either the operation of the flaps or the undercarriage. Thinking back to WWI and those occasions when German fighters attacked British aircraft as they were about to land or take off, the same 'sneak' attacks could be used against the Blenheim.[10]

Cockpit of a Blenheim MkI. The only part to which some consideration was given to the pilot's task was the RAF standard flight instrument panel. The other instruments and controls were figuratively thrown in and allowed to settle where they might. (British Aerospace)

Guns or speed?

Many new aircraft looked good on paper and when the shining prototype, unburdened by bombs, guns, radios and armour, cavorted above the spectators at an air display. However, once the new aircraft entered squadron service and were used in exercises a number of shortcomings become apparent. The results of mock engagements between Hurricane fighters and Blenheims were not published. In a dive and close to clouds, a Blenheim might be able to throw off a pursuer but if forced to stand and fight, the single gun in the turret was not going to deter a determined opponent. It is a thought-provoking exercise to question the policy at the time concerning the design of light and medium bombers, such as the Blenheim. Were they expected to defend themselves against multi-gun fighters? Should the policy, as already touched upon, have been one of using speed as the best form of defence, for example as argued by de Havilland ?

Blenheim performance

The Blenheim's performance with two 840 hp Mercury engines, was well up to the standards of other twin-engine bombers: five minutes only needed in which to reach 10,000 ft with 1,000 lb of internally stowed bombs and a range of 1,000 miles; 265 mph at 10,000 ft, but not up to the speed of the latest fighters. One rival design was the French Breguet 690 light-attack bomber. This was intended, when it eventually received its engines, to have similar cruising speed and time to 10,000 ft. However the 690 carried a smaller load of bombs but a more formidable forward-firing armament of one 20mm and two 7.7mm guns; the Blenheim of 1937 having only one 7.7mm firing forward. The Blenheim's single fixed gun for the pilot, as in the Hampden and other non-fighter type aircraft, carried on a long tradition that, irrespective of the role of an aircraft, the pilot had to have at least one gun to use against targets of opportunity.

The Mercury engines of the Blenheim were not the most powerful available. The Rolls-Royce Merlin of 1,000 hp might have been a better choice. However, it was likely that Bristols wanted to use their own 'home-grown' engines such as the Mercury and the Pegasus and, possibly, they were hoping that their new sleeve-valve fourteen and eighteen cylinder twin-row radials would soon be proved.

To raise or not to raise?

The experiences of 114 Squadron with a new type of aircraft produced some interesting observations by the pilots. For example the undercarriage of the Anson was rarely retracted for local flying because of the need to hand wind it up and down. In contrast, it was standard procedure for the wheels of the Blenheim to be retracted. However it was reported that some Blenheim pilots were not retracting the undercarriage during 'circuits and bumps'. However this was not recommended because should an engine fail soon after take-off the extra drag of the undercarriage could prove fatal.

The Blenheim's climb-out performance on one engine was marginal. The pilot had his hands full with moving the propeller control of the dead engine into coarse pitch, trimming out the rudder load and completing all the other vital actions needed for a successful one-engine climb. Of course if the port engine failed then the undercarriage could not be raised.

A spectacular arrival

On 10 March all eyes at RAF Wyton were on 114's first new Blenheim to arrive. It circled the airfield and then turned into wind. The undercarriage was lowered, the flaps moved down to the landing position and the propellers put into fine pitch. The landing was a good one and the new Blenheim rolled along the turf and slowed down preparatory to turning towards the hangars. Suddenly the tail came up higher and higher and over went the Blenheim to slide and thump on its back to a stop. Fortunately it did not catch fire and the pilot survived the dramatic arrival but, presumably did not survive the interview with his commanding officer.

Miles Magister ab initio trainer. Along with the Tiger Moth the Magister in the UK provided the embryo pilot's introduction to flying. (Peter Ottery)

Spares and repairs

On 1 April 1937 twelve new Blenheims were delivered to No 114 Squadron. Despite the date they all landed safely. However before July was out one of the new aircraft was extensively damaged when its undercarriage was inadvertently retracted as it was being taxied. Before much longer 114's inexperience with modern aircraft began to show, as also did the undeveloped state of many of the Blenheim's systems. The squadron was unable to operate effectively because of the poor serviceability and the difficulty of getting hold of spare parts.

The operation of new types of aircraft, particularly high-performance monoplanes with complex systems, coincided with an unusually severe winter. In a snowstorm a 114 Squadron Blenheim pilot was unable to maintain control. He decided that the aircraft might have to be abandoned. However he then lost control and was thrown out when it became inverted. Corporal T. E. Barnes, alone in the nose of the aircraft reached the controls. He recovered control and effected a crash-landing near Hinckley thereby saving the life of the other member of the crew; for which action he was awarded the Air Force Medal. The importance of this accident and its investigation to the history of the expanding years of the RAF is in the findings of the Court Martial that included the decision that the pilot flew in cloud conditions that were outside those for which he had been authorised and he abandoned the aircraft without warning the crew. Apparently there were standing flight orders in 114 Squadron prohibiting flight above cloud in a Blenheim for all but the more experienced pilots. From the Court Martial came

Blackburn B.2 side-by-side ab initio trainer. This was an alternative to the tandem cockpits of the Tiger Moth and the Magister. (British Aerospace)

the caveat that 'Until certain modifications have been made, the Blenheim is not considered suitable for casual cloud flying'. It also emerged that the pilot's instrument flying experience consisted of eleven hours dual and only two and a half hours solo. All this emphasised that the pressure of the international situation was forcing the service to run before it could walk in order to have an adequate supply of first-line aircraft and competent pilots.[11]

Ab initio

Two main types of aircraft were used for *ab initio* training: the Tiger Moth and the Magister. There was a third type, the Blackburn B2 side-by-side biplane trainer, but this was used at only a few schools. The Tiger Moth started its service life in February 1932. It was a modified version of the successful de Havilland Gipsy Moth. The principal changes being the inverted engine to improve the forward view, the cabane structure further forward and the wings swept back to allow easier exit from the front, instructor's, cockpit when wearing a parachute. Although the Tiger Moth's performance was modest, nevertheless it demanded a high standard of precise control on the part of a pupil pilot. It cruised at 93 mph, achieved 109 mph and could climb at 675 ft per minute.

The Magister was the final development of the 1935 Miles Hawk Major designed at Philips and Powis of Woodley. This was also a rare instance of a woman at the top of a design staff: Blossom Miles. The Magister, like the Tiger Moth, had to have a number of modifications to its civil-school original. For example, the cockpits had to be enlarged to make room for seat-type parachutes. Also the spinning characteristics were modified and there were a number of detail changes. The de Havilland Gipsy

Major engine of 130 hp was also used in the Tiger Moth. Because of the Magister's monoplane configuration and lower drag it could cruise 25 mph faster than the Tiger Moth but had a lower landing speed (42 mph). Perhaps the most significant difference between the two aircraft were the split flaps of the Magister.

On leaving the Elementary Flying Training Schools (EFTS) successful pupils required training on aircraft having more advanced performance. The step from the *ab initio* to, say, the Blenheim or Hurricane was too great and therefore there had to be an intermediate stage of training with suitable aircraft.

Single to twin

Converting pilots from single-engine *ab initio* aircraft to twin-engine types often had to be done 'in squadron'. For example, the pilots of No 114 Squadron, who were about to receive Blenheims in place of their single-engine machines, had to use the Ansons of 206 Squadron in order to obtain the twin-engine endorsement stamp in their log books. The pilots of 114 were not all that impressed with the Anson as a step towards flying the Blenheim because the two aircraft had little in common. The Anson had a flat approach to land, whereas the Blenheim had a steeper approach with a tendency to undershoot rather than overshoot as with the Anson. Importantly the Anson had fixed-pitch propellers and a manually-operated undercarriage in contrast to the variable-pitch propellers and power operated undercarriage of the Blenheim. The Anson was also not demanding enough. It did not prepare a pilot adequately for the 'less-forgiving of mistakes' characteristics of the new multi-engine types about to enter service. To meet the bomber-trainer and the fighter-trainer roles, two new aircraft types were needed. One had already been put into production, the Airspeed Oxford, and the other, the Master Trainer, was being considered.

Airspeed Oxford

The Oxford, which entered service at the new SFTSs (Service Flying Training Schools) in November 1937, was another example of a civil aircraft, the Airspeed Envoy, adapted to meet Air Ministry requirements. The Oxford was designed to specification T23/36 for an advanced flying school twin-engine trainer. Because it was primarily of wooden construction it economised on metal components and was therefore less expensive to produce. The Air Ministry was well aware that in the event of war production would have to be sub-contracted outside the traditional airframe builders and there might well be a shortage of materials.

In many respects the Oxford was in advance of the twin-engine training aircraft of other airforces; albeit there were few foreign types with which to make a comparison. A retractable undercarriage, flaps and a well-equipped cockpit were features intended to give trainee pilots a sound introduction to the problems and tasks to be faced when flying first-line twins such as the Blenheim, Whitley and Wellington and, further in the future, the large four-engine bombers then on the drawing board or at the prototype stage of development. Although the Oxford's Cheetah engines had fixed-pitch propellers nevertheless the design office provided a dummy propeller pitch control. This enabled a pupil pilot to become familiar with the required cockpit drill for first-line aircraft based on a mnemonic, such as 'HTMPFFG' for Harness, Trim or Throttle friction, Mixture, Pitch, Fuel, Flaps, Gyro or Gills.

Although the Oxford is referred to as a derivative of the Envoy, the metamorphosis from civil aircraft to RAF trainer was not a smooth one. There were months of argument over the detail design changes required by the Air Ministry. Airspeed had to keep re-negotiating the contract. By the time all the changes were incorporated, the Oxford had moved a long way on from the Envoy. The Directorate of Technical Development (DTD), that had imposed the changes, was being opposed by the ministry who wanted to put the Oxford into production with the minimum number of changes from the Envoy. Airspeed sat in the middle.

Adding to the company's problems was uncertainty over which of three possible engines types would be agreed to by the ministry: the Lynx, as used in the Envoy, the Cheetah or the Wolseley Scorpio.

Miles Kestrel two-seat fighter-trainer as first submitted to the Air Ministry. (Adwest Group plc via Julian C Temple)

The Scorpio became the victim of the differences between the government and Lord Nuffield. Lord Nuffield had disagreed with the government over the Shadow Factory Scheme and withdrew from the engine sector. In the end the Cheetah was selected.

The Oxford is also important in the history of aircraft production because of the flow-line system of production introduced by Hessell Tiltman of Airspeed. Contributing to component interchangeability and ease of maintenance was Tiltman's photo-lofting technique, whereby profiles of the structure were reproduced photographically. This ensured a high degree of accuracy.[12] Many aircraft companies continued with the lofting technique derived from ship building whereby long flexible splines were moved and held in position by heavy 'shoes'. The splines were then used as a guide for marking out the lines of a hull directly onto wood or metal master patterns.

Miles Kestrel trainer

F.G. Miles of Philips and Powis had tried since 1936 to convince the Air Ministry of the need for a high-performance monoplane, two-seat, trainer which would enable pilots to convert from the biplane trainers and fighters to the Hurricane and Spitfire. Therefore, Miles designed the M.9 Kestrel and built one as a private venture. The Kestrel was a graceful, sleek aircraft powered by a Rolls-Royce Kestrel. The engine company had a financial interest in Philips & Powis and the Kestrel engine, of which there was an adequate supply, could be put to good use. The prototype was flown by F.G. Miles for the first time on 3 June 1937; less than a year after the start of the design process which occupied only 400 man-weeks. The top speed proved to be nearly 300 mph at 14,500 ft. This was only about 15mph slower than the Hurricane. The handling characteristics, as intended, were similar to those of both the Hurricane and the Spitfire. Nevertheless, despite its promising performance, the Air Ministry continued to hesitate over giving Miles an order.

In the meantime the Air Ministry had encouraged the development of another fighter trainer, the DH Don, but the resulting aircraft proved unsuccessful and therefore the Miles Kestrel was ordered to become the Master of Training Command. However a number of major changes had to be made to the original design. The windscreen, cabin top and fuselage aft of the cockpits were modified. These changes were in order to match the aircraft to its role with Service Flying Training Schools. The prototype was powered by a Rolls-Royce Kestrel XVI of 745 hp. The production version had the Kestrel XXX of 715 hp and the 'chin' radiator re-positioned under the centre section. These modifications reduced the top speed.

On your own

Pilots at flying schools did not have the benefit of radio-telephonic communication with the ground.

Apart from the downward-pointing recognition signalling lamp and reading the Aldis lamp instructions from the Duty Pilot, a pupil pilot flying solo was more than on his own. Once away from the airfield circuit during night flying and over sparsely populated regions it was very easy to become lost. This handicap persisted well into WWII and may have contributed to the number of pupil pilots who crashed after attempting to find their way to an airfield at night or in poor visibility.

In the Cockpit

In the 1930s very little was written about the relationship between the controls and instruments of the cockpit and the pilot. Among all the world's aircraft types, including both civil and airforce, there appeared to be little standardisation of the position of the controls or of the relative positions of the instruments on the panel in front of the pilot.

The many different cockpits occupied by the pilots of the RAF reflected more or less the current level of thought on the subject. As with airframes and engines and other equipment, cockpits and their fittings were not necessarily the best available. Specifications issued three or four years before a new aircraft type entered squadron service predicated instruments and controls available at the time the specification was issued. Those items of cockpit which were modern were usually modifications introduced after the aircraft had entered service. For example: although the RAF was to have the collimated reflector gunsight as standard equipment, few, of the Hurricane or other fighters were intially equipped with it because of production delays. As mentioned they had to make do with the long-established ring-and-bead.[13]

Common to most RAF cockpits were: seats which accommodated a parachute; Sutton harness, with forward release so that the pilot could reach distant control levers and switches; and increasingly the provision of the Basic Six arrangement of the important instruments on one standard design of panel.

Owls and Fools

More advanced designs of instruments and controls were becoming available at this time. However the Air Ministry often refrained from adopting them in order that aircraft production would not be delayed. 'Only owls and fools fly at night' used to be a common expression among aviators. It fell into disuse as more and better 'blind flying' instruments and techniques became available. In the USA in 1929, Kollsman and Sperry instruments enabled Lt Doolittle in a Consolidated two-seat biplane to take off, complete a circuit of the airfield and land the aircraft back at the starting point without being able to see out of the cockpit. From the special set of instruments developed for that important flight in the history of aviation evolved a succession of better and better 'blind flying' instruments. Parallel work in Britain, notably by W.E.P Johnston and Reid and Sigrist, who developed the turn and bank indicator, led to the RAF's Basic Six instrument panel.

The investigation into the disastrous forced-landing of six Heyfords in March 1937, that had become lost in poor visibility, concluded that the lack of adequate space and equipment for the navigators was a contributory factor. The Harrow about to enter service needed a proper station for the navigator and better flight instruments. Another last-minute modification was the protection of the fuselage against lumps of ice thrown off by the propellers.[14]

In the 1937 edition of *Air Publication 129* Chap. III there is the statement: 'Instruments in the future will be grouped together'. The Basic Six panel contained the airspeed indicator, the artificial horizon, the rate-of-climb indicator, the directional gyro and the altimeter. The climb indicator, which also indicated rate of descent, was the progenitor of the modern vertical speed indicator. The Basic Six panel was a logical arrangement compared with the seemingly muddled arrangement of instruments used by other airforces, particularly American. This was strange when we consider the advances made in the theory and practice of instrument flying in the USA in the 1930s; as exemplified by the books of Assen Jordenoff.[15]

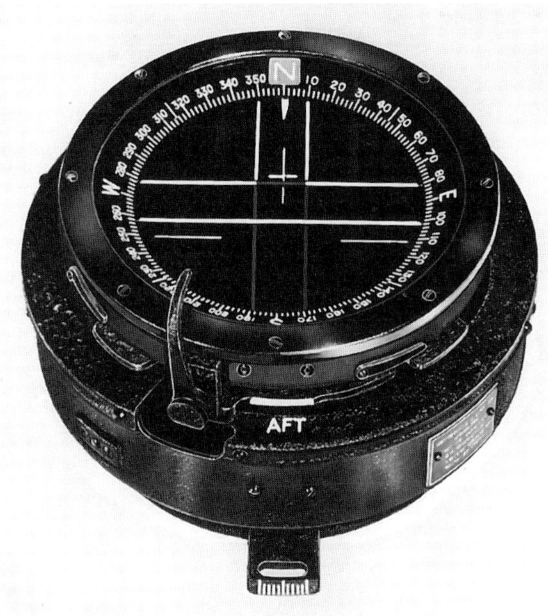

P Type aperiodic pilot's compass. This along with the gyro directional indicator (bottom middle on the RAF Basic Six panel) was the principal non-electronic heading guidance system. It was also one of the distinguishing features of a British cockpit. (Smiths Industries)

An important instrument common to all RAF cockpits was the pilot's magnetic compass. The type P4, for example, was usually mounted in front of the pilot's knees or to one side of the cockpit. It was the primary navigational instrument. The compass had a rotating grid ring graduated over 360 degrees with north marked by a red arrow. When the pilot needed to alter the aircraft's course onto a new heading he rotated the grid ring until the required course was set against the lubber line that represented the fore and aft axis of the aircraft. The aircraft was then turned until the grid wires were lined up with the magnetic needle and with the red arrow set against the northern crosswire of the needle. The operation was simple but there was always the danger that the pilot might inadvertently align the black, south, arrow against the needle. If that happened a reciprocal course would be flown. The use of the magnetic compass is described in some detail because it is a good example of an instrument that required some manipulation on the part of the user before it provided the required answer. Today we expect an instrument to display information unambiguously and not be capable of inducing errors on the part of the user.

Efficient cockpit design was often inhibited by the reluctance on the part of aircraft manufacturers to depart from their established standards. What had sufficed for the previous type would do for the next; that is provided it met the Air Ministry specification. However such a broad criticism of designers deserves an explanation. The private aircraft companies were often severely restricted by a shortage of money. There were over thirty companies in Britain. Some were small both in size and financial capital. Therefore they could not afford to indulge in research into better cockpit equipment and arrangements. In order to make the most of the few crumbs of contracts, which had to be shared out, they tried to win those which would allow them to adapt existing designs and to incorporate existing equipment. The need to share the few contracts among the many is emphasised by the fact that once WWII began many companies were saved. They retained their financial strength until the end of the war when they numbered 31 aircraft and 15 engine companies. As an example of the struggle that many aircraft companies had remaining solvent in the 1930s is Airspeed Ltd's reluctance to give a night demonstration of the Envoy. With the company's accounts over £4,000 in the red they could not afford to risk their only asset.

Night experience

The undoubted improvements in instrumentation were not being used to the advantage of Bomber Command pilots. In 1937 only 84 had their log books endorsed as qualified for night flying. The annual flying hours for the command were about 130,000 day and only 8,700 night. In two years flying the command's crews made 478 forced landings after failing to work out their position.[16] Following his tour of inspection of squadrons, Sir Edgar Ludlow-Hewitt, C-in-C Bomber Command reached the conclusion that 'the command was entirely unprepared for war and unable to operate except in fair weather'. In retrospect, it is obvious that the weak condition of Bomber Command arose from the limitations on flying hours, insufficient training and lack of suitable equipment; especially for night flying.

After the Hurricane

Early in 1937 Hawkers at Kingston started to scheme a successor to the Hurricane. They had in mind a faster and heavier armed single-engine fighter. The wing for the new aircraft was configured to accommodate twelve 7.7mm Colt Browning guns; a 50 per cent increase on the firepower of the Hurricane. The 'private venture' design initiative on the part of Hawkers was independent of any Air Ministry plans for future fighters. The Air Ministry, at the time Hawkers were designing the twelve-gun fighter, issued Specification F 18/37 for a four-20mm gun, single-engine, fighter to complement the twin-engine Specification F 37/35 of 1935 that led to the four 20mm-gun Westland Whirlwind. Eventually Sydney Camm, Chief Designer of Hawkers, was persuaded to postpone further design work on the twelve-gun fighter and wait for F18/37 to be officially distributed to the ten on the ministry's list of favoured companies. The specification, including the operational requirements, arrived at Kingston in January 1938. Apart from the four 20mm-gun requirement Camm's 12-gun proposal came very close to the requirements of F18/37.

In 1937 any advance in performance and all-up weight could be achieved only by installing a more powerful engine: recourse could not be made to innovative aerodynamics; either because they were not available or, if available, not enough was known about them to justify incorporating them into a new aircraft. Therefore 'the devil you know', in the shape of contemporary fighter design, had to be married to an engine capable of developing 2,000 hp. The ball was in the engine designer's court. Potential '2,000 hp' engines included Napier's Sabre (24-cylinder H), Rolls-Royce's Vulture (24-cylinder X) and Bristol's Centaurus (18-cylinder two-row radial) .

A summary of developments in the mid 1930s, particularly of new aircraft types, might give the impression that the individual aircraft companies concentrated their efforts strictly in accordance with the Air Staff's demands and ideas. In reality most of the design offices produced numerous projected aircraft. For example, in addition to de Havilland, G.R.Volkert, the Chief Designer at Handley Page, proposed an unarmed bomber. This was three-man crew, twin Sabre-engined, bomber of 37,000 lb auw intended to achieve a top speed of 400 mph.[17]

Great Circle northabout

In 1937 an airfield was built at Gander in Newfoundland. Eventually this became, with Prestwick in Scotland, a staging post for a northabout Great Circle route between Canada and the United Kingdom along which aircraft were ferried from factories in the USA. In view of the isolationist policy of the United States at the time, this was an uncertain plan, because its future success would depend on a significant change in that government's attitude to becoming involved in a European war. At the time the distances involved on the proposed trans-Atlantic routes seemed immense. For example the southernmost west-to-east, Dorval in Canada to Prestwick in Scotland, was over 3,150 nautical miles. The northernmost, staging at Reykjavik in Iceland and closer to a Great Circle (i.e. shortest distance between two points on the surface of the globe), was about 2,900 nautical miles.

The Last Pageant

The 1937 RAF Pageant at Hendon was to be the last. In some ways the decision to end this annual display and replace it with open days at selected RAF stations on Empire Day reflected the changes taking place throughout the service: changes prompted by the continuing volatile international situation.

A new threat

In Germany the Junkers 88 was emerging as a twin-engine, multi-purpose machine whose 'paper' per-

Napier Sabre 24-cylinder engine installed in a flying test bed Battle. After a protracted development programme the Sabre went on to power the post Spitfire/Hurricane generation of fighters such as the Typhoon and Tempest. (Derek James)

formance was impressive. Its design owed much to ideas from the USA and to the American, Alfred Gassner, working with Junkers. It was, however, with 1,340 hp engines and a bomb load of 3,000 lb, a bigger and more powerful aircraft than the Blenheim and the Breguet 690. Its 'paper' performance of 1937 was more than justified in WWII when it proved a formidable and versatile opponent.

Avro Anson. The first production aircraft went to 48 Squadron in March 1936. It served in Coastal Command, on general reconnaissance duties, and as a trainer and communications aircraft throughout WWII. This photograph shows clearly the Avro type cupola with a balanced gun mounting for a Lewis gun. (Aeroplane Monthly)

Chapter Four

1938/I

Aware that the German airforce was the most likely potential enemy the basic policy relating to the balance between offensive and defensive squadrons was revised. Previously more funds were allocated to the provision of bombers. Now it was the recently formed Fighter Command that was to have priority.

Defence priority

When considering the overall defence needs of the United Kingdom the RAF 'lobby' was strong. It argued for both offensive and defensive strength in the air. It has since been suggested that the greater threat was the German Army not the *Luftwaffe*. The former was formidable and therefore the British Army should have received a larger slice of the 'defence cake'; as events were to prove in 1940. Another air defence factor was the strength, or rather the lack of strength, of the French airforce. In 1938 this was estimated to have 250 fighters and 320 bombers. The airforce's Chief of Staff was quoted as saying that the aircraft were 'of doubtful performance' and that he expected 40 per cent casualties in the first month of war and 64 per cent by the end of the second month.[1]

Faced with the realisation that Germany might attempt to subdue Britain by sending over mass formations of bombers then there would have to be more fighter than bomber squadrons. The fighters would be equipped with eight-gun Hurricanes and Spitfires. The former were in squadron service but the latter were slow to arrive because of production problems at Vickers Armstrongs Supermarine factory at Southampton.

Spitfire production

The few Spitfires delivered to No 19 Squadron at Duxford were still subject to modifications. When production orders were first placed with Vickers Supermarine works the Spitfire was essentially a very 'clean' high performance monoplane. Reginald Mitchell and his successor, Joseph Smith, had designed a fighter having low drag, moderate wing loading and a good power-to-weight ratio. The elliptical planform wing was aerodynamically very efficient. A pilot could 'throw the Spitfire around the sky' without it shaking and rocking and going out of control.

At the A&AEE Martlesham Heath its performance and handling characteristics were evaluated by the service test pilots to verify that it met the contract specification and was capable of being flown by the average pilot. The aircraft tested at the A&AEE was without guns, gunsight, radio, armour plating and many items needed to equip it for operational flying as an interceptor. At this time Sqn Ldr Stainforth, of record-holding Supermarine S6B fame, was writing the Pilot's Notes for the Spitfire.

In theory the Spitfires should have entered squadron service much earlier. This was prevented by the many snags to be overcome and by the need to find and approve numerous subcontractors. The manufacturer and the RAF had to keep two parallel lines of development and improvement under way: one, the many modifications to engine and airframe as the hours flying experience built up and, two, the introduction of 'fighting' equipment. Vickers Supermarine works were able to develop and build the prototype and supply a pre-production batch. But the works were not equipped for large-scale production. Overall the company lacked large-scale production expertise. In many ways this was symptomatic of the British aircraft industry as a whole. For nearly twenty years the industry had led a hand-to-mouth existence. It had to survive on the occasional production order. With war threatening the industry needed to be re-organised, and to tool-up for production quantities not seen since 1918.

The Air Ministry's policy was to avoid getting all its aircraft and engine production 'eggs' from one basket. Orders were distributed among the large manufacturers. However, the smaller companies were sometimes left out because the Air Ministry continued the policy insisted on in the 1920s by Frederick Handley Page of restricting orders to the select 'family' of companies which formed the SBAC. As it was, the Air Ministry's limited funds were supporting no fewer than sixteen design teams.[2]

To help the industry to gear up for large scale production the government decreed that defence contracts had priority and the nation's commerce was no longer to be free from disruption by defence interests.

Shadow Factory politics

In May 1938 Lord Swinton was relieved of his responsibility for the RAF and replaced by Kingsley Wood. Swinton was one of the principal architects of the RAF expansion programme. Churchill later commented on Swinton's dismissal as follows:

> We were both sacked for the two best things we ever did. I was sacked for the Dardenelles. You were sacked for building the air force that won the Battle of Britain, and they couldn't undo what you did.

In 1938 the Prime Minister, Neville Chamberlain, allowed the Air Minister Kingsley Wood to take the Castle Bromwich Spitfire factory away from Vickers Armstrongs and give it to the Nuffield organisation. It was done not for technical reasons but for political expediency and would have serious consequences in the future for production . If war had started in autumn 1938 the potential output of Spitfires from Castle Bromwich would not have been realised. In 1940 it was estimated that another 1,000 Spitfires could have been available had the Castle Bromwich factory remained under the direct control of Vickers.[3]

The companies who operated shadow factories were: Austin, Daimler, Rootes (Hillman, Humber & Commer), Rover and Standard. Bristol and Nuffield (Austin) shared Mercury engine production. Nuffield, originally allocated fighter production, also took on the building of Battles. Blenheims were built at Speke by Rootes Securities Ltd who were also responsible for one of the engine factories. Altogether there were eleven shadow factories. Rolls-Royce established its own engine factories at Crewe and Glasgow independently of the shadow scheme because it considered that automobile factories were incapable of making aircraft engines to the required standards of quality.[4]

Rolls-Royce reservations about the automobile industry's standards were not without foundation. The motor industry found there were unexpected and very special problems involved in the production of aero-engines. Sir Maurice Dean was of the opinion that the government was not even taking the subject seriously in the summer of 1938.[5] In June 1938 Sir Ernest Lemon of the LMS railway was appointed as Director-General of Production and introduced a policy of sub-contracting among the aircraft and engine companies and others: a policy that had been resisted by the industry.

Defence of UK

Every day Fighter Command and its scientists working at Stanmore, Bawdsey, and Biggin Hill were getting closer to perfecting methods and equipment that would enable a controller to position fighters within a few miles and above an enemy bomber formation. The first part of the chain of radar stations was being built to cover the Thames estuary and a scheme of allocating specific areas or sectors to an individual fighter control room was worked out.

During the August home defence exercises it became clear that the CH stations could not detect aircraft at an elevation angle of less than 1.5 deg. This meant that an aircraft flying below 12,000 feet would not be detected until it was within about 50 nautical miles of a CH station. Therefore development of what was to become the CHL (Chain Home Low) radar was given greater priority.[6]

An interesting aspect of these research and trial flights, under the orders of a controller, was the presumption that German bomber formations would approach the English coast line flying approximately on a compass heading of 270 degrees. The most likely targets were London and industrial centres in the South East and Midlands and therefore they would attempt to cross the coast north of Dover and south of the Wash. It was not anticipated that they would be accompanied by an escort of fighters because none of the German fighters, such as the Bf109 or 110, had adequate range.

In 1938 the RAF did not have a high performance, heavily armed, fighter able to operate against enemy bombers flying at night. The radio location scientists and those developing and proving the detection and reporting system, realised that at night and when there was overall cloud cover, the defences would be 'blind' once an aircraft had passed over the coastal-located Chain Home stations. The location of aircraft by the observer posts using sound alone was an uncertain technique. There was also a need for a long-range fighter able to penetrate enemy airspace.

A potential answer to both the night-fighter and the long-range 'penetration' fighter requirement was the Bristol Aircraft company's private venture design. However the Air Ministry rejected the twin-engine fighter proposal because it did not satisfy all the requirements of Specification F9/37 or of F11/37. Undeterred the company submitted a design that incorporated major components from the Beaufort; such as wings, aft fuselage and empennage. A redesigned forward fuselage section and higher-powered engines (Hercules) completed the new proposal. A significant feature was space in the roomy fuselage for re-loading the four 20mm guns. At the time the Hispano 20mm gun was fed by a 60-round 'drum 'magazine that had to be lifted into position in the cold and dark.

The basic layout also permitted the optional installation of a dorsal turret. There was also a proposed 'slim' fuselage variant that would have provided an alternative to the Westland Whirlwind whose slow development was worrying the Air Ministry. The Bristol aircraft was designed to accept 1,600 hp Hercules VI engines giving it twice the thrust of the Whirlwind's two Peregrines.

The Bristol night-fighter eventually became the Beaufighter. Its development was expedited because it evolved from the Blenheim via the Beaufort. The importance of the Beaufighter's early years is as an example of how existing aircraft designs were blended by a private venture initiative in co-operation with the Air Ministry so as to produce a 'flexible' aircraft that in later years was able to undertake many important roles at the sharp end of the RAF.

Bomb the bombers

Research was undertaken at the Royal Aircraft Establishment into a bombsight that would enable a defending aircraft to drop bombs on a bomber attempting to attack a city or industrial centre. Specification F11/37, for a two-seat, twin-engine, twin 20mm-gun turret, day and night fighter included the requirement for carrying a 500 lb load of aerial mines intended to be dropped on a formation of enemy bombers. This was an interesting idea, provided the bombers below held a straight course. Even if the aiming problems had been overcome there was the more difficult problem of controlling the defending 'bomber' so that it was in the right tactical position and above the intruder. Airborne interception radar had yet to be fully developed when the scheme was mooted. Such an aircraft had to have a fighter-like rate of climb and a good margin of speed. Even with control from the ground the pilot depended on visually detecting the enemy over the last few miles if a successful interception was to be made. One question that did not appear to be raised is: what happens if a bomb or bombs miss their intended target and carry on earthwards?[8]

Taking a weapon to the enemy is often the most difficult task of many.

Arming and fuelling

In 1938 Fighter Command started to train its ground crews in rapid re-arming and re-fuelling of aircraft. To some extent however realism was being compromised because many of the Hurricanes and the few Spitfires had only four guns in place of the intended eight. The re-arming and servicing of aircraft under simulated gas attack was an important part of the training programme. Not until airmen had experienced the hot and confining effect of their gas masks when working did they and their masters realise how difficult it would be to work for long hours under such conditions.

400 mph the target

Ever since the Supermarine S6B gained the Schneider Trophy outright for Britain, 400 mph was the design target for the eight-gun, monoplane fighter. Although the advertised top speed of both the Hurricane and the Spitfire was less than 400 mph, the RAF recognised that, with the help of the elements, a squadron-standard Hurricane could be flown from Edinburgh to Northolt at an average speed of 400 mph. Sqn Ldr Gillan's high speed flight not only made the headlines in the lay press but also aroused comment in the technical press. The validity of the 408 mph average was challenged. Some writers argued that the speed claimed was not possible with a Hurricane. However some of the doubters were not aware of the strong tailwind that persisted for the greater part of the flight. Also, they may not have been aware that the organisers made sure of a favourable meteorological forecast before the flight.

Rolls-Royce Merlin 12-cylinder, nominal 1,000hp, engine. The principal in-line, liquid-cooled engine in 1938. (Rolls-Royce)

The RAF did not respond to the doubters and did not publish any details of the flight.

Snow, ice & fog

An interesting fact of life in the RAF was the habit of organising air exercises mostly during the summer months. However, this did not test men and machines in the rigours of flying and maintaining equipment in arduous conditions. In a Northern Europe winter, guns, for example, became soaked by condensation at ground level which could then freeze once an aircraft climbed to above a few thousand feet. In the winter of 1938/39 the service was tested by severe snowfalls and low ground temperatures that provided a foretaste of the 'Arctic' conditions of Northern France a year later.

Blenheim problems

When the Blenheims tried 'battle' climbs to 30,000 feet men and machines were subjected to the extreme cold of high altitude. The Cellastoid transparent panels cracked in the intense cold, making them difficult to see through and letting in blasts of refrigerated air. Because of the effects of high altitude Blenheims were limited to 18,000 feet or minus 25°C. Radio and intercom equipment failed because of the ingress of moisture. Although the Blenheim's 'paper' performance included a ceiling of 31,000 feet it often failed to get above 29,000 feet.

Other Blenheim problems came to light following a flying display by 114 Squadron from Aldergrove. When taxying over rough ground to their dispersal sites, tail wheels and stern frames were damaged. The Blenheim had been in service for some time but trouble was still being experienced with the retractable undercarriage; either because of mechanical defects or pilot forgetfulness.

The single-engine performance of the Blenheim was no better and no worse than that of other twins. The service was still losing Blenheims and crew in take-off accidents following the failure of an engine at the critical point. For example K7037 of 114 Squadron crashed on take-off, following failure of the starboard engine, killing the crew of one pilot officer and two aircraftmen.

Essentially the major problem facing a pilot when an engine failed on take-off was the need to maintain height: but at the same time power had to be reduced on the good engine in order to maintain direction against the asymmetric thrust. The Blenheim did not have feathering propellers. These were still at the development stage. Moving the 'dead' propeller into coarse pitch was about the only remedy open to the pilot; followed by adjusting aileron and rudder trim. All those vital control actions had to be executed in a cockpit whose design and position of controls took no account of the pilot's difficulties. The failure of an engine or both engines just after take-off usually resulted in a fatal crash. As mentioned, the arrangement of the controls in the cockpit did nothing to improve a crew's chances of surviving mechanical problems.

The Blenheim is an example of the significant difference between what we would now call 'the cutting edge of technology' and the general level of technology achieved in aircraft design. For example, the early production Blenheims had some of the engine instruments mounted not in the cockpit but on the inboard side of each engine nacelle. This was a common practice in the 1920s in multi-engine aircraft. It was in stark contrast to the all-metal, monocoque construction, the retractable undercarriage, flaps and variable-pitch propellers that together made up one of the world's most advanced military aircraft. It emphasised the way in which accessories, such as instruments, were failing to keep up with the advances being made in the first half of the 1930s in engines, structures and propellers. Radio equipment, guns, gun turrets, electrical generators and night-flying equipment, like instruments, were still in the process of being developed to standards that were compatible with the new aircraft about to join the RAF.

As with the Heyford in 1936, the Blenheim in 1937 represented a collection of parts and equipment that was not adequate to the tasks for which it was selected. The Blenheim was contributing to a large proportion of the incidents and accidents that were a feature of service life. Although the aircraft was aerodynamically better than the aircraft types it was replacing, it was far less forgiving of pilot errors.

Vickers Wellington.

Wellington production that had started at the end of 1937 was getting underway. The production version differed considerably from the prototype. Although Vickers had come close to the Air Ministry's requirements they found that the prototype had to be extensively re-designed before it was acceptable. The bulbous tail gun position abaft the fin had to be replaced by an entirely new design of power-operated, twin-gun, mounting. This is often referred to as a 'turret'. However it was not a turret in the true meaning of the word; it was more akin to the casemate mounting of an early Dreadnought's guns. Vickers used the term 'windscreen'. These mountings were replaced in 1939 by proper power-operated turrets in which the gunner, guns and sight rotated as one unit.

An interesting feature or omission was the lack of self-sealing fuel tanks and armour plate for the pilot's seat and other vital areas. As noted, the Air Staff's policy concerning the use of the Wellington was for large formations to operate over enemy targets in daylight. Such a policy raised the questions: could a formation of Wellingtons, with guns having limited traverse on the beam, be defended against determined and agile fighters able to attack from all sides and not just from astern?; or, was reliance for success being based on the assumption that 'The bomber will always get through'?

The geodetic construction[9] principle, as used for the Wellesley, was claimed, by Vickers and its designer Barnes-Wallis, to give great strength for minimum weight. Fabric covering was used over the greater part of the fuselage, wings and tail surfaces. Whether or not such a method of construction was better than all-metal stressed skin or monocoque was a debatable point at the time. As it happened the geodetic construction resisted battle damage surprisingly well during WWII. At the time the Wellington I gave the appearance of great potential for striking at an enemy. But the question remained: was the equipment provided for accurate navigation and the aiming of bombs, especially at night, going to be effective? If war had started in 1938 the few Wellington squadrons along with the Whitleys would have represented the sharp end of Britain's air power. Irrespective of the Wellington's lack of equipment for accurate navigation, target-finding and bomb-aiming, pilots liked the way it handled.

Armstrong Whitworth Whitley

The Whitley was conceived as a 'heavy' bomber and ordered by the Air Ministry in 1934. In 1938 it was recognised to be obsolete when compared with the expected performance, defensive armament and offensive load of the 'new' generation of long-range bombers, such as the Handley Page and Short Brothers four-engine bombers. Like the Wellington, the Whitley was in the heavy bomber class. The appellation 'heavy' related to the 'medium' classification of the Blenheim and the 'light' of the Battle. As noted, production was temporarily slowed while consideration was being given to cancelling the programme in anticipation that the new generation of bombers would soon be available.

Whitley dustbin

In August 1938 some Whitley IIIs were equipped with a ventral, power-operated, twin-gun, extendable turret. The Nash and Thompson FN 17 turret was not much bigger than a domestic dustbin. It closely confined the gunner, guns, ammunition tanks, hydraulic system, elevating and training controls and a reflector sight. Only a narrow vertical window was provided for sighting an attacking fighter. The gunner had to rely on other crew members to give him an indication of the quarter from which the fighters were attacking. A similar ventral turret was being fitted to Wellingtons.

Extending the turret from its retracted position required a sequence of actions on the part of the air gunner. Standing on the turret's seat, the gunner

Armourers installing one of the four 7.7mm Browning guns in the FN-4 tail turret of a Whitley V bomber. (R. Wallace-Clarke)

first raised the turret from its retracted position sufficiently to release the up-locks. With the locks held clear, the turret was then lowered to the fully extended position beneath the aircraft. The gunner lowered himself onto the seat and then wound down an enclosure for his legs.

The ventral turret could only achieve the following speeds of actuation: elevation 14 deg/sec; depression 19 deg/sec; rotation 58 deg/sec. With modifications these figures were improved and became respectively: 29 deg/sec; 34 deg/sec; 60 deg/sec. The twin 7.7mm Browning guns could be elevated or depressed over an angle of 70 deg. The 'walking pipes' which conveyed hydraulic power to the rotating service joint (RSJ) of the turret were replaced by armoured flexible hoses.

The single Vickers K or Lewis tail gun of the Whitley I, II and III was mounted in an AW Type 38 balanced, manually operated, 'turret'. The Air Staff was very critical of the provision made for the tail gunner. 'The turret (sic) was cold and draughty and could not be used for high altitude flights.' In contrast Whitley IIIs were fitted with a Nash and Thompson (FN) power operated turret in the nose mounting a single Vickers K gun. An AW manual gun cupola in the nose would have been untenable. As it was the FN turret also let in icy blasts of air as well.

Whitley IV

At this time Air Ministry reached the conclusion that it was not going to be possible to fit guns heavier than 7.7mm into tail turrets. Therefore, the decision was taken to encourage the development of dorsal and ventral turrets armed with 20mm guns. However the development of turrets with 20mm guns took longer than expected and therefore the new long-range bombers were equipped with 7.7mm guns in the dorsal and ventral positions. The Whitley IVs had the NT four-gun power turret in the tail. This was the world's first example of a four-gun turret in the tail of an aircraft. The turret was at the end of a long lever, the fuselage, and therefore subject to large accelerations when the pilot took extreme evasive action. This made it difficult for the gunner to track an attacking fighter. As with the earlier versions, the Whitley IV's interior had been designed with little thought given to the comfort of the crew or to eliminating sharp, harness-catching, projections. In this respect the Whitley was little different from the other bomber types in service with Bomber Command. Flying at above 15,000 feet required the crew to use oxygen and to have an adequate supply of hot air for heating and electrically-heated flying clothing.

Four-engine bombers?

C.G. Grey, editor of *Aeroplane*, writing on 27 August 1938 continued to criticise the Boeing Flying Fortress.

> . . . the big four-engine bomber is the silliest aeroplane that anybody ever imagined, one lucky shot from an ordinary machine-gun and away go four motors, some tons of bombs and several good men.

His comment must have been of particular interest to the Air Staff in the light of the earlier decision to develop Bomber Command into a 'four-engine' force.

Germany the target

The Cabinet was told by the Air Staff, when discussing the use of the RAF as a strategic weapon, that the industrial heart of Germany, the Ruhr, could be destroyed by one month of bombing operations. Fifteen hundred bomber sorties in daylight would be sufficient to halt Germany's war production.

Assuming that losses were not made good or some of the 300 aircraft available were not needed elsewhere, then after 30 days of sustained attacks the bomber strength would be halved by enemy action and from other causes, such as engine failure. Not only would nearly 150 aircraft be written off but about 800 trained aircrew would be prisoner, injured or dead. With no adequate and comprehensive system for replacing the experienced pilots lost or for training observers, wireless operators and air gunners, the loss of personnel would have been as hard to bear as the loss of aircraft. A year later the C-in-C Bomber Command told the CAS, that if his command were ordered to make an all-out offensive against Germany, he estimated that the Blenheim squadrons would be destroyed in less than four weeks and the Hampden, Wellington and Whitley squadrons in less than eight weeks.[11]

Bomber Command, in theory should have been able to drop around 100 tons of bombs for each day of operations. However as the bombs were unlikely to be larger than 500 pounders they would have had little effect on industrial targets. Observers of air raids during the Spanish Civil War noted the comparative ineffectiveness of bombs. Admittedly a 500 pound bomb exploding within a housing block caused severe damage and many casualties. But these medium size bombs only caused significant damage to industrial plants and to public utilities if they struck a vital part: otherwise once the dust had settled and the damaged structure cleared away, production equipment, such as machine tools, was back in use within a few days.

Another matter that exercised some people was the morality of bombing civilians. *Flight* for 22 September 1938 included the following:

> We may be sure, however, that British bombers will not be used for attacks on civilian populations. The wise commander aims

Loading a bomb into a Whitley I of No.10 Squadron in 1937. (Aeroplane Monthly via: J. Goulding)

always at winning the war, not making himself spitefully unpleasant to the enemy people.

Bombs

Even if RAF bombers were able to navigate to distant targets and score direct hits most of the bombs were ineffective. As mentioned in Chapter Two, bomb design and production were serious problems that had to be overcome. The design and quality of British bombs had changed little since 1918. Precious weight was still being wasted on excessively thick casings and fuses were rudimentary and unreliable. The situation had not been helped by the Air Ministry's lack of direct control of design and production over the preceding 20 years. Fortunately bomb design and production was reorganised in 1938 with the Air Ministry exercising full control.

Bombing potential

Was the bombing potential of the RAF deliberately exaggerated as part of the 'battle' with the Treasury over funds? Furthermore was the bomber in general an overrated weapon? Was the belief in the potential of the bomber blinding it to the need for better navigational techniques and equipment and to the need for target identifying and bomb-aiming systems? Without such aids the finest bomber in the world would be of little use. At command and squadron level many officers voiced their concern over the lack of target-marking bombs and target illuminating flares.

Although there was some improvement in the accuracy of navigation in general in 1938 there was still much room for improvement. Since the end of WWI, navigation of long-range aircraft was usually the responsibility of the second pilot. However with the introduction of aircraft, such as the Hampden, without provision for a second pilot, more observers, whose primary task was navigation, had to be trained.

The navigation of long-range aircraft, particularly over the ocean, required the application of astro-navigational techniques. A specialist astro-navigation course had only been in existence for a year. An essential item besides a bubble sextant was a transparent astrodome through which the navigator could 'shoot' the stars. Using a sextant from an open cockpit was not an ideal arrangement.

Landing aids

Irrespective of the need for target-finding equipment, aircraft crews were still having difficulty in locating specific airfields at night or in poor visibility. Even if a crew was successful in correctly identifying the destination airfields, they may have had difficulty in landing. At night or in poor visibility much depended on the skill of the pilot and his wireless operator.

A common cause of accidents in the 1930s, and in other decades, was what we now euphemistically call 'controlled descent into high ground'. In other words, a pilot uncertain of his position descends through the overcast in order to verify his position. Frequently this ended in disaster.

A basic technique for making an approach and landing, depended on careful mental dead reckoning from a position overhead the airfield. On receipt of the signal from the ground 'Engines overhead' the pilot executed a series of timed runs on different headings as he received a succession of bearings. This method was refined and became the ZZ Approach method. On the final approach to the landing the pilot may have had the visual guidance of gooseneck paraffin flares set out in a pattern. There may also have been a powerful Chance floodlight to illuminate the touchdown area. Standards of airfield lighting varied from one station to another. Once again there was great inconsistency in the technical level achieved among the many different systems and equipment which were essential if the maximum potential of an aircraft was to be realised. In general there had not been much advance on the airfield equipment of the Independent Force of 1918 that even included electric-lamp 'flare' paths.

Lorenz

The German company Lorenz developed a beam approach system. This was sufficiently accurate to enable aircraft to land in poor visibility. In the mid-1930s the RAF adopted a modified version of the Lorenz system.

The RAF's Lorenz used two VHF radio beams: one to the right of the approach line transmitting a series of Morse dashes: the beam to the left transmitted a series of dots: where they overlapped they produced a continuous sound in the pilot's headphones. The pilot flew the aircraft so as to intercept the beams and then turned towards the airfield so as to keep in the steady note sector. There were two vertical 'fan' marker beams whose signals indicated to the pilot, as the aircraft passed through them, that he was passing through the outer marker fan and therefore two miles from the touchdown point: the inner marker fan beam indicated that the aircraft was close to the edge of the landing area. If a pilot used this beam approach technique correctly he would pass through the outer marker at 1000 feet above the ground and be at about 100 feet when passing through the inner marker fan beam. Lorenz system was first used in the United Kingdom in 1935 at Croydon for civil aviation. A modified version later became the RAF's Standard Beam Approach System.

Given the erratic variations in visibility which persist for much of the time in the British Isles, a landing aid was most important if the RAF was required to fly irrespective of the meteorological conditions. In the USA, the same principle of overlapping radio beams formed the radio range system which then covered large areas of the country. This gave the pilot Morse letter As to the left and Ns to the right of the steady note of the centre line. The radio ranges provided the long distance flyer with a succession of beams along which to fly. It was not adopted by the RAF because it did not want to be restricted to a number of fixed radio range stations and quadrature tracks in the event of war.

Night training

Despite the continuing uncertainty over the international situation and the realisation that war was now likely to start, if not within a month, at least within a year, night flying training hours were still too low. For example, 224(GR) Squadron moved to Eastleigh for night flying either because the home airfield was unsuitable or because of objections from residents who lived close by. Out of the total flying hours of just over 1,620 only 280 were at night. A pilot of a GR squadron aircraft needed to have the experience of much night flying if he was to make a safe landing after a long patrol.[12]

Night flying accidents continued to take their toll of men and machines. Typical is a Battle of 63 Squadron whose pilot became confused when trying to find and then identify the flashing beacon at Odiham. He came down too low and the aircraft crashed into a wooded hill. The pilot along with a corporal and an aircraftman was killed. Few pilots or their commanders, appeared to be aware of the dangers of flying over sparsely populated country at night with only a few pinpoints of light showing. (*Pace*: St-Exupéry).

Coastal Command

The Air Staff, having looked to the future of Fighter and Bomber commands, was now seeing what needed to be done to bring Coastal Command up to date. Essentially the command was made up of ten Anson GR squadrons, range only 750 miles, and a few squadrons of biplane flying boats. Sunderland squadrons were still 'working up' As usual the Admiralty and the Air Ministry rarely agreed when studying future aircraft needs.

Sir Frederick Bowhill, C-in-C Coastal Command, continued the expansion policy of his predecessor and was very aware of the need to advance the technologies needed for long-range ocean patrolling and equipment for finding and attacking submarines. A Coastal Anson carried only a modest bomb load 500 lb and could not carry a torpedo. The tasks Coastal Command would have to face in war can be viewed against those performed by the RNAS in the Great War. There were four distinct types of operations: anti-U-boat patrols using airships, float planes and flying boats; single-seat fighter sorties in support of the army; single-seat night fighters, long-range heavy bomber operations. But what the RNAS did not pursue was the development of long-range ocean patrol aircraft operating from airfields.

In December 1937, the Air Ministry decided on the primary roles of Coastal Command in war: trade-protection, reconnaissance and co-operation with the Royal Navy. However no specific mention was made of attacking warships or for that matter merchant ships. Not until the outbreak of war would a more urgent approach be made to the methods of attacking ships and submarines. Bombs, torpedoes and depth charges were weapons for which there had been limited research and development in the inter-war years. Minelaying as a weapon was delayed until April 1940. The Admiralty and the Air Ministry forgot all about the lessons learnt during WWI on how to protect shipping. Both the convoy system and air escorts for merchant ships were neglected during staff studies. The Royal Navy was going to rely on ASDIC[13] for protection against submarines. It concentrated its planning for war on the menace of the commerce raider; in turn this influenced the potential role of Coastal Command.[14]

On 14 June six Ansons set out from Bircham Newton. Their crews were briefed to find the aircraft carrier HMS *Courageous* that was somewhere out in the North Sea. A combination of poor visibility and lack of practice left the ship undetected. Contributing to the failure to find the carrier were navigational errors. Over the sea these were likely to average five miles in every 100. The lack of practice was one of the consequences of a restriction on flying hours in order to conserve engine life. Engine spare parts were in such short supply that each Anson was limited to fifteen hours flying each month. If war had started what then?

More exercises

The number of air exercises increased as the service prepared for war. In the rapid deployment exercises of 1938 Coastal Command had to give up its peacetime establishment and routines. When the exercises required squadrons to move away from their home stations their 'tails' were failing to keep up with the van, both geographically and administratively. Only with the unofficial help of squadron wives were some units able to deploy in accordance with operational orders.

The flying boat squadrons of Coastal were finding difficulty, compared with the 'land-based' squadrons, in moving at short notice to another operating base. Flying boats required specialised handling equipment, slipways and marine craft for their support. Maintenance, particularly of engines, was more complex than with other aircraft types. Altogether a flying boat squadron needed a larger number of personnel and support equipment than other squadrons. In September six Singapore flying boats of 209 Squadron left Felixstowe, the ancestral home of RAF flying boats, for Invergordon. This was a positioning flight to demonstrate rapid deployment in the event of war. Of the six that set out, only one arrived at Invergordon; the remainder succumbed to a variety of mishaps on the way. One out of six, 16 per cent may not seem significant but when related to the few aircraft available at the time to the command it did not auger well for its wartime potential.

And all the time the menacing clouds of war were growing larger with each passing day.

Vildebeest replacement

There was an urgent need for a replacement for the Vildebeest. This large, single-engine, biplane had an all-up weight with torpedo of 8,000 lb. The span was nearly 50 ft. Pilots were instructed not to exceed 120 knots otherwise the tail might break off. A stop-gap decision intended to keep the Vildebeest in front-line service for a few more years, or at least until the new torpedo-bombers arrived, was the Mk IV. This had the new Bristol Perseus sleeve-valve engine and was the first of its type to power an RAF aircraft. Specification M15/35 for a Vildebeest replacement was answered by Bristol and Blackburn. The former developed the Beaufort and the latter the Botha. These were twin-engine, monoplane torpedo-bombers. However, neither was ready by September 1939.

Flying boats

Throughout the history of the service up to the end of WWII, including that of one of its precursors, the RNAS, the flying boats maintained an air presence when airfields suitable for large landplanes were not available because of the nature of the terrain or because of political limitations to their establishment. The flying boat found its own landing area and therefore was independent for a short time of fixed installations. However, for sustained operations a flying boat required extensive beaching and maintenance facilities.

For long-range operations over water the flying boat was preferred over the landplane because of its ability to take off with a greater all-up weight by taking advantage of large areas of water. However, the flying boat was aerodynamically less efficient than the landplane because the hull was a compromise between the needs of air and water.

Saunders Roe test flew its four-engine A33 flying boat that was designed to meet specification R2/33. The A33 had the high wing layout favoured by Sikorsky with the fuselage not integral with the wing and with sponsons in place of wing floats as used on the Martin M130 and the Boeing 314. The initial series of flight tests revealed poor water performance with porpoising and excessive wave forces on the sponsons. Eventually, a flight attempted in choppy sea conditions ended in failure of the wing and with one of the propellers piercing the hull. That was the last outing for the A33. The Lerwick was also being flight tested in Autumn 1938. It too tended to porpoise and it also produced a bow wave that struck the propellers. The rudder loads were excessive and the take-off in even a benign sea was too long unless the operational load were reduced. Even if it got off the water the cruising speed was 12 knots below the 'paper' performance.

Short Sunderland

The flying boat chosen to enter Coastal Command service in 1938 was the Sunderland. It was the largest of the new type entering the Command at that time and it also continued the RAF flying boat tradition.

The structural technology used for the Sunderland was derived from Short Brothers experience with the C Class four-engine, monoplane, civil flying boat. Like the A33 it was designed to meet the requirements of Specification R2/33 for a long-range flying boat. It was intended from the start to have power-operated, multi-gun, turrets. The 'sting' in the tail was the Nash and Thompson four-gun turret. Within the current upward march of technology the Sunderland represented a significant step. In place of the part fabric covered biplanes, such as the Singapore III, the Sunderland was an all-metal monoplane. Without doubt Short Brothers successfully moved from the mixed metal, wood and fabric era into the all-metal age and developed a range of large flying boats having excellent sea-keeping qualities as well as the ability to stay on patrol for many hours. The deep hull provided ample room for a galley and rest bunks for the crew. There was also room to house the 2,000 lb bomb load internally. The bomb racks could be winched out under the wings from their stowage position in the hull. Like all flying boats, the Sunderland's apparent strength was deceptive. The planing bottom was clad with duralumin less than 2mm thick. Therefore, great care was needed when trying to alight in heavy seas. A stall following a bounce could result in failure of the hull and the loss of the aircraft.

Short Sunderland four-engine flying boat that entered service with Coastal Command in the summer of 1938. (Derek James)

The Sunderland, which was progressing well, the A33 and the Lerwick, which were not, were being developed against the ominous background of Imperial Airways continuing loss of its passenger flying boats from various causes.

Anson Replacement – the Hudson

In 1938 it was apparent that a replacement for the Anson was required urgently. To this end Air Commodore A.T. Harris led a purchasing mission to the USA. The Air Ministry had come to accept that the expansion of the service could not be achieved without help from outside the UK.

The purchasing commission looked at the Lockheed Model 214. This was based on the successful civil airliner the Super Electra in service with a number of airlines, including British Airways. It had the potential as a general reconnaissance aircraft for Coastal Command. Lockheed's order book was nearly empty therefore the Burbank plant in California responded eagerly to the commission's interest and built a mock-up of the proposed type 214 in five days. After inspecting the mock-up and studying the Lockheed proposal documents an order was immediately placed for 250 aircraft. However the 214 had to be modified to meet RAF requirements. For example the civil type, two-pilot, cockpit was altered to a single pilot's position. This was on the port side, as with the majority of new aircraft types in the RAF. The navigator's position in the mock-up, abaft the cockpit, had inadequate views outward for a general reconnaissance aircraft therefore it was moved to the nose. The wireless operator's position was placed behind the pilot and the fuselage structure was redesigned to provide a large hole for a dorsal turret.

Of particular interest, in the light of the re-armament programme, was the decision to accept Hudsons minus much of their operational equipment. One reason for this was the absence of suitable power-operated multi-gun turrets in the United States. Also, on arrival in the UK, the aircraft were fitted with RAF type radios and other equipment special to British practice.

One condition in the contract for the supply of 214s was that they had to be referred to as 'training aircraft' in order to comply with United States policy relating to the provision of warplanes to a foreign power. The 214 became the Hudson and enabled Coastal Command to take the war to the enemy with much effect during the early months of WWII.

The contract awarded Lockheed in June 1938 was one of the largest placed by Britain in America.[15] The Society of British Aircraft Constructors (SBAC) sent a strongly worded protest to the government over the purchase of airframes and engines from the USA. It argued that the orders should have been placed in Britain. The SBAC was also engaged in an acrimonious debate over whether or not Australia be allowed to set up its own aircraft industry.

NA-16 Harvard

In addition to the 214, the purchasing commission selected the North American NA-16 to fulfil the advanced, 'single-engine' training aircraft requirement. This was done to avoid being dependent on just the Miles Master.

The purchasing commission's interest in the NA-16 was strengthened by the knowledge that several versions of the NA16 had been delivered or were on order for Australia and the air services of the USA as well as for those of other countries. The production line was well established and the commission was satisfied that once an order was placed the aircraft could be delivered quickly. At about £10,000 each the NA16 was not the cheapest among the aircraft types being considered as an advanced trainer. The initial order was for 200 of the 1E version. The Commonwealth Aircraft Corporation of Australia ordered 40 North American NA16s, the majority of which would be built under licence in Australia.

NA16s were delivered to No 3 FTS at Grantham in June 1939 and given the service name of Harvard. They become a familiar sight and a familiar sound at other FTSs. The ungeared propeller achieved high tip speeds that produced a harsh and distinctive sound.

The orders for the Hudson and the Harvard were important not just for the RAF but for the USA. They revitalised two American companies and enabled them to expand in time to meet the tremendous demand for aircraft in World War II.

Transport aircraft

In the other half of the RAF, the overseas squadrons, Valentia biplane bomber-transports were still in the first line of the Order of Battle. Although they performed many different tasks with some degree of effectiveness, the RAF was not gaining experience from the operation of all-metal, monoplane transport aircraft able to carry heavy loads over long distances. The only transport aircraft of more advanced technology and performance were the Bombay and the Harrow. However they were deficient when it came to 'load flexibility'. They could carry a number of soldiers along with their rifles and packs but larger and more bulky loads, such as field guns and mules, could not go easily through the narrow access doors.

Had the expected war started in 1938 then the RAF would have had no suitable transport aircraft either to meet its own needs or those of the army. There were also few communication aircraft. The DH 89M Rapide lost out to the Anson when competing for the general reconnaissance contract. The Rapide (Mk I) was then ordered as a trainer for the Electrical and Wireless Schools and as a communications aircraft (Mk II). Up to ten passengers or a ton of freight could be carried but no bulky loads because at its maximum cross section the cabin was only 4′ 3″ wide by 5′ high and the door 2′ 6″ wide by 4′ 6″ high.

The RAF needed the equivalent of the Ju52 or a version of the DC-3. In the event of war there were plans for the impressment of civil aircraft. However, little was done to encourage the design of a versatile transport aircraft that would have been of great

Hampden cockpit. The high set position of the basic six-instrument panel and the control wheel relative to the lower edge of the forward windows emphasises the extremely good view afforded the pilot. A small detail is the rather crude mechanical interlock between the engine ignition switches and the undercarriage control (left-middle). (Crown Copyright)

value to all three services. One of the reasons for this dreadful omission can be found in Trenchard's doctrine that the RAF should not invest in types of aircraft which might be used as an ancillary service by the army and the Royal Navy. Another was the lack of interest in the development of civil land planes from which airforce transports might have been derived.[16]

Incidents and accidents

As the RAF expanded there were more aircraft and increased flying hours. In consequence the number of incidents and accidents increased in proportion. As in the previous year they prompted questions by MPs and editors.

Attention was given to the lack of 'blind flying' instruments. One of C.G. Grey's targets for criticism was the Royal Aircraft Establishment at Farnborough. He accused it of obstructing the development of blind flying instruments. He proposed that no new equipment for the RAF be given to the establishment because its predominantly left wing staff would always sabotage progress. Only many years later would C.G. Grey's very pro-right-wing opinions come to light. To some extent the

Cockpit of a Gladiator. This is the 'Sea' version but in general is typical of 1930s design. The bilges are in full view, ready to trap any rubbish, including tools. There is the standard RAF panel of six essential flight instruments, an aperiodic compass between the pilot's legs and an optical reflector gunsight with range and enemy wingspan setting controls. (Shuttleworth)

development of the useful Basic Six Panel of instruments refuted Grey's criticism of the RAE.

In August 1938 the C-in-C Bomber Command wrote to the Under-Secretary of State at the Air Ministry emphasising the need for formalised cockpit drills that would reduce the number of mistakes made by pilots. The C-in-C Mediterranean went further and urged that aircraft designers adopt a standard arrangement of engine controls for all aircraft. The RAF Basic Six Panel of instruments was standard for all first-line aircraft and for the Oxford twin-engine trainer. However the Air Ministry decided that its funds did not allow it to retrofit the older types of aircraft with the standard panel.

CHAPTER FIVE

1938/II

Fearful preparation in September 1938, with war expected any day, was matched by urgent gathering of the RAF's strength. An all-out assault on Britain from the air was everyone's expectation. The nation was resigned to waking up to a scene from the film of H. G. Wells Things To Come *with cities silent, smoking and buildings ruined.*

Munich

Together the two allies had a formidable navy. The French had a large and well-equipped army. However, it was anticipated that the war would open in the air. The French airforce was good in parts but overall was weak. It did not have a sufficient number of fighter squadrons equipped with high-performance aircraft. Also, it did not have an effective system of radar. Therefore the greater burden of defending the eastern border of France against bomber raids and chasing off reconnaissance aircraft would fall on the RAF.

In war the RAF could be faced with a demand for a wider range of air operations than those envisaged at the start of the expansion programme. For example, no provision was made to provide anti-submarine air-escorts for merchant ships. Twenty years earlier air-escorts had proved effective in deterring submarine attacks. However, neither Coastal or Fighter commands had sufficient aircraft in 1938 to provide both offensive, deterrent and reconnaissance operations. At the insistence of the Admiralty, Coastal Command proposed to concentrate on reconnaissance with emphasis on finding the German Fleet and commerce raiders should they venture out. Therefore Coastal Command Ansons practised interception of ships passing from the North Sea into the Atlantic. The operations room at the command's Bircham Newton station went on 24 hour watch.[1]

If the second great German war had started in late 1938 the RAF would have only had 93 eight-gun fighters. Most of the Hurricanes had only two-blade, fixed-pitch propellers and were without their

The Lockheed Electra used by Prime Minister Neville Chamberlain in 1938 to fly to Germany to negotiate with Hitler. A similar aircraft was used by Sidney Cotton for covert photographic sorties over Germany before WWII. (Derek James)

Hurricanes of No 17 Squadron. Note the two-blade, fixed-pitch propellers and the airmen using the hand-cranked starting gear. (Aeroplane Monthly)

full complement of eight guns. The eight-gun Spitfires had only just arrived at 19 Squadron Duxford and were not fully operational. One authority gives the strength of Fighter Command in October 1938 as 406 first-line aircraft in 29 squadrons.[2]

With only five of the 29 squadrons equipped with Hurricanes and the sector control organisation limited to the east and south-east coasts, Fighter Command was still not up to strength. The command needed more aircraft and extensions of CH radar coverage.[3] In addition to the Hurricanes the RAF had a few hundred obsolescent biplanes to stem the expected assaults by over 500 German bombers. There were also 17 squadrons of Blenheim medium bombers. Each could be modified to become a fighter equipped with five fixed, forward-firing, 7.7mm guns plus the single gun in the turret.[4]

September war preparations

Indicative of the change from peace towards war conditions was the order from the Air Ministry to all fighter squadrons: 'Use the wing span dimensions of German aircraft for range estimation'.[5] This referred to the scale at the base of the reflector sight against which a rotating mark could be set by the pilot to correspond to the wingspan of the target aircraft.

Among other preparations for war were the important full-load fuel consumption test flights by Blenheim squadrons. These made medium-range sorties across the North Sea. They also took part in exercises by flying out to sea and then turning back to simulate hostile bombers.

The gun turret of the Blenheim continued to give mechanical trouble and it was not being used effectively by air gunners because of their lack of experience. The training of observers and gunners was still not fully organised and there was a shortage of specialised training equipment. Even though it was out of date the TR9B radio-telephone, hitherto reserved for fighters, was being issued to some bomber squadrons.

Post-mortem

The rapid deployment in the spring and the stand-to in September at the time of the 1938 Munich crisis passed. There was a breathing space before the next international crisis. However, although the British public relaxed the airforce could not. The faults and shortcomings of the period of intense activity, with the service expecting to be at war within a few hours, were studied and eliminated wherever possible in the October exercises. The chain of radar stations was increased from three to five.

Sir Maurice Dean, Private Secretary to the Chief of the Air Staff in the late 1930s, listed the reasons why Britain did not go to war in 1938 as:[6]

1. Re-equipment of Fighter Command had barely begun.
2. The radar chain was half completed.
3. Of the forty-five fighter squadrons deemed necessary at the time only twenty-nine were mobilised and all but five were obsolete.
4. The five modern fighter squadrons could not fire their guns above 15,000 feet.

The last item highlights the difficulty of ensuring that every aspect of aircraft design and operation advanced in step with all the others.

One outcome of the post-mortem on the year's exercises and the stand-to in September 1938, was a suggestion by the Air Staff that fighter aircraft be fitted with guns able to fire upwards at an angle. The suggestion was not followed up; although four guns in the Defiant's turret could be elevated when attacking an aircraft from below. Later an experimental version of the Mosquito was equipped with a mock-up of a dorsal gun turret that included upward arcs of firing. The two requirements, turret-fighter and night-fighter, prompted a number of proposed aircraft designs.[7]

Cockpit of a MkI Spitfire. A ring sight has been fitted to the reflector sight mounting. The black lever on the right is the hand-operated pump for raising and extending the undercarriage and the flaps. This required the pilot to change hands on the controls after take-off. Although it was criticised at the time, other companies also tried to get away with this arrangement. (Vickers)

The records of the aircraft companies from the 1930s include many examples, sometimes a dozen or more, of innovative fighter aircraft designs. Tricycle undercarriages, twin-boom arrangements, pusher propellers, and 12 guns or more. Out of the plethora of schemes only one or two proceeded as far as a flying prototype. There were many reasons for having to abandon what seemed at the time to be the answer to all the Air Ministry's hopes. A stumbling block might be the unavailability of a suitable engine type or guns. There was also the question of fitting a new type, particularly a revolutionary one, into the overall structure of the RAF. There were the training of maintenance personnel and the provision of specialised support equipment to be considered.

Hawker Hurricane

A detailed description of the Hurricane published in the technical press included an interesting comment on the two-blade, fixed-pitch, propeller.

> Many had expressed surprise that the Hurricane was not fitted with variable-pitch airscrews (sic). The answer is that it has such a tremendous reserve of power that even with the airscrew stalled at the beginning of the take-off run the acceleration is reasonably good, and the wooden airscrew is, of course, a great deal lighter.

'Reasonably good' was not good enough for a fighter which had to be capable of getting into the air as quickly as possible. Fortunately the splined output shaft of the Merlin engine could accept a metal, three-blade, variable-pitch propeller when they became available.

A comment on the operational use of Hurricanes referred to 'patrolling for invading bombers'. This was related to the ability of the Hurricane to patrol 'on very little throttle', thereby conserving fuel. Apart from the help of radar, to avoid standing patrols, which could not be disclosed, the comment on 'little throttle' was misleading. Going for maximum miles per gallon flying at low revolutions could result in the generator failing to meet the demands of the electrical system.

The Hawker design team did not use, as some other companies did, the all-metal stressed skin form of construction. They applied the latest ideas in aerodynamics to the type of structure with which they were familiar: metal frame with wooden formers and stringers covered by fabric. Had they gone for stressed-skin then the designing and production of the necessary tools and jigs would have delayed output. The method of construction used for the Hurricane may be compared with that of the Spitfire: the former metal-framed, fabric-covered (the forward fuselage was all-metal); the latter virtually all-metal. It took 170,000 man-hours of design, development and modification time to get the Hurricane ready for squadron service. The Spitfire took 300,000 man-hours. Another set of statistics compared the two aircraft on the basis of the effort needed in design hours per each pound of weight: 60 for the Hurricane, 150 for the Spitfire.[8]

Concern was expressed over the resistance of the fabric covering to speeds in excess of 300 mph. Hawkers were confident that the special method adopted to trap the fabric by a metal strip, secured by bolts in channels formed for the purpose in the structure, was acceptable. The article in *Flight* magazine noted that the fabric covering had given no trouble. However after further experience gained in squadron service the fabric wings were replaced by an all-metal version.

Flight's contemporary comments on the Hurricane suggested that pilots new to the aircraft had found no difficulty in handling it after a 'brief' training on Miles Magisters. It acknowledged that the aircraft had to be treated with respect; particularly as it very rapidly picked up speed in a dive. The contemporary biplane fighters had plenty of built-in drag in the shape of struts and rigging wires, as well as a fixed undercarriage, and therefore did not go 'downhill' at the same rate. The reference to 'brief training on the Magister' was written without the knowledge that many of the new high-performance aircraft, including the Master, could 'get away' from their pilots. There was therefore an urgent need to get the Master and the Harvard into the training schools.

Night fighting

Of the many shortcomings highlighted by the Munich crisis one of the more important was the continuing lack of a high performance, heavily armed, fighter able to operate against enemy bombers flying at night. Already mentioned, the realisation that at night and when there was overall cloud cover, the defences would be 'blind' once an aircraft had passed over the coastal-located Chain Home stations. There was also a need for a long-range fighter able to penetrate enemy airspace. The Beaufighter had yet to fly.

The tension and heightened preparations for war highlighted the absence of an effective night fighting force in Fighter Command. The Hurricane squadrons took part in night exercises but without an effective system of target finding at night these were limited in their success. The 'biplane' squadrons tried to improvise night fighting techniques and equipment. Even though, for example, the Furys of Nos 1 and 43 Squadrons at Tangmere did not have navigation lights and were not equipped for night flying. Each squadron was given two Hawker Demon two-seat fighters for night flying. These were used for night operations pending the equipping of the Furys with a lighting system adapted from bicycle lamps. This was a local squadron modification. Irrespective of whether or not the biplane fighters were able to operate at night, they were not fast enough to catch the Blenheims playing the part of the 'enemy' in exercises.

Cathode ray tube

The cathode ray tube (CRT), at that time usually only to been found in a laboratory or television set, was acquiring an increasingly important place in the technology of the RAF. It was the primary display component of the radar chain and of the fighter HF/DF system. It was also part of the experimental airborne radar sets for detecting ships and other aircraft. The demand for CRTs to meet the needs of the RAF, let alone for the Royal Navy and for the army, was met by the radio industry. Fortunately the industry already had CRT production lines for domestic television sets following the start of the BBC's television service in 1936.[9]

Although the radio industry had been organised to ensure the production of CRTs they and the airborne radar sets, of which they formed a vital part, would be useless without an adequate electrical supply. Already mentioned is the RAF's standard 28 volt 500 Watt engine-driven generator. In a twin-engine aircraft, such as the Blenheim, there was usually only a generator on one of the engines. Realising that something had to be done quickly E.G. Bowen persuaded Metropolitan Vickers to design an alternator which would fit onto the existing DC generator mounting on an engine. This became the standard alternator for British and many American aircraft throughout WWII, thereby ensuring that there would be adequate electrical power at the different voltages needed for airborne radar. This is an example of the importance of an apparently insignificant component to the success of a system.[10]

Filtering information

Between the time of the first echo of a hostile aircraft appearing on the CRT of a radar station and when a sector controller issued steering and height instructions to the intercepting fighters there was a complex analysis and filtering procedure. Essentially the problem was that of sorting out conflicting and irrelevant information. Therefore the complete fighter control system of Fighter Command was equipped with every possible electrical and mechanical device to speed information processing. As mentioned in Chapter One, the CH stations used an electro-mechanical device, the 'fruit machine', devised by G.A. Roberts of the Bawdsey research station. This rapidly converted an echo on a CRT to numerical co-ordinates of position. This system used the standard Post Officer Strowger Hudd rotary selectors used in automatic telephone exchanges. The co-ordinates and other data were transmitted to a filter room, filtered and passed upward to the Command and Group fighter control rooms. After further analysis, the track and height of the hostile raid were passed to a sector operations room to be displayed on the 'table'. The sector controller then issued course and height instructions to the interceptors. The target to which the scientists and the RAF operations staff were working was two minutes between an echo appearing on the CRT of a CH station and the raid symbols being placed on a sector table.

Albemarle

When the Bristol Aeroplane Company schemed a replacement for the Blenheim, they chose a tricycle undercarriage to simplify landing and taxying. The majority of service aircraft had tail-wheels that required a particular set of ground handling procedures. A tricycle undercarriage aircraft could be moved nose first by attaching the tow bar to the nose leg.

The Bristol Type 155 also included a ventral and a dorsal turret, each with twin 20mm guns even though the successful development of the turrets was not certain.

Before the Type 155 could proceed further than the drawing board the Air Ministry and industry considered that in the event of war there would be a shortage of skilled labour and special alloys. Therefore Specification B18/38 was issued in September 1938 for a twin-engine medium bomber similar to the Type 155 whose construction would minimise the use of materials that might become difficult to get in war conditions. The Bristol design was re-worked to allow for rapid production and the minimum use of special alloys and skilled labour. However on the 9 November responsibility for the design and development was transferred to Armstrong Whitworth and the design reclassified as a reconnaissance bomber. Extensive use was made of welded steel tubes and plywood so that a wide range of sub-contractors, including, as with trainer aircraft, furniture manufacturers. The resulting Armstrong Whitworth AW 41 was a twin-engine design powered by two Bristol Hercules XIs each of 1,590 hp. An alternative engine type was the Rolls-Royce Merlin. It was intended to carry 1,500 lb of bombs at 320 mph at 20,000ft out to a target 750 miles away. Defensive armament was concentrated in a four-gun dorsal turret. The ventral turret of the Type 155 was deleted.

Bristol Hercules 14-cylinder sleeve-valve engine for the new generation of 'heavy' bombers and the Beaufighter. (John Heaven)

A new company, A.W. Hawksley, was formed for development and to control production. The extensive changes that had to be made to the original design and subsequently by Hawksley delayed the aircraft's entry into squadron service until 1943 and then as a target tug and paratroop transport and called the Albemarle. It is a good example from the late 1930s of 'too many cooks' and lack of direction.

Martin-Baker MB 2

James Martin (later Sir James) ventured nearly £30,000 on the design and building of a prototype 'easy-to-maintain' eight-gun fighter. This was the MB 2 designed to meet the requirements of specification F5/34. It flew for the first time on 3 August 1938. To justify the appellation 'easy-to-maintain' Martin incorporated a number of innovative details such as good access to the guns, easily removable fuel tanks and easy access to the back of the instrument panel. Unfortunately for Martin-Baker the MB 2 did not meet with the approval of the Martlesham Heath test pilots. The aircraft was also handicapped by having to use a Napier Dagger III engine and not, as intended, the more powerful Merlin. With the Merlin engine it was expected to match the performance of the Hurricane and Spitfire as well as carrying eight 7.7mm guns.

Martin Baker MB 2 was an attempt to design an eight-gun fighter with a performance comparable with that of the Hurricane but of simpler construction and with emphasis on ease of servicing and maintenance. (Martin Baker)

Short four-engine bomber

Shorts built a half-scale flying prototype in 1938 to determine the handling characteristics of the full-size aircraft then being designed to meet specification B12/36. This would become the Stirling.

In the meantime Vickers were having trouble with the structure of the production version of the Wellington. There had been a number of changes to the shape of the fuselage and much re-designing of structural components. A not uncommon problem at the time related to the method adopted by the designer to reduce the effect of air-loads on the elevators. Should they be aerodynamically balanced using inset hinges or horn balances, or have servo-tabs to reduce the load on the pilot's arms? Vickers were in dispute with the RAE whose aerodynamacists favoured inset-hinge balancing. Throughout its life the Wellington exhibited a significant change of longitudinal trim when the flaps were lowered or raised. All the doubts and changes of mind delayed the introduction of the aircraft into squadron service.

Westland Whirlwind

F37/35, with which the Westland Whirlwind complied, was one of 41 specifications issued in 1935 by the Air Staff as part of a concerted effort to advance aircraft technology. F37/35 was, for its time, significant because it specified an armament of four 20mm guns. The emphasis on a greater weight of armament, either as number of guns or in calibre, reflected the universal move toward larger all-metal fighters with the required room and strength.

The remarkable Westland Whirlwind flew for the first time in October 1938. The adjective 'remarkable' is used deliberately. W.E.W. Petter maximised

Cockpit of a Westland Whirlwind. For its time, the instruments and controls were mostly positioned to a logical arrangement. The windscreen frame and the one-piece blown plastic canopy afforded the pilot all round arcs-of-view. (Derek James)

the potential of two engines in a small elegant airframe and introduced a number of unusual features. For example, extensive use was made of thick magnesium for the monocoque fuselage and the radiators were integral with the leading edge of the wing. Another interesting feature was the one-piece blown 'bubble' cockpit canopy which afforded the pilot a wide field of view. The nose housed the four 20mm guns required by the specification where there was plenty of room for the ammunition drums and easy access for armourers.

However, not all the Whirlwind's advanced details and equipment were without criticism. Servicing personnel found many things to complain about. The hydraulic and pneumatic systems were particularly difficult to maintain in good order; twelve man-hours were needed to change one wheel; the Exactor hydraulic engine controls, as in other aircraft types, were difficult to maintain and were also disliked by pilots. The exhaust from each engine was ducted internally through the fuel tanks to the rear of the nacelle. This arrangement was viewed with some reservations because of the proximity of the hot ducting to the fuel tanks and to the aileron control rod. The one-piece high-lift Fowler flaps that extended from aileron to aileron were interconnected with the radiator flow control flaps. Although most new aircraft required some changes and adjustments following the first flight, the Whirlwind needed many changes to improve the aerodynamics and handling.

Rolls-Royce produced a new V-12 engine for the Whirlwind based on the Kestrel. The 860 hp Peregrine was a compact design matching the fine lines of the nacelles but was plagued by problems. There was also the problem for Rolls-Royce of having to provide for another production line when it was already committed to the Merlin and the development of the new 24-cylinder Vulture.

There was even a proposed 12-gun version of the Whirlwind. However the idea got no further than a mock-up of the nose. It had to be larger than the original in order to accommodate twelve 7.7mm guns and 6,000 rounds.

A comment by a Westland manager indicated that:

> although the Whirlwind had great potential its engines never came up to expectation; there was also a lack of effort and understanding by the production staff of what was needed to progress from a prototype to a production aircraft; and there were too many new ideas tried in one new aircraft design.

Nevertheless, considering that design work started in 1935, figuratively amid a generation of single-engine fighters of which many were biplanes, Westland made a significant contribution towards advancing aircraft design in general.

Engine developments

The development of engines of at least 1,000 horsepower, as already noted, was essential for the fighters and bombers of the expansion programme in the 1930s. The British aero-engine industry had only been able to devote time to engine development since 1926. Before that year the demand for engines for the RAF and for the airlines was too small to justify investment in other than modest research projects. Already mentioned was the contribution made by the Schneider Trophy competition to the development of powerful engines. The development of suitable engines for the new generation of aircraft was being undertaken by five companies: Rolls-Royce, Bristol, Armstrong Siddeley, Napier and de Havilland. Of these only Rolls-Royce and Bristol before 1939 were able to develop engines of 1,000 hp or more; although Napier had great hopes for its projected 2,000 hp Sabre 24-cylinder 'H' liquid-cooled engine.

Increased power could not be achieved just by increasing cylinder swept volume, boost pressure, by minimising obstruction of inlet and exhaust gas flow and using higher octane number fuel. Better lubricating oils had to be found and the metallurgists had to contribute stronger and lighter metals for crankshafts, connecting rods and pistons. Nickel-chrome steel became an important element. Important components not developed sufficiently to match the new high-power engines were ignition systems and spark plugs. The latter had been improved very little over those used in WWI. Those available in 1938 were not fully resistant to the effects of higher combustion chamber temperatures and 100 octane fuel.

The new 1,000 hp engines enabled the aircraft companies to meet the demands for high-speed fighters and large, twin-engine, bombers; the latter able to carry 3 to 4,000 lb bomb loads for 1,000 miles or more. This reflected the fact that the design factors mentioned above had all reached roughly the same stage throughout the engine world. Interestingly the principal German V-twelve and the 9 and 14-cylinder air-cooled radials were within the same 800 to 1,000 hp bracket of British engines. In one important respect German engines differed from their British counterparts. This was the use of direct fuel injection. Injecting the fuel directly into each individual cylinder was considered by the Germans to be better than the alternative of using a carburettor system. One drawback of the Rolls-Royce Merlin, when used in fighters, was the tendency to cut-out when subjected to negative G; such as in an aerial dual. Fuel-injection had been tried in Britain. The Bristol engine company developed a direct injection fuel system for the experimental 9-cylinder Draco radial of 1932. (The 8-cylinder Antoinette engine of 1908 also had direct fuel injection.)

Two-stage superchargers

The RAE had been at the forefront of supercharger development. The two-stage supercharger was essential for high altitude operations; as demonstrated in 1937 by Bristol. The Armstrong Siddeley Tiger VIII engine, fitted to Whitley IIs, was the first in RAF service to have been equipped with two-stage superchargers. It could develop 845 hp for take-off and 780 hp at 14,000 feet. In 1938 AW was developing a 21-cylinder, three-row radial engine, the Deerhound, intended to deliver 1,500 hp.

In the years immediately after the WWI the RAE had investigated the feasibility of adapting the exhaust gas-driven turbine to aero-engine supercharging. The Air Ministry showed little interest. The development of exhaust-driven turbo-superchargers continued in the USA where they were installed in experimental high altitude bombers and in the P-6E and P-30 fighters.

The Air Ministry tended not to take sides when considering the relative merits of in-line liquid cooled engines and air-cooled radial types. However, by 1935 a preference emerged for close-cowled, liquid-cooled, in-line engines for fighter aircraft. This may have been a subjective impression that suggested an in-line engine with separate coolant heat exchangers (radiators) caused less drag than a radial air-cooled type. In reality a carefully designed air-cooled engine with aerodynamically contoured cowling would produce no more drag than a liquid-cooled in-line engine when the drag of the latter's heat exchangers was included.

On the subject of engine drag, a small but important design feature was coming into production for fighters. This was the ducted, thrust-producing, heat exchanger. By enclosing the radiator block in a carefully shaped duct its drag was offset by the thrust of the exiting heated air; the energy of which was increased during its passage through the matrix of the radiator. Both the Hurricane and the Spitfire were fitted with the thrust-producing radiators; with the former aircraft the oil-cooler matrix was integral with the main radiator block. Irrespective of the competing merits of liquid and air-cooled engines, the principal concern was to avoid unnecessary delays to aircraft production should a particular type prove unsuitable. Therefore Rolls-Royce, Bristol and Napier were encouraged to develop high-powered engines for both fighters and bombers. Also aircraft companies were required to design for alternative engines.

The Bristol engine company adopted an entirely different approach to the design of high-powered engines when compared with Rolls-Royce. In 1927 they started to develop the Burt-McCollum sleeve-valve mechanism as an alternative to the poppet-valve. Four sleeve-valve engine types were developed during the 1930s culminating in 1938 with the 890 hp 9-cylinder Perseus, the 14-cylinder 1,400 hp Hercules, the 14-cylinder 1,130 hp Taurus and the smaller 600 hp 9-cylinder Aquila for civil aircraft. Subsequently the Hercules became, along with the R-R Merlin, the power backbone of the RAF. Armstrong Whitworth was not able, through force of circumstances and Air Ministry policy, to achieve 1,000 hp with the 14-cylinder Tiger in production for the Whitley.

The Society of British Aircraft Constructors looked into the feasibility of having a set of standard design details applied by the different engine manufacturers that would permit unrestricted interchangeability among engines of similar power. This study was at the instigation of the Air Ministry which was always looking at schemes that would avoid too many eggs in one basket in the event of war.

Co-operation on design standards and practices was not, as might have been expected, a feature of the aircraft engine industry as a whole. Each company tended to be secretive about important design details and production techniques. This had some unfortunate results. For example, had Bristols allowed Napiers to adopt their sleeve-valve barrel design then the Sabre engine might not have been so troubled by lubrication problems in its early years.[11]

Propeller developments

Constant-speed propellers along with automatic boost and mixture controls were specified for the engines of all first-line aircraft. However, it took

Bristol Taurus 14-cylinder sleeve-valve engine. Applications included: Albacore, Beaufort, Gloster F.9/37. (John Heaven)

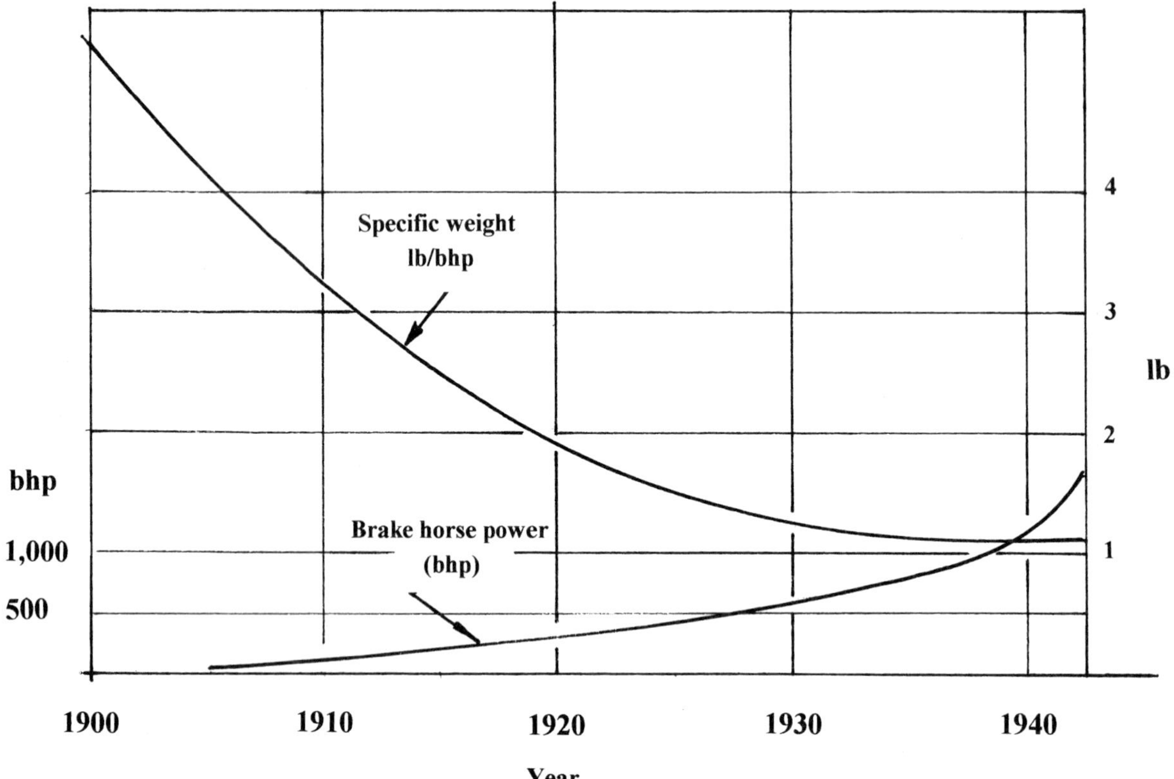

Engine Brake Horse Power & Specific Weight

time to implement these important standards. The Hurricanes and Spitfires joining Fighter Command at the end of 1938 had two-blade, fixed-pitch propellers that restricted their performance.

The variable-pitch propeller, from which derived the constant-speed type, was the result of parallel development work during the 1920s in Britain, the USA and Canada; albeit its origins were in the 19th century. Both hydraulically and electrically-operated mechanisms had been developed. The fixed-pitch propellers of the RAF's fighters may have been the result of a lack of foresight on the part of the Air Ministry. W.H. Barling of the RAE did development work on a variable-pitch four-blade propeller as early as 1915. However, by 1921 the work was shelved because the ministry argued that there was no benefit to be gained from variable-pitch. It considered that the improvement in performance offered was outweighed by the complexity and weight of the variable pitch mechanism; particularly as at that time the speed range of aircraft was only 2 to 1. However, by 1924 the speed range had expanded to make variable-pitch a more useful device.

Included in the 'experts' opposition was the personal animosity to Professor Hele-Shaw, the principal 'variable-pitch' innovator in Britain. As with Pollen when the Admiralty refused to recognise him as the true inventor of the navy's fire-control predictor system, some in the Air Ministry had an aversion to anyone who tried to make a profit out of innovation.

The 'variable-pitch' story was clouded by the fact that although 'experts' in the Air Ministry either deliberately delayed progress or were indifferent, others actively encouraged development because in 1924 industry was asked to submit designs for variable-pitch mechanisms. In 1926 Forsythe's hydraulically-operated constant-speed propeller was tested on a R-R Condor engine. Hele-Shaw and Beacham, co-inventors, described their variable-pitch propeller in a lecture at the Royal Aeronautical Society in 1928. Their reception was so hostile, particularly from representatives of the RAE and H.C. Watts of the Metal Propellers (fixed-pitch) company, that the aeronautical press was moved to comment on the unfairness of the audience.

As late as 1934 parts of the Air Ministry were still pursuing an anti variable-pitch policy. However attitudes changed when de Havilland obtained a licence in 1936 to make the Hamilton Standard variable-pitch propeller. The first DH variable-pitch propeller was bench tested on a Gipsy Six engine.[12]

Engine-control

The principal engine companies, in association with the accessory manufacturers, developed automatic boost and mixture controls. These essential accessories relieved a pilot of the need to watch constantly the boost pressure gauge and adjust the mixture controls during rapid changes of altitude. Along with constant-speed propellers, automatic mixture control (AMC) and automatic boost control (ABC) enabled a pilot to make the most effective use of an aircraft's engine or engines. In this respect the RAF was in advance of other airforces. For example, as late as 1942 American fighter pilots were having to keep a close watch on boost pressure; particularly during take-off. Interconnected throttle and pitch levers were evaluated in a Hurricane I. This modification included a 'pull-to-open' movement, as with French and Italian aircraft.[13]

In Germany at the time not only were engine designers moving away from the float chamber/carburettor in favour of direct-injection but were developing 'single-lever' control for the DB 601, Jumo 211 and the BMW 801. The one lever would integrate control of fuel flow, boost pressure, propeller pitch, and supercharger gear change.

Extended range operations

The usual method of extending the range of an aircraft was to carry more fuel by sacrificing some of the useful load of passengers, freight or bombs. However an airforce was usually reluctant to reduce an aircraft's nominal bomb load. Therefore a number of ideas were considered and even tried in flight, that would increase range without diminishing the useful load. Of these the Mayo Composite proved of considerable interest not only for air mail work but for bombers. The idea of launching one aircraft off the back of another had been demonstrated by Porte, of flying boat fame, in 1916 when a Bristol Scout was carried aloft by a flying boat. In 1935 the Air Ministry gave Short Brothers a contract to develop a 'composite' consisting of a four-engine seaplane carried on the back of a large flying boat.

In January 1938 the Mayo Composite consisting of *Maia* the lower component, and *Mercury*, the upper component, was tested at RAF Felixstowe, the Marine Aircraft Experimental Establishment. *Maia* was a modified version of the Short Empire class commercial flying boat. *Mercury* was a special long-range float plane designed to be carried into the air on the back of *Maia*. At the full operating load of fuel for 3,000 nautical miles and a useful payload, *Mercury* could not take off unaided. *Mercury* was released from *Maia* over Foynes on 21 July 1938 and reached Montreal in 22 hr 22 min. Although the payload was small, only 1,000 lb, nevertheless had *Mercury* been a bomber it could have struck a psychological and unexpected blow far into enemy territory.[14]

Alternatives to the Mayo were already being investigated at Farnborough: such as: catapult assisted take-off for the forthcoming heavy bombers: and in-flight re-fuelling. In-flight re-fuelling research had interested the RAE since 1924 and Sir Allan Cobham's Flight Refuelling company since 1932.

Specification B 1/35 for a heavy bomber originally

included provision for in-flight refuelling and when Vickers started on the design of the successor to the Wellington this requirement was taken note of. However, it was decided instead to increase the size of the fuel tanks and use more powerful engines.

In 1938 the Air Ministry requested Flight Refuelling Ltd (FRL) to study the possible benefits in performance and useful load. The Stirling was selected as an example aircraft. FRL reported that its take-off run would be significantly reduced and the initial climb rate improved. Bomb load and range could be increased. After take-off the Stirling would be 'topped-up' to bring the maximum take-off weight 15 per cent above the normal. If it was the intention to operate a squadron or even two squadrons of bombers from a common airfield then there were a number of serious problems to be overcome; apart from the difficulties of passing the hose at night from tanker to bomber. How were the tankers going to find the bombers? If a link-up was missed because of navigational and visibility problems the bombers might have to land back. Air exercises had demonstrated that the taking off and the landing of large numbers of aircraft at night posed a number of difficulties. Mayo had argued in 1932 that refuelling in the air was only a fair weather operation; his Composite was the better method.[15]

In January 1938 the Air Ministry loaned an AW 23 to Interair Ltd to try Flt Lt Atcherley's air refuelling system. The trials involved joining the AW 23 to an Imperial Airways flying boat by a hose through which fuel was transferred in flight. Although, ostensibly, the purpose of the experimental flights was to extend the range of the civil flying boat the co-operation of the Air Ministry indicated an interest in extending the range of bombers and flying boats.

While the trials with *Maia* and *Mercury* and in-flight refuelling proceeded, the Wellesleys of the Long-Range Development Unit (LRDU) attempted a 7,000 mile non-stop flight from Ismailia in Egypt to Darwin without any unusual aids.

The Pegasus XXII engines of the Wellesleys were fitted with long chord cowlings and automatic boost and mixture controls as well as constant-speed propellers. 100 octane fuel was used. Three aircraft took part in this notable endurance feat; particularly on the part of the crews. On 5 November 1938 the aircraft took off from Ismalia in the Canal Zone to fly to Australia. One aircraft flew non-stop for 7,162 miles to Darwin in 48 hours averaging 148 mph. The navigational skill displayed, over a route with only a few ground-based navigational aids, was all the more remarkable considering the generally low standard of navigation in the RAF at that time.

Balloon Command

The 1,000 or more balloons that were being produced for RAF Balloon Command, were little different in design from those of twenty years earlier. However there had been improvements to the design of the cable, so that it would part when struck so that its weight and inertia would cripple the colliding aircraft. Each balloon was tended by its handling crew, a powerful motor-winch truck and a trailer for the hydrogen gas cylinders. Each barrage balloon was large. It was 63 feet long and 31 feet high. The fabric and harness weighed 550 lb. When inflated it contained 20,000 cubic feet of gas and needed a handling crew of ten.

The 1936 experiments to determine cable dimensions and the possibility of including lethal devices, such as explosive charges, confirmed that the desired operating height of 15,000 feet could not be achieved. Therefore the balloon barrages were used as a deterrent to enemy aircraft flying below 5,000 feet.

Along with the fighter sectors, anti-aircraft gun batteries and the network of observer corps posts, the balloon barrages were a key element in the defence of the United Kingdom. Unfortunately London, for example, was defended by only 142 balloons instead of the planned 450.

The people of Britain, particularly in London, became used to seeing the RAF balloons. In many of the parks the RAF balloon barrage crews went about their interesting task of inflating and raising their ungainly charges. The other parts of Fighter Command were not in the public eye: the CH stations and the network of filter, operations and

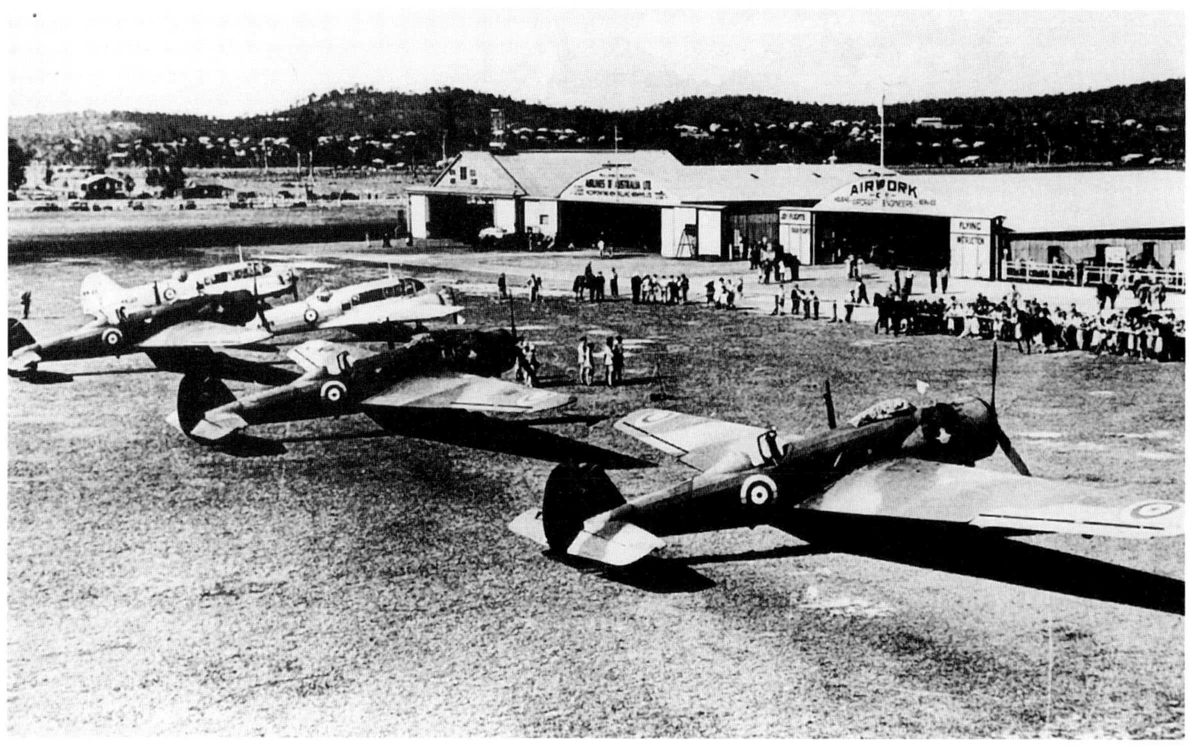

Long-range Wellesleys used for the Ismailia-Darwin record flight. (5-7 November 1938). Seen here during a subsequent tour of Australia. (Derek James)

sector rooms were out of sight. Fighter Command's other 'eyes', the Observer Corps posts were either out in the country or on top of tall buildings and therefore not usually seen by the public. There was a mood of great determination throughout the service. Calibration exercises were arranged for the Observer Corps. Some of them took place at night so that the observers could develop their aural techniques for estimating the height, heading and type of aircraft. However, except between Croydon and the east coast, there were few opportunities to listen for German aircraft.

Curate's egg

At the end of 1938, the RAF became less like the curate's egg. The production of first-line aircraft in Britain had advanced to within 42 per cent of that of Germany and of all types to 54 per cent.

Chapter Six

1939/I

At the beginning of 1939 the expansion programme accelerated even faster as the international situation became even more hopeless. Few had any confidence that war could be avoided.

War tomorrow

Those who had been working to the different 'war in 20, 10 or 5 years' plans had to adapt quickly to a new scenario that assumed war could start at any time. Even were it postponed, the autumn of 1940 was the foreseeable limit. The Air Ministry, the Air Staff, commands, stations and squadrons were all well aware of the need to complete, as soon as possible, preparations for a fierce air war. However, despite the imminence of war, there were still many things that needed to be done or provided. As Germany seized Czechoslovakia on 15 March, the shadow factories were approaching their maximum production rates and the radar stations were on 24-

In May 1939 Members of Parliament visited RAF Northolt to see for themselves how the money they had voted for was being spent. In the foreground a Fairey Battle with a Hurricane in the background. (Aeroplane Monthly)

hour watch looking seawards for 120 miles over arcs of 120 degrees. In March, squadron identification markings were painted out and the national markings made less conspicuous. Squadrons were identified by code letters. Aircraft were dispersed away from the inviting targets of large hangars, even though hangars and buildings were covered with netting to break up their outlines.

Future needs

Although both the four 20mm-gun fighter and the four-engine bomber were established programmes, their progress towards production at a rate which would match an assumed attrition rate was an unknown factor. Particularly when related to the uncertainty over exactly when the second German War would start. However, it is important to note, in the light of criticism at the time and some histories, that aircraft production in the UK by 1939 had at least equalled that of Germany.[1]

The supply of 20mm guns from the Grantham factory of the British Manufacturing and Research Company was uncertain at the beginning of 1939. Therefore, although there were a number of promising '20mm-gun' fighter prototypes and proposed designs, such as the Gloster F9/37, see below, the problems of 20mm gun production prompted concentration on fewer different types of aircraft. The prototype four 20mm-gun Beaufighter flew for the first time on 17 July.

Engines were also a problem at the beginning of the year. The Peregrine, for the Whirlwind four 20mm-gun fighter, and the Taurus for the Beaufort were delayed by production problems. The engines were also alternative installations for the Gloster F9/37.

Gun sights

Another serious problem at the time was a shortage of Mk II reflector sights for Hurricanes and Spitfires. As mentioned, many aircraft had to be fitted with the old-fashioned ring-and-bead sight pending an improvement in the supply of reflector sights. Fortunately at the time of the Munich crisis of 1938 the Air Ministry persuaded Barr & Stroud to seek a production agreement with a foreign company. Goerz of Austria was selected and 700 Mk II sights were delivered before the start of WWII despite the *Anschluss* imposed by Germany on Austria.[2]

Gloster F9/37 proposed day and night 'heavy' fighter with provision for mounting up to five 20mm guns. This is the version with R-R Peregrine engines. (Derek James)

This is the version of the Gloster F9/37 with Bristol Taurus engines demonstrated before MPs at RAF Northolt in May 1939. Gloster proposed a derivative powered by R-R Merlin engines. (Derek James)

Spinning

Fatalities and injuries from crashes following persistent spins from reasonable heights as well as spins at low altitude, particularly when approaching to land or taking off, continued as in earlier years. Most, if not all, Service Flying Training Schools prohibited intentional spinning. One of the most important acceptance tests for a new type of aircraft was a thorough investigation of its stalling characteristics at different weights and CG position. The results of the spinning tests enabled the appropriate advice and instructions to be included in the Pilot's Notes for the type. When an NA 16 (later to be named Harvard) was delivered to the Aeroplane and Armament Experimental Establishment at Martlesham Heath for assessment it was equipped with a spin recovery parachute. N7000 was put through its paces by Sqn Ldr R. Cazalet and flight test observer R.P. Alston on 16 February 1939. It was put into a spin at 3,000 feet and allowed to make a few turns before the recovery parachute was streamed from the tail. This stopped the spin. Unfortunately, the parachute was then either released or broke away and, as often happened, the aircraft entered another spin. With only 1,500 feet in which to stop the spin the crew had no chance of escape once the Harvard started to spin at over 200 degrees per second

Presumably the spinning characteristics of the Harvard were not included in the discussions between the Purchasing Commission and the North American Company when the order was placed in 1938.

Aircrew training and experience

Already mentioned was the lack of night flying experience compared with day hours in pilots' and observers' log books. The reasons for this arose from a combination of causes. One was bad weather, particularly the severe winter of 1938/39, that curtailed both day and night flying. At some stations, night flying was restricted in order to avoid upsetting the local residents.

The lack of night flying hours among the pilots of many squadrons and the wide variation in skills between the senior pilots and those who had just joined, added to the reluctance of commanders to order night exercises. In any event night flying tended to disturb the domestic life of a station. Night flying was sometimes put off until the annual practice camp. In this respect the

North American Harvard trainer. Along with the Miles Master, the Harvard provided the important upward step in performance, leading to the first-line fighters such as the Spitfire and Hurricane. (Peter Ottery)

Cockpit of a Miles Master I advanced trainer. A considerable upward step in complexity from that of the Tiger Moth and the Magister but very close to that of the Hurricane and the Spitfire. (Miles Aircraft)

RAF tended to exhibit an ambivalent approach to war. As long as the expansion of technology, skills and experience could be limited to daylight then there was plenty of enthusiasm. Observers were not trained to a sufficient standard before joining a squadron. Wireless operators were given too much training in the theory of radio rather than concentrating on 'hands on' experience of maintenance and operating. Few had the opportunity of studying complete aircraft wiring systems so as to understand what went where and what did what.

Speed records

On 24 February 1939 Flt Lt H. Purvis piloted a special 'speed' version of the Spitfire to 408 mph.

The Speed Spitfire was assembled from components intended for the 48th production Spitfire Mk I. The attempt on the speed record started at the

The Speed Spitfire of 1939 with a four-blade, fixed-pitch propeller. In November 1940 the aircraft, as K 9834, was fitted with a standard Spitfire Merlin XII engine, cooling system and a three-blade Rotol, constant-speed, propeller. (Vickers Archives – Cambridge University Library)

end of 1937 after a special version of the Bf 109 had taken the record with an average speed of 380 mph. The 48th Spitfire, K9834, was diverted from the standard production line. Guns and their associated equipment, radio and other military items were left out. The skin was flush riveted and all joints filled. A skid replaced the tail wheel. The special cockpit canopy was much lower and more streamlined than the standard. Airframe and wing drag was reduced as much as possible. The standard wing span was reduced to 33 ft 8 in.

Rolls-Royce developed a special 2,000 hp 'speed' version of the Merlin with a modified and enlarged cooling system. Dissipating the tremendous heat developed at a boost pressure of over 2 Atm. (29 psi) at 3,200 rpm required trials with a number of different cooling systems; including using the main fuel tank as a heat sink. The standard Spitfire propeller was replaced by a special four-blade, fixed-pitch type.

Bomber Command problems

Sir Henry Tizard and his team of scientists studied the operational deficiencies of Bomber Command. The team visited a number of bomber stations at which the aircrews were asked to explain their problems. A wide range of subjects was discussed; such as finding the target, hitting the target and handling complex aircraft.

The Tizard tour, and subsequent analysis of many problems encountered by bomber crews, underlined the general unsatisfactory position of the command. The scientists, in view of the imminence of war, arrived late on the scene. Nevertheless they saw and heard enough to make a number of recommendations. These included improving navigational equipment and techniques, improving the defensive armament of aircraft and the need for a gyroscopically stabilised high altitude bomb sight. The last item, designated SABS Mk II, was in the final stages of development and proving at the RAE in September 1939.

Although future bombers would have conventional power-operated gun turrets consideration was given to the development of remotely-mounted and operated guns for bombers. Among the arrangements considered were guns on an arm projecting from the tail of an aircraft: another proposed locating guns in the rear of the engine nacelles.[4]

Beam guidance

The most damning sentence in the Tizard report on Bomber Command was in the opening paragraph:

> . . .with proper training it would be possible to be pretty certain of being within one's objective by a distance of ten to fifteen miles, even if one could not see the ground.

During the discussions with staff officers and with aircrew the suggestion was made that a radio beam might be directed to pass over a target and thereby provide guidance for a bomber. In view of the low standard of navigation, referred to in the report, the guiding beam idea needed urgent investigation.

Live bombs

In March 1939 Battles dropped live bombs during close-support exercises with the army. Diving in formation, each Battle released two 500 lb bombs. In another attack each aircraft dropped four 250 lb bombs. Unfortunately, England's special weather took part in the exercises forcing a reduction in the size of the formations so as to reduce the chance of collisions. The poor visibility also prevented some pilots from finding the target: one of the factors studied by the Tizard team. Blenheims were also used during the exercises with the army. They dropped 20 lb and 40 lb bombs.

Gun ships

A popular feature of American 'pulp' aviation magazines in the 1930s were illustrations and articles on the subject of the bomber escort. These were usually twin-engine aircraft carrying a number of guns and intended to fly in formation with bombers so as to protect them from attack.

The Wellington was one of a number of types considered as a potential heavily armed escort for bomber formations. Those who advocated such a role for the Wellington did not appear to have considered the tactical problems. For example, should the escort keep station on the wing of the formation or should it guard the tail? Or would attacking fighters ignore the escort? The alternative had already been demonstrated in Spain. This was for fighters to escort the bombers. The Defiant might have been adapted to the escort role if it had some forward-firing guns. The Air Staff was obviously concerned about the defence of bomber formations because it instructed the A&AEE to evaluate and report on the Seversky SEV-2PA 'Convoy Fighter'. Major Seversky piloted this two-seat, single-engine, all-metal, monoplane during some of the flights from Martlesham Heath. An A&AEE observer was in the gunner's cockpit. The A&AEE's own pilots flew the aircraft.

Although the SEV-2PA was advertised as a 'convoy fighter' neither the A&AEE nor Fighter Command had time in which to assess its effectiveness as an escort for a formation of bombers. It could be they were more interested in the aircraft's general performance and handling. It was a well endowed machine having a 1,100 horsepower Pratt & Whitney R-1830 Twin Wasp, using 100 octane fuel, driving a three-blade, constant-speed propeller. The top speed was about 50 mph slower than that of the Spitfire. However, the Seversky was designed to meet the American long-endurance requirement: speed and rate-of-climb, as with European fighter specifications, being of less importance. The advertised endurance of 11 hours at 236 mph was of particular interest as it indicated a fuel tank capacity of at least 330 gallons. Earlier, in 1935, Martlesham Heath had tested a Northrop long-range, monoplane, all-metal, light-bomber that gave a clear indication of the way aircraft design was developing.

First four-engine bomber

L7600 the prototype of the new Short four-engine bomber, to specification B12/36, made its first flight on the 14 May. Powered by the new Bristol Hercules II 1,375 hp engines the aircraft performed well and exhibited no serious handling problems. The landing back at Rochester airport presented no problems. However near the end of the landing run L7600 suddenly swerved to one side, the gawky undercarriage collapsed and the aircraft was destroyed. The cause of the disaster was attributed to the brakes seizing on one wheel.

When the half-size prototype was tested at the A&AEE Martlesham Heath in 1938 it was recommended that the wing angle of incidence relative to the fuselage fore and aft datum line be increased from 3.5 deg. to 7.5 deg. in order to keep the take-off and landing run distances within reasonable limits. Faced with having to re-design completely the wing/fuselage structure, the decision was taken to 'skate round' the problem. The solution adopted was that of lengthening the undercarriage legs. This solved the incidence problem at the expense of an absurdly, gawky, complicated and heavy undercarriage. The second prototype flew on 3 December 1939 with a re-designed undercarriage.

When the Stirling entered squadron service in August 1940 the ungainly undercarriage elected unfavourable comment, such as: 'Never had so many men, four engines and tons of metal been needed to carry such a heavy undercarriage so far.' It has been suggested that the Stirling had the wing of the Sunderland flying boat. This was the original intention. However when the Air Ministry stipulated that the aircraft had to fit inside a standard RAF hangar then the span had to be limited to 100 feet. Limitations were also placed on the size of the principal production elements so that they could be carried on the RAF's road vehicles.

The original version of the Stirling included three power-operated gun turrets: FN5 in nose, FN20A in tail and an FN25 ventral. Although the FN ventral turret went to war in the Whitley and Wellington it was removed from the Stirling before it entered squadron service. The FN25 was reported to be unreliable and cramped. Perhaps the main reason for removing the turret was to reduce drag. The Stirling was already handicapped in performance by having to carry a heavy and complicated undercarriage. Eventually a dorsal twin-gun turret was fitted. As with the Whirlwind, the Stirling was equipped with Exactor hydraulically operated throttles for the Hercules engines in place of the conventional rod or cable systems of other aircraft types. The system proved unsatisfactory in both aircraft.

The designer of the Stirling unfortunately did not anticipate that in the future the RAF would use bombs larger than 2,000 lb. The bomb bay was divided into short fore and aft compartments that eventually prevented the carrying of 'block busting' 4,000 lb bombs and the even larger types which were to follow.

Bombing ranges

At last the RAF received permission to establish bombing ranges on a large scale. Salisbury Plain, on which the army has been making explosions and firing live shells for 100 years, was denied the RAF until 1939. In the inter-war years landowners and rural authorities in general opposed the establishment of bombing and firing ranges. Hence the recourse to simulated bombing using the Hills Mirror: which also economised on bombs. However in those years there were no effective substitutes for live ammunition fired at real targets.

Grass and runways

The majority of service airfields were grass covered; only the 'aprons' in front of the hangars were of concrete or tarmacadam. 'Hard' runways had been advocated for some years but the Air Staff objected to their use because it made airfields too conspicuous.

A significant influence on aircraft design by the extensive use of grass surfaces was on tyre dimensions and inflation pressure. Tyre pressure was limited to 35 lb psi for operations from grass airfields. This meant that aircraft had to have 'balloon' tyres. In turn this restricted wheel diameter. With increasing aircraft weight the brake shoe area, severely restricted by the small wheels, was inade-

Whitley used by the Royal Aircraft Establishment to determine the maximum wheel loading for use on grass airfields. The aircraft was taxied with various loads carried on the steel structure mounted between the main undercarriage legs. (Derek James)

quate. This resulted in the brakes fading after a fast landing and heavy application of the brakes. Also the tyres crept round the wheel rims.

The new long-range bombers were designed for all-up weights exceeding 50,000 lb. The HP 57 prototype bomber, fitted with tyres inflated to 35 psi, was flown at an all-up weight of 55,000 lb. Eventually the HP 57, the Halifax, had tyres inflated to 55 psi to allow for a 50 per cent increase in all-up weight.

To investigate the effect of heavier tyre 'footprints' on grass surfaces the RAE conducted a series of tests. These involved the Whitley prototype fitted with a steel beam attached to the main undercarriage legs. The beam was loaded with steel plates to increase the footprint loading. The standard wheels of the Whitley were replaced by specially made oversize Dunlop wheels. The aircraft was taxied on grass at different weights. At 40,000 lb, nearly double the normal weight, the tyre tracks were six inches deep. Nevertheless the RAE concluded that operations from grass surfaces at that weight were feasible. However, someone in the Air Ministry had reservations and by 1939 nine RAF bomber stations had 'hard' runways or were about to complete their construction.

Fighter Aircraft

Gloster F9/37

A new twin-engine monoplane with twin fins and Bristol Taurus 14-cylinder, sleeve-valve engines was demonstrated in May 1939 to MPs at RAF Northolt. This was the Gloster F9/37 single-seat fighter. The fuselage was designed to accept mountings for 20mm Hispano guns. The guns were mounted at a positive angle of about 20 degrees. Apparently, this upward angle was not intended to facilitate attacking bombers from astern and below. It was necessary to allow the guns in the upper decking of the fuselage, behind the pilot, to fire over the top of the cockpit. A second prototype had R-R Peregrine engines. The aeronautical press was not able to find out much about the new aircraft and had to assume that it was a fighter.

Development of the Gloster twin-fin fighter was in parallel with that for the Bristol Beaufighter. At the time there was definitely room for two heavy twin-engine fighters in the airforce. This also acknowleged the overall policy of not putting all the eggs in one basket. The Gloster design team lead by W.G. Carter, like other teams, was able to produce a number of alternative arrangements of the principal aircraft components aimed at meeting the published specification. Production of the airframe was not anticipated to be a particulaly difficult task. Stressed skin monocoque fuselage and all-metal wings and empennage technology was sufficiently advanced to present no particular problems. However, engines were another matter. Three engine types were available to Glosters: R-R Peregrine and Merlin XX and the Bristol Taurus. None of the three was ideal. The Peregrine was limited in power and the Taurus not fully developed. The Merlin XX was already earmarked for other aircraft already in full scale production and therefore its availability could not be guaranteed. The MAP also questioned whether the F9/37 would be the best way to make use of the Merlin XX

The importance of the F9/37 to the history of the expansion programme is the innovative approach displayed by Glosters. The design approach was comparable to that of Westland's Whirlwind. Neither of the two companies had prior experience of designing high-performance twin-engine aircraft. In contrast, Bristols arrived at the Beaufighter via the Blenheim and the Beaufort.

Had the F9/37 gone into production with satisfactory engines then it would no doubt have helped to bolster the RAF's big-gun fighter strength. In its five 20mm-gun version it would have caused immense damage to enemy aircraft at night. That is provided room had been found for an AI interception radar and an operator/gun-loader.

Derivatives of the Gloster F9/37 were being prepared. These had the same wing, but with Rolls-Royce Merlin or Bristol Taurus engines and alternative armament. One of the alternative designs being prepared by Glosters included a single-seat fighter with four 20mm and eight 7.7mm guns.[5]

Among the possible fighter configurations not adopted was the pusher. The RAF had no pusher fighters since WWI. However, from time to time during the late 1930s designers considered the pusher in order to meet a fighter specification. They were particularly attracted to the freedom it gave to concentrate a large number of guns in the nose.

The monoplane, twin-boom, pusher with the engine behind the pilot as well as needing a tricycle undercarriage had to have some means of enabling the pilot to abandon the aircraft without being killed by the propeller. The ejection seat not having been perfected then recourse had to be made to a jettisonable propeller or a ventral escape hatch as in the Beaufighter.

The 'drawing board' pushers included the Gloster F18/37 to be powered by either a Napier Sabre or a R-R Vulture. The proposed armament of twelve 7.7mm Colt-Browning guns would give a heavy concentration of bullets on a target.

Although Carter and his team at Glosters exhibited considerable ingenuity in a number of designs for fighters they were not the only ones. J. Smith at Supermarine submitted a design for a twin Merlin-engined fighter whose advanced features included twelve 7.7mm guns in the wings and a tricycle undercarriage. Another arrangement not adopted was the engine amidships driving a tractor propeller through a shaft passing beneath the pilot's seat. In 1934 there was one example flown. This was the Westland F7/30 biplane fighter in which the pilot was positioned ahead of the upper wing. This aircraft anticipated the development of 'Gatling' multi-barrel guns for aircraft in the 1950s. At the time a multi-barrel gun with the Accles-type positive feed was being considered at the A&AEE Martlesham Heath by H.S.V. Thompson. However neither the aircraft nor its gun was adopted. Also, as mentioned in the previous chapter, Martin Baker's MB2 was another fresh approach to the single-seat fighter; albeit of a conventional shape.

It is unfortunate that the need for the utmost secrecy meant that few outside the aircraft design offices knew of the forward-thinking applied by British design teams. Within two years American magazines would include information and illustrations about prototype fighters that incorporated many of these revolutionary features along with the implication that only the USA could nurture such advanced concepts.

Westland Whirlwind

During a test flight of the Whirlwind on 10 June 1939, Harald Penrose found that the exhaust pipe on one side had burnt through the adjacent aileron control rod but, fortunately, not through the wall of the fuel tank. The aileron on that side went full up so that Penrose had to use full up aileron on the other side to level the aircraft. He effected a safe landing. After the near loss of the prototype and a valuable and experienced test pilot, the exhaust arrangement was changed to the conventional position at the sides of each nacelle.

Brewster Buffalo

In 1939 the British Purchasing Commission in the USA decided to order 180 Brewster type 339 (Buffalo) single-engine fighters.

The 339 was not a success even though it had all the right ingredients: a powerful and usually reliable engine, four 12.7mm guns plus other features common to American radial-engine fighters of the time. But the 'mixture' was not right and the aircraft's performance fell below that of the figures in the sales brochure. Both the USMC and the RAF made a poor choice. However, in fairness to the UK purchasing team, they were under orders to get what fighters they could, as quickly as they could, in order to enhance the strength of the RAF: a case of quantity not quality. Although outside the span of this book, it is worth recording that the first Buffalos arrived at 71 Squadron in July 1940 for evaluation. They were rejected. Applying the long-established policy of 'anything will do for the overseas squadrons' the Buffalos were shipped off to Singapore. This decision may have been influenced by the assumption that anything that flew would be far better than any Japanese aircraft.

More formations

Bomber Command continued to practise defensive formation flying. For example, in July Wellingtons of 149 Squadron, operating from Manston, simulated a daylight raid on Marseille. Formation flying was a sign to the taxpayer that the RAF was a disciplined and highly professional force. Formation flying was also intended to enhance the effectiveness of a bomber's guns when attacked by fighters through a combination of Lanchester's square law and the Gestalt).[6] The basic formation element was the 'vic' of three aircraft.

Among the evasive tactics which Bomber Command intended to use if attacked in daylight was the 'rotating vic'. On the command of the leader of the vic of three bombers, the aircraft to each side changed places: one passing downward behind the leader, the other passing above and behind. The 'rotating vic' was intended to confuse attacking fighters. Whether it would confuse the enemy was questionable. With big aircraft in close formation the manoeuvre could be dangerous, particularly when the pilots were already coping with attacking fighters.

Number 9 Squadron of Wellingtons devoted twenty hours to formation flying in preparation for a fly-past over the 25th International Aviation Exhibition at Brussels. Twenty hours within the flying limitations imposed on Bomber Command at the time was generous.

Interception exercises

The exercises during July when fighters were scrambled to intercept Bomber Command aircraft, resulted in No 11 Group controllers and pilots achieving an interception rate of 60 per cent. The de-briefing of bomber crews emphasised the need to increase the defensive armament of the Hampden. Twin Vickers K guns were not fitted to both gunners' positions until Spring 1940. However, just doubling the number of guns did not overcome the built-in handicap of the poorly designed gun positions.

After each of the major defence exercises of 1938 and 1939, Fighter Command complained about Bomber Command's lack of enthusiasm and its use of 'game' rules that often made the exercises useless. The C-in-C Bomber Command was asked to deploy formations of bombers against the defending fighters and not send lone aircraft. In peacetime a single aircraft became confused with civil traffic or aircraft from other commands. By August 1939 the complaints from Dowding and his staff could no longer be ignored and thereafter Bomber Command used

Air Exercises 1939. Hurricanes of No. 17 Squadron preparing to move out for take-off. (Aeroplane Monthly)

formations of bombers to make simulated attacks.

The radar stations and reporting and control networks took every opportunity to sharpen their techniques. Despite the ability of the seaward-looking radar stations to detect approaching aircraft at ranges of 100 miles, Bomber Command did not like sending its single-engine aircraft more than ten miles out to sea before they turned back to simulate an incoming raid. This state of affairs suggest that somewhere along the evolutionary line of bomber development from 1930 onward someone in authority could not envisage the need for overwater flying.[7]

Sir Henry Tizard observed that: 'The side which develops the greatest transmitted power on the shortest wavelength will win the war.' By 1939 the radar scientists had already developed transmitters operating at a wavelength of 1.5m (200MHz). When compared with the nominal 10m (30MHz) of the CH system this was a significant advance toward Tizard's target.[8]

Seminal to the development of higher transmitted power at high frequencies was Watson-Watt's invitation in the Spring to Professors Oliphant and Randall and Dr Boot of Birmingham University to spend their vacation at radar stations. This gave them first-hand experience of the problems that needed to be solved. In the next six months they developed the resonant cavity magnetron. This seemingly inert lump of machined metal, only a few inches in diameter, developed the high power at the extra high frequencies required for airborne radar transmitters. Following a visit by Watson-Watt to the Cavendish Laboratories at Cambridge, a list of potential radar scientists was drawn up. Groups of scientists were allocated to the various radar stations. From then on academic scientists began to flood into radar research.[9]

In the summer of 1939 Alexander Korda was busy with his *The Lion Has Wings.* He was a very able producer and with Hungarian determination

Typical East Coast CH station. The tall towers supported the transmitter antennae arrays. The group of four towers supported the receiver antennae. (GEC Marconi)

'poked' the cameras into every corner. Not until the Air Staff saw the completed film did they realise that Korda had somehow penetrated and exposed for all to see one of Fighter Command's sector operations rooms. Shots of the plotting table, if seen by an expert, would reveal much about the working of radar and the associated reporting and control system. Therefore, some scenes had to be cut.

Subsequent studies of the Battle of Britain emphasised that the *Luftwaffe* took some time to realise that RAF fighters were appearing at the right time at the right place to intercept raids because of a control system based on radar. Yet Korda's film was available to the *Luftwaffe* from which to deduce that Fighter Command did not just rely on standing patrols or uncontrolled fighter sweeps.

Syko

In July 1939 wireless operators were given Syko encrypting machines for greater security of signals. This was a mechanical device into which the signal was entered, one character at a time. The encrypted or de-crypted characters were then read off the machine and transmitted or noted down. A card of random characters was slid into the machine before use. The Syko cards were changed every twelve hours. Messages were simplified by using the RAF's general code book and the international Q code for aviation.[10]

Boulton Paul Defiant

The first production version of the Boulton Paul Defiant flew for the first time in July 1939. In some respects the Defiant was forced on Fighter

A resonant cavity magnetron developed by Randall and Boot that produced the high power at ultra high frequencies that enabled Britain to make a significant technological leap ahead of the Germans with centimetric radar. (GEC Marconi)

Command. Four hundred and fifty were on order in June 1938. The Vice-Chief of the Air Staff, Sholto Douglas, informed Dowding, the C-in-C Fighter Command, that he had to form nine Defiant squadrons. That would have needed about 150 aircraft. It is suggested by some historians that Ludlow-Hewitt proposed the use of the Defiant because the Bristol two-seat fighter of WWI had been so successful. The latter had a forward-firing gun for the pilot in addition to the one or two Lewis guns for the observer. The Defiant had no forward-firing guns for the pilot. Not unexpectedly Dowding objected to the imposition of Defiants. They were heavier and slower than the Hurricane and their possible role in the order of battle was uncertain. Despite those reservations, Dowding was overruled by the Air Staff. However, in June 1939, in response to growing doubts about the wisdom of ordering a fighter having no forward-firing guns, the number of Defiant squadrons to be formed was reduced to six. As it transpired, only two Defiant squadrons were formed.

In 1938 Churchill advised Chamberlain, the prime minister, that: 'latest developments favoured the turret type (aircraft)'. The records do not indicate on what evidence Churchill based his advice. At that time none of the world's airforces was fielding a 'turret type' fighter.[11, 12]

There was more to the arguments for and against

The Boulton Paul Defiant two-seat fighter conceived with World War One in mind rather than the air war of the future. This example is equipped with airborne interception (AI) 1.5m radar c 1940. The transmitter antennae are on the side of the fuselage: the receiver antennae on the leading edge of the wing. (Derek James)

the Defiant than just its performance. The power turret needed well-trained gunners to make the most effective use of its fire power. The training of air gunners in general was not properly organised until late 1939. It also needed skilled servicing personnel to maintain the complex mechanism of the turret. Already in 1938 the increased level of activity among fighter squadrons in particular had emphasised the need for more skilled servicing personnel.

Rolls-Royce Vulture

On 25 July 1939 Avro's new twin-engine bomber, the Manchester to specification B13/36, took off for the first time. The engines were the recently developed Rolls-Royce 24-cylinder, 1,760 hp Vultures. This was to be one of the new generation of bombers able to carry up to four tons of bombs. A contract had been placed in 1937 for 200. The Handley Page Halifax was also designed to have Vulture engines but when it became clear that Rolls-Royce was having problems, the Halifax was re-designed to take four Merlin engines: later there would be a Hercules-engined version. In the meantime Avro had to press on with the Vulture. Today's engines have such low rates of failure that twin-engine aircraft very much larger than the Manchester operate regular airline services across the oceans. In 1939 engine reliability was poor and twin-engine aircraft were frequently lost following the failure of one engine. The Manchester was, for its time, big and the sudden loss of half the thrust placed the crew in an often lethal situation. The four-engine version, the Lancaster, on the other hand could usually overcome the loss of one engine. A simple matter of 50 per cent for one and 25 per cent for the other.

Bristol Beaufighter

The 7 July 1939 is important in the history of night-fighting aircraft because this marked the first flight of the Beaufighter. As described in Chapter 4, design started in 1938 as a private venture by Bristol on a high-performance, long-range fighter using many components of the Beaufort; such as the wings and empennage. When the prototype was inspected by the Air Ministry the design was adopted and Specification F 17/39 was issued, along

Rolls-Royce Vulture 24-cylinder X configuration engine, nominal 1,800 hp, intended for the RAF's next generation of bombers to replace the Wellington, Whitley and Stirling. It was not as succesful as the Kestrel and Merlin and only entered squadron service with the AVRO Manchester. (Rolls-Royce)

Bristol Beaufighter, whose comparatively large fuselage provided space for the 'black boxes' of airborne interception radar as well as four 20mm guns. (Aeroplane Monthly)

with orders for four prototypes and 300 production aircraft.

The importance of the Beaufighter to the expansion and re-equipment of the RAF was the size of the fuselage. Its large cross-section, inherited from the Beaufort, gave the second crew member space in which handle the 60-round drums when re-loading the four ventral 20mm guns. When AI radar became available the Beaufighter provided more space and easier access to the 'black boxes' than the cramped fuselage of the Blenheim. The Beaufighter is an example of an aircraft whose design anticipated the needs of night fighting and whose potential was realised by those who controlled expenditure. The Beaufighter and AI radar developed along parallel and, as far as is known, separate programmes. Bowen refers to unsuitability of Blenheim as a night-fighter and to a visit to Bristol in late summer 1940 to see one of the early Beaufighters and the realisation of its potential for AI radar. This suggests that at the time none at Bristol knew of AI radar. Both just made it in time to meet the *Luftwaffe*'s switch from day to night attacks on Britain in 1940.[13]

Hudson

In the summer of 1939 No. 224 Coastal Command squadron received its first delivery of Hudsons to replace the Ansons. The expression 'As like as chalk and cheese' is apt. The Hudson was very different from the Anson.

By those pilots familiar with the Anson and its gentle flying characteristics the Hudson was viewed with some concern. Although the expansion programme had already introduced pilots to twin-engine fast aircraft, such as the Blenheim, none was quite like the Hudson. Its cockpit equipment, variable-area Fowler flaps and flying characteristics, particularly on landing, were somewhat different from other aircraft. ,[14]

With a top speed similar to that of the Blenheim, the Hudson crews considered they had one of the world's most advanced aircraft. Compared with some of its contemporaries the Hudson was comfortable and less likely to fatigue its crew. The cockpit could not be mistaken, even on a dark night, for other than an American design: comfortable seats, adequate heating and ventilating for example.

Hudson I of 206 Squadron Coastal Command. (Derek James)

So many British aircraft cockpits were either too hot or too cold and full of icy draughts.

The engine starting procedure required considerable dexterity on the part of the pilot. Press the starter and booster coil buttons. At the same time hold the spring-loaded engine selector (port or starboard) switch and operate the engine priming pump and the wobble-pump lever to pressurise the fuel system. When the engine started the idle cut-off lever had to be released and the throttle advanced to keep the engine running. On a cold day the pilot had to continue operating the priming pump and pressing the booster coil button. A one-armed paper hanger would have understood the problem.

During the take-off the pilot had to watch the boost gauges because automatic boost controls were not fitted to American engines. Also they did not have automatic mixture control, as with British engines, so the pilot had to keep an eye on the exhaust gas analyser instrument and manually adjust the mixture setting. An interesting aspect of Hudson flying was the drill used when the hydraulic system failed to lower the undercarriage. First partly lower the flaps using the hand pump if there was total hydraulic failure, then reduce speed to about 90 knots by raising the nose and slamming the throttles shut and finally push the control column forward. The resulting manoeuvre was intended to swing the undercarriage legs forward and down and, hopefully, lock.

100 Octane fuel

Sometimes missing from the wealth of aviation technical literature is the story of 100 octane fuel and how it arrived just in time for the RAF. Without 100 octane fuel both the Hurricane and the Spitfire would have been at a disadvantage when tackling Bf 109s during the first year of war.

The octane number of a fuel indicates its resistance to detonation. The higher the number the greater the resistance and therefore the higher the permissible boost pressure before detonation occurs. When the Hurricanes and Spitfires first entered squadron service their Merlin engines were limited at 3,000 rpm to 6.25 psi boost pressure because only 87 octane fuel was available. With 100 octane fuel the engines could be operated at 12 psi

* The Anson's Vne was only 170 knots. The Hudson's Vne was around 300 knots.

Air Exercises 1939. Hurricane of No 17 Squadron with attendant three-hose refuelling vehicle. The double (yellow) disc sign above the vehicle was intended to indicate its position to pilots who otherwise might not see it when taking off and landing or even when taxying. The gun ports in the wing leading edge are concealed by fabric. (Aeroplane Monthly)

(54 in. mercury) boost. In terms of power this represented an increase of 300 bhp; which in turn improved both the rate of climb and the top speed. Although samples of 100 octane fuel had been produced before 1938 it was not until that year that the Air Ministry placed a contract for engine tests using ESSO 100. Both Rolls-Royce and the Bristol Engine Company were involved with the trials that were conducted in association with the Royal Aircraft Establishment and Esso.

The RAF was going to need tens of thousands of gallons of 100 octane fuel; not just the few hundred used for the tests. It was not until June 1939 that a substantial quantity arrived from the Netherlands West Indies. On the 6 July a Hurricane was used to verify the improved performance of the new fuel. From August onward supplies continued to arrive and the RAF was able to stockpile sufficient 100 octane for sustained operations: enough in fact to last throughout the Battle of Britain. Had the Esso, BP and Trinidad refineries not gone 'on stream' in time then there might have been another 1940 post-mortem factor to consider. Meanwhile the Daimler-Benz 601 engine of the Bf 109, despite having fuel injection, was limited in power because Germany only had 87 octane fuel available in 1939.[15]

100 octane was reserved for the high power engines, such as the Merlin, Tiger and Pegasus used by operational squadrons. Other units, such as training, continued with 87 octane. One outcome of having two fuel standards was the ever-present danger of someone putting the wrong fuel into the tanks of an aircraft. To distinguish between the two the 100 octane was coloured green and the 87 blue.

In-flight refuelling

The trials of flight refuelling that had started in 1938 continued into 1939. The flexible hose method of linking the Harrow tanker and the S.30 flying boat proved to be practicable. However there were problems with jettisoning fuel in the event of trouble soon after take-off. Fuel tended to be sucked into the hull through the drift-sight hatch and the refuelling hatch in the tail. In addition to the hazard of the fumes that lingered in the hull there was the lengthy time taken to dump fuel. Only about 50 per cent of the fuel load could be jettisoned. The time taken to empty the tanks exceeded ten minutes. Therefore in the event of having to descend at 1,000 ft per minute from the operating height of 11,000 to 12,000 ft the aircraft was still over the maximum landing weight. Nevertheless, on 5 August 1939 Imperial Airways inaugurated a transatlantic mail service with Short S.30 flying boats refuelled in flight from Harrow tankers. As already noted, such a method of extending range or useful load would present difficulties if applied to the operation of a large force of bombers; particularly at night; and particularly if circumstances prevented the specialised training of pilots and hose-handlers. Furthermore, the provision of a fleet of tanker aircraft would impose an additional burden on aircraft production resources and on the training facilities.

Mobilisation

Full mobilisation of Bomber Command was ordered on 1 August 1939 and war establishment exercises were started. Wellington squadrons flew sorties on the 8th to 11th to simulate enemy bombers as part of the full scale Home Defence Exercise. Once again Fighter Command continued to complain that Bomber Command was imposing conditions that were making the exercises of little value.

During the exercises with Fighter Command, two of 149's Wellingtons were lost in the North Sea. The list of crew members in one of the Wellingtons lost emphasised the current establishment and the number of non-career aircrew: a sergeant pilot as captain, a pilot officer as 2nd pilot, an acting sergeant as observer (navigator) and the wireless operator, air gunner and armourer/air gunner who were all Aircraftmen 1st class part-time aircrew.

The French airforce took part in combined exercises with Fighter Command during August. Seven formations of bombers, fighters and reconnaissance aircraft 'raided' Harwich, Manchester, Liverpool and northern towns. Other raids were against the Midlands and the West Country. A raid on London by a large formation of bombers with escorting fighters was intercepted when crossing the coast. These exercises provided a useful rehearsal for the future air war.

Radar reconnaissance

Early on the morning of the 3 August the airship *Graf Zeppelin* came across the North Sea on an electronic intelligence sortie. The *Luftwaffe* radar experts on board were required to record the characteristics of any high frequency transmissions from coastal stations. The airship arrived off the Bawdsey radar research station and then turned north to fly the length of the eastern shore of Britain. It went as far north as Scapa Flow. Throughout the flight no transmissions were picked up. It has been suggested that none of the east coast radar stations detected the airship, although fighters were scrambled to identify it visually. During a previous and unsuccessful radar reconnaissance, in May, the *Graf Zeppelin* had been detected by the CH stations.[16]

Had the high frequency detection equipment in the Zeppelin worked then it is possible that the lack of radar coverage at low level would have been revealed. Whether or not the *Luftwaffe* would have concentrated on low-level 'below radar' sorties is debateable. The majority of air generals were ex-WWI pilots, imbued with the principle that 'He who has the height advantage wins'.[17]

30 minute readiness

On the 17 August, the traditional month in which European wars usually started, Spitfires of 19 Squadron scrambled to intercept a co-operating French bomber flying toward Birmingham. All Fighter Command squadrons were at 30 minute readiness with the aircraft dispersed around the edge of the airfield.

A large part of Britain was subjected to a trial

'blackout' on the 24 August. Those RAF crews airborne at night and who had not flown much over uninhabited areas, realised the importance of being skilled at navigating without reference to the ground.

Friend or Foe?

In 1939 IFF (Identification Friend or Foe) was used for the first time in air exercises. An improved version, the Mk II, was already in production and scheduled for installation in September.

The IFF receiver/transmitter in an aircraft was triggered whenever a radar pulse detected the aircraft. The IFF unit amplified the pulse and re-radiated it. This altered the blip on the ground radar CRT so that it could be distinguished from other echoes. Without IFF a radar operator would have been unable to distinguish 'friendly' from 'unfriendly' blips.[18]

Communications developments

Irrespective of the accuracy and information content of radar observations, they were of little use to fighter controllers if they could not be made available with the minimum time lag. Good and secure communications were the life blood of battle. Therefore since 1935 the Post Office had been building up a network of telephone and teleprinter links for use by Fighter Command and other commands. This included the Defence Teleprinter Network (DTN). Redundancy of links, so as to provide alternative circuits, was assured by the fact that the majority of teleprinter circuits were shared with the voice telephone system.[19]

Airborne Radar

As with the previous years, research and development in airborne radar for interception (AI) and for ship detection (ASV) continued at a pace. By 1939 both the scientists and the Air Staff realised that a pilot could not on his own fly the aircraft and operate the radar set. There would have to be a three-man crew: one to fly the aircraft, one to navigate and the third to operate the radar. Although airborne interception (AI) sets were evaluated in Fairey Battles and an order was even placed for fifty aircraft to be modified, twin-engine aircraft would have to be used. Therefore the Blenheim was selected as the first AI aircraft. In July two were allocated to Martlesham Heath for AI trials. On the 17th of the month the prototype Bristol Beaufighter was airborne. Just over a year later came the first night interception, using AI radar, of a German bomber.

Radio

During the year Marconi continued with the development of an 'all-wave' general purpose receiver/transmitter set to replace the TR1082/1083 equipment with its awkward-to-use plug-in coils. The new set was being designed to have pre-set tuning; as with many domestic radios. The receiver would combine improved communication and direction-finding functions including a visual homing indicator for use by both the wireless-operator and the pilot.

The new transmitter and receiver were intended for application to all types of aircraft except single-seat. Eventually the production versions were classified as transmitter T1154 and receiver R1155. The design of both units was not finalised until after the outbreak of war and production did not start until June 1940.[20]

Radio-telephone

The TR9, high frequency (HF), radio-telephone equipment in use for communication with fighter aircraft was frequently subject to interference, distortion and insufficient range. In 1928 research had started at the RAE into very high frequency (VHF) sets. However progress towards the design of suitable equipment was slow. It was not until 1935 that the first stage of development was completed and the engineers could turn towards the problems of manufacture. Interestingly the selection of different frequencies was to be through push-buttons and not by selector levers. With a war likely to start at least

Receiver Type 1082 (left) and transmitter Type 1083. Until the advent of the Marconi all-wave, general purpose radio receiver and transmitter in 1940, these two radio units were the standard communications equipment in RAF aircraft. (Phil Racher)

Marconi general purpose transmitter type T1154. This one made by E. K. Cole. (GEC-Marconi)

Marconi general purpose receiver type R1155. The standard receiver, along with the transmitter type T1154, for the majority of RAF aircraft from mid-1940 onwards. (GEC-Marconi)

by 1940 there was an urgent need to get the new communication sets into production. This took longer than expected and a revised, less demanding, specification had to be applied.

In 1937 development started at the RAE on what was to become the TR1133. The first TR1133s were ready by August 1939 but it was not until October that trials could start using the Spitfires of No. 66 Squadron at Duxford. An improved version was put into production, the TR1143. However production delays continued and Fighter Command had to work to two different radio standards; with some squadrons using the HF and others the VHF. It would be another year before 16 of the fighter squadrons were re-equipped with VHF radio.[21, 22]

Among the list of those items essential to the expansion of the RAF and its re-equipment to fight a modern war, VHF radio is one that came too late. There was also delay in providing adequate means of communication between aircraft and troops on the ground. This was an area of technology that lagged behind others throughout WWII. Lysanders were equipped with message pick-up hooks. This slow method of collecting messages was still being demonstrated to the press as late as May 1939. It was as if the lessons of WWI, when radio links between air and ground and vice versa were used, were forgotten.

Flying boats

At the beginning of 1939 the civil class G flying boats of Imperial Airways were earmarked for Coastal Command. John North of Boulton Paul advised on the defensive armament to be fitted. He recommended that there should be two BP Type A dorsal turrets and a third in the tail. When the turrets were installed early in 1940 the tail turret caused severe aerodynamic problems and a number of different fairings at the base of the fin had to be tried before a satisfactory installation was found.

At the Marine Aircraft Experimental Establishment (MAEE) in the summer of 1939 the RAF was evaluating a twin-engine Consolidated PBY-4 flying boat. The aircraft was flown from Botwood in Newfoundland to the MAEE at Felixstowe, a distance of 2,130 nautical miles. The PBY-4 was given a high assessment rating by the MAEE. Its potential for Coastal Command was enhanced by its use for the long-distance survey of the Imperial Reserve Air Routes across the Pacific that confirmed its reliability and ability to land in different sea states.

Orders for aircraft

The road to war in 1939 was marked by the many contracts for more aircraft. They were ordered in numbers undreamt of in the aircraft industry's years of stagnation. For example: 200 Whirlwinds from Westland; 225 Hampdens from English Electric and 1,500 Ansons from A.V.Roe. The existing orders for Hurricanes and Spitfires were increased and more Hudsons and Harvards were ordered from the USA.

Chapter Seven

1939/II

In August the days of peace were hurrying to their end. Those in the know and those who read the signs correctly, were certain that Britain and France would be at war with Germany within a few weeks.

Battles to France

The crews of the Fairey Battle light bomber squadrons, that moved into French airfields on the 25 August 1939, were well aware that their aircraft were obsolescent. They were obsolescent when they received them in 1937. They were the victims of a governmental policy that decreed that having established a shadow factory scheme then it had to make aircraft; any aircraft. In the absence of more suitable and modern aircraft, production continued with the Battles. It is not clear how the RAF in France intended to use the light bombers. Would they be used in large formations in daylight against an advancing German army? Or would they be used to attack enemy airfields? What happened if they encountered heavy and accurate light anti-aircraft fire or Bf109 fighters? Overall the RAF's first-line strength was made up of too many light bombers of doubtful value.

Dispersing

In August Fighter Command stations implemented arrangements and dispositions for war. Aircraft were dispersed around the perimeters of the airfields with their pilot's tent within twenty-five yards of the aircraft. Pilots and their aircraft were at five minutes readiness status. Tannoy loudspeaker systems were in use for relaying commands from the sector operations rooms and from station headquarters.

The monotony of waiting 'For the balloon to go up' was literally interrupted by taking off to shoot down barrage balloons that had broken free. As they rose rapidly to around 30,000 feet the Hurricane pilots found out how sluggish their aircraft were at that height. Incidentally, barrage balloons that broke free from their moorings were to cause more disruption to the national grid, by dragging their cables across the high-tension wires, than German bombs.

Restrictions on civil flying

Hitler sent an ultimatum to Poland. With the *Luftwaffe* dominating the skies, German troops crossed the Polish frontier on the 31 August.

An immediate consequence was that the UK control and reporting network went on 24 hour watch. The movements of all aircraft were plotted, particularly those flying in from the continent of Europe. Its task was simplified to some extent by the Air Navigation (Emergency Restriction) Order effective at midnight on the 31 August. Essentially the Order prohibited flights by civil aircraft over the eastern half of England and most of Scotland. It also included a list of other specific areas over which civil aircraft must not fly. Other conditions specified that landplanes might only enter the United Kingdom at Shoreham Airport, Belfast Harbour Airport, Bristol (Whitchurch), Liverpool (Speke) and Perth (Scone). Civil aircraft were also prohibited from flying between sunset and sunrise and had to fly within view of the ground and not above 3,000 feet.

The parts of the Order prohibiting flying at night and not above 3,000 feet related to the difficulties of observing aircraft once they had passed

A Gloster Gladiator in the 1938-39 black and white undersurface colours. The wheel discs and propeller spinner were still painted yellow when a squadron of Gladiators moved to Croydon aerodrome at the outbreak of WWII. (Peter Ottery)

through the chain of radar stations. Only aircraft flying in daylight and below cloud could be tracked and identified by the Observer Corps with certainty.

The British civil aircraft fleets moved from Croydon to Bristol. As they moved out, Gladiators of 615 Squadron and Hurricanes of 3 and 17 Squadrons flew in. The Gladiators still displayed some of their peacetime colouring: yellow wheel discs, full red, white and blue roundels and the lower wing surfaces white on one side and black on the other. Despite the Air Staff's dispersal orders, so as to avoid a knock out blow, about sixty fighters gathered at Croydon.[1]

Covert activities

For some time the German airline Deutsche Lufthansa and British airlines had been involved in covert intelligence gathering. RAF pilots had been seconded to British Airways to gain experience of high-speed long-range flights and, whenever there was an opportunity, of observing German airfields, communication centres and industrial areas from the air. Lufthansa had ceased to operate from Croydon on a purely commercial basis. The day services were doubled and sometimes trebled and there were frequent night services advertised for cargo carrying. Many of the night flights were carrying only 200 lb of cargo. As with the day flights, they carried supernumerary crews, ostensibly 'learning' the route.

It so happened that two important RAF stations lay approximately on the route between Croydon and Germany. Whenever the wind direction allowed, Lufthansa crews made sure they flew directly over these Fighter Command airfields. One inquisitive German transport aircraft flew low across Biggin Hill. The duty pilot fired a signal flare across its bow. The Germans did not complain.

General mobilisation

The signal for general mobilisation went to all RAF units on the 1 September. As an example of Bomber Command's potential, 149 Squadron had twenty Wellington Mk1s and three Mk1As. The latter had FN, twin 7.7mm-gun, power-operated nose and tail turrets in place of the Vickers casement type mountings. Both types of Wellington were sometimes fitted with the FN17 extendable ventral turret. At the time few doubted that with their six Browning guns, each able to fire at 1,000 rounds per minute, they could beat off attacking fighters. As with other squadrons, 149's war establishment was twelve aircraft. The remainder were moved to the Group Pool training squadrons.

As the signal for general mobilisation came off the RAF's teleprinters, the BBC's television transmitter at Alexandra Palace in North London shut down in mid programme. This was done to deprive German aircraft of a convenient radio navigational beacon. However, radio transmissions continued because each service was transmitted from more than one station.

Scatter

On the 1 September 1939 Bomber Command squadrons and some Fighter Command squadrons were dispersed away from their home stations to avoid a surprise 'knock-out' blow within minutes of war starting. This was a defensive measure that unfortunately, because of the disruption, reduced the ability of the RAF to attack.

There were a number of 'scatter plans' for moving squadrons so as to render obsolete any data the Germans may have gathered on squadron locations. As an example: 90 and 101 Squadrons moved from Upwood and West Raynham respectively to Weston-on-the-Green, where they were joined by 104 and 108 Squadrons from Bicester. The records are not clear on the question of why so many bombers had to be concentrated on one airfield considering the perceived fear of a pre-emptive blow by the *Luftwaffe*.

During the first few weeks of war the dispersion of squadrons away from their home stations resulted in wasteful aircraft movements and frustrated crews. An unnecessary burden was imposed on maintenance crews and the aircrews often were deprived of regular meals and settled accommodation. For example: four Wellingtons were flown on the 8 September from Upper Heyford to Newmarket. From there they went on to Mildenhall to enable the operations and intelligence officers to 'interview' (sic) the crews. For some reason the operations staff were unable to travel the short distance, even by road, to Newmarket.

Second Great German War

War was declared between Britain and Germany at 1100 on 3 September 1939. This was just a formality: the Royal Navy and the RAF had been virtually at war since the Munich crisis. Britain and France together had about 3,400 first-line aircraft and about 3,800 in reserve for operations in Europe.[2]

The Western Air Plans, of which there were 16 of importance, included draft operational orders that could be sent to Commands and onto groups and squadrons. They included a wide range of targets and enemy activities agreed between the Air Staff and the politicians. The list emphasised the significant number of different types of operations that the airforce was expected to carry out.[3]

The RAF had two primary tasks. The first, at the insistence of the Admiralty, to augment the search for the main German fleet; the second, all available fighter squadrons to stand-to ready to repel an expected knock-out blow by the *Luftwaffe*. However, the expected knock-out blow by waves of bombers and fighters was more in the minds of the politicians than in hard facts. Unless Germany immediately invaded and established airfields in the Netherlands, Belgium and Northern France the flying distances involved weighed against such an attack being decisive. Although German bombers could reach as far as Birmingham, for example, an escort of fighters would have had to turn back before reaching the target. At the time not every one appreciated that a bomber was mostly fuel and bombs and designed to cruise on a steady course, whereas a fighter was all engine and not much fuel and designed for violent manoeuvre at full throttle. It would be another four years before fighter design progressed sufficiently, as with the P-51, to provide long-range escorts.

The formal declaration of hostilities meant that restrictions on the arming of bombs were removed. However, the service had a special restriction hung round its neck by the War Cabinet. This was the prohibition against attacking enemy ships if they were close to an inhabited shoreline, such as when in harbour. Even the formidable lobby of the Sea Lords could not persuade the Cabinet to remove the embargo.

Within minutes of the declaration of war, an 'unidentified' aircraft crossed the coast near Shoreham. Wing Commander W. Pretty, duty controller in Fighter Command's 11 Group operations room at Uxbridge, ordered the air-raid alarms to be sounded. Although this was a false-alarm it made the command's adrenaline flow and, unintentionally, emphasised the gravity of Chamberlain's announcement.

Bristol Blenheim IV medium twin-engine bomber powered by two Bristol Mercury engines. (Peter Ottery)

Over Wilhelmshaven

Coastal Command had been keeping a watch on the movement of German ships since September 1938. As war was declared, London flying boats of 201 Squadron were already out on patrol from their base at Sullom Voe.

Those directing the war were anxious to determine the strength of the German fleet off Wilhelmshaven; the nearest naval harbour to Britain. Coastal Command Hudson aircraft were ready to take off. However, the operational signal went to the Bomber Command station at Wyton and not to a Hudson squadron. A Blenheim IV took off at 1201 to photograph the German naval base and to report back by radio the disposition and classes of ships in the harbour. The crew was: F/O McPherson (pilot), Cdr Thomson RN (Navigator), Cpl Arrowsmith (wireless operator).

The outbound flight was uneventful: that is if we ignore the extreme cold inside the unheated and draughty aircraft. Steadily climbing, the Blenheim arrived over the naval base at 24,000 feet. This was the first British aircraft to cross the coast of Germany since war was declared. Seventy photographs were taken. The opposition was ineffective. A signal was prepared but it could not be sent because the wireless set was frozen and inoperable. Although height was reduced once away from the coast, the transmitter remained out of action. The vital information in the sighting report did not reach the Admiralty until after the aircraft landed back at Wyton. When the photographs were developed they showed the German ships raising steam: some of them already heading out into the Schillig Roads.

Someone had blundered. The Blenheim and its crew used for this first operational sortie of the war had been standing by for two days. Therefore the flight was no last minute decision. There had been time in which to perfect all aspects of the sortie. Some provision should had been made to prevent the radio equipment failing or being affected by low air temperatures. Exercises in which Blenheims and other aircraft flew at heights above the freezing level resulted in condensation affecting the radio equip-

Blenheim IV cockpit. Items of particular interest are the P Type aperiodic compass (to the left above the rudder pedals) and the right-thumb-operated brake control lever on the control spectacle. Forward of the instrument panel can just be seen the observer's (navigator) chart table; the seat is folded up on the right. This photograph also shows the complex shape of the nose, compared with that of the Mk I Blenheim, needed to give the pilot a clear view forward over the navigation position. (British Aerospace)

ment. Furthermore, considering the possibility of radio failures, why was only one aircraft used?

Attack the German fleet

Various plans prepared in the event of war were opened. These included attacking German warships. Squadrons of 3 (Bomber) Group prepared to make daylight sorties in formation Their orders included emphasis on the need to avoid casualties among German civilians and damage to industrial buildings. The government's concern for the safety of industrial buildings arose from the fact that the shareholders of the companies owning the buildings might include British subjects.

Another prohibition imposed on the bombers specified that if the targets were not reached before dusk then the bombs had to be jettisoned into the sea. They were also ordered not to attack German ships if they were in or close to the territorial waters of Denmark or the Netherlands.

Hampdens in echelon to starboard. The upper and lower gun positions for the manually aimed Vickers 7.7mm K guns had restricted fields of fire. On the upper part of the nose of the nearest aircraft can be seen the single, fixed, Browning 7.7mm pilot's 'targets of opportunity' gun. (Derek James)

Armed reconnaissance

On the 3 September an 'armed reconnaissance' in force was ordered. This was made up of eighteen Wellingtons and eighteen Hampdens. Three aircraft of 149 Squadron were airborne at 1835 and set off eastwards to look for German warships. As they set course from Mildenhall another nine Wellingtons were preparing to take off but were recalled at the last minute. Three of the Wellingtons left before the recall signal arrived. They found no ships and therefore dumped their bombs in the sea.

The next day another reconnaissance sortie to Wilhelmshaven was ordered. The same Blenheim and crew as the first sortie flew at 300 feet across ships lying off Wilhelmshaven and in the Schillig Roads. The aircraft also flew up the Elbe estuary to photograph ships lying off Brunsbuttel, the southern end of the Kiel canal. This time the radio worked, but the signals were corrupted during encryption. Staff officers waiting for information concerning the location of German warships, so that operational orders could be prepared, had to wait until the Blenheim landed back at RAF Wyton.

Searching in formation

Between the 4th and 19th of September Bomber Command made seven attempts to search for and attack German warships. Wellingtons and

Hampdens flew in formation for two reasons. One, they hoped to defend themselves better against fighter attacks and two they could make a concentrated attack when they found enemy ships. Although aircraft of Coastal Command sighted German ships on at least six occasions they were so far away that the bombers, on reaching the reported position, found no worthwhile targets. The sorties failed because of a combination of:

time in which to transmit the sighting report and brief the bomber crews
time to assemble the bomber force
time to reach the reported position; inaccurate position reporting and poor navigation.

Another adverse factor may have been the inadequate radio communication between aircraft of each formation that prevented them spreading out to widen the search area. There was also the psychological factor imposed on the crews who realised that, after two hours or more flying, the enemy ships were far from their last reported position and on their way to the safety of harbour. The crews were also mindful that the German warships were reasonably safe from attack in harbour because of the strictures placed on Bomber Command about attacking ships when there was a possibility that civilians and private property might be damaged.

On the 4th fifteen Blenheim IVs and fourteen Wellingtons took off to attack German warships lying in the Schillig Roads and off Brunsbuttel. The Blenheims attacked at the former location. The fuses of the 500 lb bombs were set with an eleven second delay so that they could be dropped from mast height. Of the ten Blenheims that found the targets five failed to return. Of the eight Wellingtons of 149 Squadron that set out for Brunsbuttel only two crews were able to find the target. The other Wellingtons squadron did no better.

Why were so few crews able to find such clearly defined targets as warships in daylight? The answer must lie with inadequate training in navigation. When aircraft arrived over the north west coast of Germany only those crews familiar with the many small islands, inlets and indentations could distinguish one from another. Readers of Erskine Childers' *Riddle of the Sands* will appreciate the problem.

Leaflets

Wellington and Whitley squadrons tested the air defences of Germany and reconnoitred potential targets. In accordance with an agreement with France, no bombs were dropped. The Allies were worried lest the Germans reacted to lethal aerial attacks before they were ready to counter them. The French air defence system was in no condition to prevent massive air raids against the cities of the eastern departments. Many of its aircraft were obsolescent. The most lethal weapon was the propaganda leaflet. The leaflets exhorted Germans to overthrow their government and abandon the war. As the German people had suffered no casualties and the war had only been on for a few days, they were not likely to take much notice of a few scraps of paper.

Over the targets the visibility was poor with haze up to 16,000 feet. Ground features could not be distinguished one from another with any certainty. There was considerable searchlight activity but no anti-aircraft gunfire.

Of the three aircraft of 99 Squadron that took off to reconnoitre Germany one returned when the pilot found the elevator and rudder controls were jamming. On landing back at Mildenhall he discovered that the bundles of leaflets piled on the rest bunk had shifted so as to foul the control rods. Another of the three aircraft had a damaged tailplane resulting from an unopened bundle of leaflets leaving the flare chute. Perhaps the airman responsible for loading the flare chute and fastening the rip cord of the bundle, decided that a heavy bundle descending at speed onto the head of a German was the better way to win the war.[4]

Extracurricula activities.

In addition to standing by for armed sweeps across the North Sea, Bomber Command provided aircraft to assist with the calibration of the CH radar station at Bawdsey. On the 12 September three Wellingtons were detailed to fly to and from a number of geographical positions. As so often happened the calibration exercise had to be cancelled because of poor visibility which prevented accurate determination of position.

Another non-operational activity involved co-operating in the making of Korda's film *The Lion Has Wings*. In the first week of war Flt Lt A.M. Small was detached from 99 Squadron to act as technical adviser.

Despite the expert advice the editors of the film decided that 'one aeroplane looks like any another'. Therefore, for example, a German night raid against London included a Condor, Ju 52, He 111, Wellington and Wellesley. The German pilots, as the 'bad guys', wore all-black flying clothing. A Wellington cockpit was used to depict a German bomber. To disguise the fact, the film was reversed left to right so that the pilot was seen sitting on the right.

The interior scenes of the forward and aft gun positions of the Wellingtons, shot in the studio, suggested that they were only equipped with a single Lewis gun. Those German fighter pilots who happened to see the film, when it was distributed in Europe, may have been encouraged by the Wellington's apparent poor defensive armament. Nevertheless the exterior shots of real Wellingtons include type IAs with twin-Browning gun turrets.

Armed sweeps

On the 26 September Bomber Command aircraft made an 'armed sweep' to find German warships. The appellation 'armed' suggests that the command also had in mind 'unarmed' sweeps; which, of course, is nonsense; or did it refer to the carrying of bombs? A formation of eleven Hampdens from 5 Group was ordered to search around Heligoland. Unfortunately the island was too close to the hornet's nest of the *Luftwaffe* fighter base on the North Frisian Islands. Unaware that their movements had been tracked by German radar they were soon in a fierce fight for survival. Any elation at having survived the flak from the island was dispelled as five Hampdens were quickly shot down by fighters. The manually aimed, drum-fed, K guns in the upper and lower gun positions were not sufficient protection. The air-gunners had to exercise skill in limiting the length of each bust of fire because each magazine only held 97 rounds. The gunners had to struggle against the G forces as the Hampden twisted and turned. With frozen fingers they had to clamp the heavy spring-driven drums into position.

Five out of the eleven Hampdens were shot down. An attrition rate close to 50 per cent might have prompted the Air Staff to abandon the armed sweep. However to do so would have lowered morale. The general opinion at the time was that the command had to gain experience and all aspects of operating a bomber force had to be tested. These included the handling of bombs, frequent changes in the type of bombs as the tactical circumstances changed from hour to hour, navigational techniques and equipment, and improved radio equipment. Nevertheless, although it was accepted that Hampdens might not be able to defend themselves in daylight against fighters, Wellingtons in formation could survive.

At this time the Whitley was the subject of a study to improve defence against fighters. A mid-upper dorsal turret was considered. Unfortunately this would have moved the aircraft's centre-of-gravity past the aft limit. The aircraft would then have become so tail heavy that no amount of elevator would compensate. For the same reason additional armour plating was ruled out.

Bomber problems

On the 18 September two Wellingtons of No 9 Squadron collided when executing a 'rotating vic' crossover. The port propeller of the right-hand aircraft of the vic cut through the fuselage of the formation leader's aircraft. This severed the tail. The stricken aircraft reared up and crashed down inverted onto the colliding aircraft. Both aircraft crashed from 800 feet with the loss of four officers and five airmen. Executing a 'rotating vic' at low level invited trouble; whether or not it was a useful manoeuvre.

The first three months of operations by Bomber Command highlighted a number of problems. Perhaps because of reports of possible danger from oxygen bottles exploding if hit by bullets or shell fragments, 3 Group instructed all its squadrons to charge the bottles only to a pressure sufficient to ensure a supply of oxygen. The instruction also required oxygen bottles to be unshipped before any flights not intended to go above ten thousand feet.

Until the 18 September, 149 Squadron at Mildenhall, for example, occupied itself with training and with modifications to equipment. It also conducted comparative trials with the FN turrets of the Mk IA Wellingtons and the Mk Is with their Vickers 'windscreen' casemate mountings. On the 18th the squadron was detailed as Group Duty Squadron. This meant that it was one of 3 Group's squadrons at two-hour readiness to take off should the German fleet venture out. Before the 30 October 149 Squadron received a succession of 'stand by to attack the German Fleet' orders. However each was followed by a stand-down signal. But on the 30th the teleprinter in the station operations room started to spell out the information 'Five enemy ships steaming at 15 knots, steering 265 degrees, true position 53.55 north, 05.08 east at 1425'. They were less than 200 nautical miles to the east of Mildenhall, about 60 minutes flying time.

At 1436, thirty-one minutes since the last sighting report, the Wellingtons of 149, plus two other squadrons in the Wing, were ordered to take off. The three squadrons were to join formation at 2,000 feet over Mildenhall at 1530, fifty-five minutes after the sighting report. Once the eighteen aircraft were in formation they were ordered to the last known position of the German ships.

The German ships had been sighted steering south of west by a Coastal Command aircraft and presumably it was calculated that in the time it would take the Wellingtons to formate and fly to the last known position the ships would have turned for home. Therefore they were ordered to sweep to the south. Assuming the ships kept at 15 knots then in the 120 minutes or more that elapsed they could have been anywhere on the circumference of a circle of 30 nautical mile radius between east and south. The only way the bombers could have found the ships was through a combination of luck and intuition. As so often happened, nothing was seen and the bombers turned back. It was dark when they got back to their home stations and it took nearly an hour in which to land all the aircraft.

This one typical sortie highlights the problems faced by Bomber Command:

- slow response time;
- lack of speed towards reported position;
- lack of search radar;
- possibility of inaccurate position reporting and navigation;
- lack of airfield equipment for handling a number of returning aircraft.

An unanswered question in retrospect is: had the aircraft found the ships and the ships had started to steam in evasive circles, would they have been hit by any of the bombs? Another among many problems that came to light in the early months of the war related to the 'paper' and actual performance of the Wellington. Pilots of 3 Group found that with a full load of fuel and bombs their aircraft only just managed to clear the edge of the airfield on take-off.

During October Wellington squadrons took part in affiliation exercises with the fighters of 17 Squadron from Debden. At the de-briefing sessions the bomber crews expressed the opinion that they could beat off attacks.

Cameras

During the 1920s and early 1930s the development of reconnaissance photography had been slow. By 1939 few aircraft were equipped with an automatic camera for use with a parachute photoflash over enemy targets at night. On the 7 October observers of some Wellington squadrons were issued with 35mm Leica cameras.

For daylight reconnaissance, Wg Cdr F. Sidney Cotton (of Sidcot suit fame) made covert aerial photographic survey flights over Europe in his modified civil Lockheed 12-A. These flights were made before September 1939. Cotton's clandestine aerial reconnaissance flights were part of a an Anglo-French intelligence operation. Operating from Heston aerodrome, to the west of London, the Lockheed 12-A was flown by Cotton at 26,000 ft over Germany. Photographs were made of parts of the Siegfried line, the area around Mannheim and the northern shore of the Bodensee. Sorties were also made from Tunis to photograph Italian airfields in North Africa. A second 12-A was acquired and extensively modified to increase its range and photo coverage. The three F-24 cameras gave an overlapping coverage of a swath of territory about 10 miles wide from 20,000 ft.

With war imminent the activities of Cotton's No. 2 Camouflage Unit at Heston became slightly more official. The Royal Aircraft Establishment and Cotton realised that high altitude sorties would be needed. They also decided that the Spitfire could make a good high-altitude photo reconnaissance (PR) vehicle. It so happened that Fg Off. M. Longbottom had written a paper on the proposed use of a small and fast aircraft that would rely on speed, rate of climb and ceiling to avoid detection. He had in mind, of course, the Spitfire. However it was not until October 1939 that a Spitfire I, which happened to be at Farnborough for repair, became available. This was specially modified for operating above 30,000 ft. F-24 cameras were installed in the wings and on the 18 November a sortie was flown over Eupen. More flights followed covering the Siegfried Line and the Ruhr Valley.[6] Later Cotton persuaded Dowding to let him have two Spitfires which were modified and equipped with heated cameras. The guns, ammunition boxes, radio and other equipment were removed thereby saving about 480 lb in weight that could be used for cameras and extra fuel tanks. They could fly at 35,000 feet and had a radius of action of over 700 miles from their advanced base at Seclin near Lille.

The two cameras fitted in the wings of the Spitfire were F-24s with 5 in focal length lenses. From 33,000 ft they gave an overlap swath of the ground 12 miles wide. The resulting films were processed and their information extracted by the Aircraft Operating Company (a cover name) of Wembley in London using a Wild A5 photogrammatic machine purchased in Switzerland.[7] The F-24 camera was eventually replaced by one giving a larger format and having better lenses, including a 36 in. focal length.

In April 1940 Cotton's unit became the Photographic Development Unit and in July 1940 was renamed the Photographic Reconnaissance Unit (PRU). The private company at Wembley became the Photographic Interpretation Unit. Both then came under Coastal Command.

The Blenheims and Battles in France were equipped with cameras for recording the disposition and movements of the German army. However, neither had the performance nor equipment to carry out their task adequately: for example, their cameras were not heated. Blenheim IVs were lost at the rate of one aircraft for every five sorties. In contrast the PR Spitfires were able to photograph twice the area covered by the Blenheims without significant loss.

The resourceful Cotton also ensured that there were mobile photo processing units available at the end of 1939 and Mobile Printing Units that provided a 'close-to-hand' service for the army in France. He certainly deserved more credit and awards than his parsimonious superiors eventually recommended. Cotton was one of those RAF officers who appreciated that an airforce was more than just aircraft. He could see the broad picture of air war; both the technology and the tactics.

Torpedo-bombers

Although a number of the new aircraft types, such as the Botha, were intended for the torpedo-bomber role only the Bristol Beaufort was in production before 1940. It was designed to meet two specifications: M 15/35 for a twin-engine monoplane with external torpedo; and G 24/35 for a general-reconnaissance bomber to supersede the Vildebeest. Eventually the Beaufort design was completed to specification 10/36. The 'off the drawing board' contract was placed in August 1936 for 78 aircraft but the prototype did not fly until October 1938. The twin Taurus VI engines gave this Coastal Command torpedo-bomber a top speed with

Bristol Beaufort torpedo bomber of Coastal Command. (Derek James)

Blackburn Botha torpedo bomber. (British Aerospace)

torpedo close to 200 knots (230 mph). A Bristol type B IV powered gun turret and one or two fixed forward-firing guns was the original gun armament. The standard 18-inch torpedo used by Coastal Command weighed 1,605 lb. This was carried in a recess under the port side of the fuselage. However when Beauforts started flying with 22 Squadron in December 1939 there were numerous faults that had to be cured before they would be fit for operational flying: in particular the Bristol Taurus sleeve-valve

Bristol Perseus 9-cylinder sleeve-valve engine for the Botha, Lysander II, Roc, Skua, and Vildebeest IV. (John Heaven)

engine suffered cooling and other problems which would take until June 1940 to sort out. As for the intended primary function, that of launching torpedoes at ships, the first such attack by Beauforts was not until September 1940.

The Botha with two Perseus 930 hp engines was underpowered and unloved and made no operational torpedo attacks.

Search and trade protection

On the 3 September Coastal Command had 53 Hudsons and more arrived over the following months. However the command was still short of aircraft and had to rely on the nine squadrons of Ansons for all short-range patrol tasks. It also meant that Vildebeests had to be used on anti-submarine patrols until December. They did not carry torpedoes. As an interim measure, until more suitable aircraft, such as long-range twin-engine fighters, were available, Blenheim Mk IVs were modified by fitting the four-gun ventral 'fighter' pack of the short-nose Mk Is. They were also fitted with IFF sets and additional radio equipment, armour plate, a reflector gunsight for the pilot and self-sealing fuel tanks. In October the modified Blenheims were allocated for 'trade-protection'. This included watching over the North Sea fishing fleet and coastal convoys. Later in the year they were transferred from Fighter to Coastal Command.[7]

Coastal convoy protection

Coastal Command did not have enough aircraft at the end of the year to fulful all the tasks it was being set by the Air Staff and the Admiralty. The Hudsons and Sunderlands looked after the long-range ocean patrols. Among the Hudson squadrons' many duties were the 'battle flights' that provided air cover for the Royal Navy sailing in Norwegian coastal waters. The Hudsons had to mix it with Ju88s, Ju87s and Do17s. In the four opening months of the war Hudson losses were heavy. They may have been less had the aircraft been equipped with feathering propellers, self-sealing fuel tanks and ventral guns to deter fighter attacks from below. Of particular interest in view of the arguments at the time over the fitting of pilot-operated guns, for targets of oportunity, are the number of occasions during which Hudsons acted as fighters. The Trade Protection squadrons (Blenheims), of which there were only four, were stretched to the limit by calls for their services. Recourse was made to the records of convoy protection during WWI. The most important fact that emerged was the effect any form of aircraft, seaplane or dirigible, had on U-boats. The mere presence of aircraft frightened them away from convoys. Therefore in December it was decided to try scarecrow tactics. Coastal Patrol Flights using unarmed Tiger Moths operated from eastern littoral airfields.[8]

If an Anson happened to come upon a surfaced U-boat, 100 lb bombs, that exploded on contact, would be dropped. Without a specialised bombsight the bombs had to be dropped from low level to ensure a hit. Unfortunately the exploding bomb's

Navigator (observer)/bomb-aimer's position in the nose of a Hampden. (R. Wallace-Clarke)

flying fragments had little effect on the thick skin of the submarine. But they did have an effect on the thin skin of the Anson. Many were badly damaged during such low-level attacks.

Hampden experiences

On the 11 September 1939 Arthur T. Harris was appointed AOC-in-C No. 5 Group Bomber Command. The majority of his aircraft were Handley Page Hampdens. Harris wrote pessimistically about the Hampden. He noted that it had been designed in 1932 and therefore was out of date. The four crew members worked in cramped, draughty and cold accommodation. It could not be defended adequately. During three attempts to attack the German fleet the Vickers K guns could not be aimed accurately when the Hampdens were attacked by Bf 109 fighters.

Italian aircraft for RAF

A proposal to order Savoia Marchetti bombers was not approved by the Commons. However, in November 1939, 400 Caproni CA311s and 313s trainers were ordered (the order was withdrawn on the 23 April 1940).

Trainer problems

The Miles Masters that, along with the Harvard, provided the step in training between *ab-initio* and

The Miles Master I derived from the more elegant but unsuitable Miles Kestrel Trainer. For many pilots this was the intermediate phase of their training between the Tiger Moth and a first-line fighter such as the Spitfire. (Derek James)

flying first-line aircraft were not allowed to be deliberately spun. They were also breaking up in the air. Structural failure of the tail surfaces was eventually found to be caused by the cockpit canopy breaking free of its hinges. The canopy, which enclosed both cockpits, was hinged on the starboard side. If it became unlocked in flight the air loads would break it off. Miles had to revert to the more usual fore and aft sliding arrangement. Another example of what seemed a good idea having to be abandoned because of other considerations.

14 and 18 December 1939

On the 14 December six out of twelve Wellingtons that attempted a daylight raid against the German fleet at Wilhelmshaven were lost. Fifteen out of 24 Wellingtons were lost attempting to attack the same target on the 18 December. The formations were more than decimated. They were cut down by over 50 per cent.

On the 18 December when the aircraft of Nos' 9 and 37 Squadron failed to keep up with the main formation they became easy prey for the German fighters. The Bf109s and Bf110s were able to inflict crippling damage. Once the 7.9mm bullets and 20mm shells punctured fuel tanks the petrol poured out at such a rate that, even if an aircraft did not burst into flames immediately, the crew had to ditch the aircraft before they were half way back across the North Sea when the tanks ran dry. The two operations have been the subject of many detailed descriptions. The key facts are: despite the three, power-driven, twin-gun turrets of each Wellington they could not deter the German fighters, particularly as the fighter pilots often chose to make 'full deflection' beam attacks from slightly above and therefore in the 'dead ground' of all three turrets; the fuel tanks were not self-sealing and there was no armour plate to protect vital areas.

After the event the self-criticism included the observation that HQ 3 Group had failed to organise exercises in formation flying by more than one squadron at a time. Squadrons were sent out in daylight without previously having flown together.

Despite the failure on the 14 and 18 December the command did not immediately, as has sometimes been supposed, abandon the daylight sortie concept. Bomber Command only postponed further large-scale daylight operations. In future they would only be ordered if they were the only way of meeting a particular, urgent and vital need.

Therefore daylight operations of the type under-

Miles Master trainer production line at Miles Aircraft Woodley in 1939. (Adwest Group plc via Julian C Temple)

taken by 3 Group, intended to test a number of operational factors and to boost the morale of the nation and of the aircrews, were no longer in the immediate war plans of the Air Staff. Of course, the overriding consideration was the simple fact that no airforce could sustain an attrition rate per operation of 50 per cent or more and remain in being for more than a few days. Even if Bomber Command at the end of 1939 had an inexhaustible supply of aircraft, to replace those lost, there was not an inexhaustible supply of trained aircrew and, what was even more important, of experienced crews. Despite the experience of the 18 December, on 2 January 1940 seventeen Wellingtons went on an 'armed reconnaissance' in formation: although they were fitted with armour plating, two were shot down by Bf109s.

Sir Arthur Harris recalled that: 'Any sustained campaign in the Autumn of 1939 would very quickly have brought us to the end of our supply of trained crews'. In another commentary he said

> What we actually had was not much good, being totally insufficient in number and with no reserves either of crews or aircraft adequate for any sort of sustained operations. Nor was there adequate organisation for

Whitley V, R-R Merlin engines. Visible are the single K gun FN turret in the nose with the bomb-aimer's window below. At the start of WWII the Whitley, along with the Wellington, represented the 'heavy' bomber strength of the RAF. (Derek James)

training crews up to the standard or in numbers required for modern war.

Whitley winter

In normal conditions the Whitley was highly regarded by its crew. The controls were light and responsive. The stall was a gentle affair and it was nearly impossible to induce a spin. The cockpit layout was better than some of its contemporaries. The pilot could reach all the essential controls without having to stretch and contort his limbs: only the emergency lever for the undercarriage extension was out of reach; as there was a second-pilot that did not matter.

Throughout the winter of 1939/40 the Whitleys of Bomber Command took the war to the enemy as best they could. Leaflets were dropped at the end of arduous outward flights in severe icing conditions; the return flight was rarely less demanding on aircraft and crew. During a typical sortie to reconnoitre southern Germany and to drop leaflets on selected cities, the crew were faced from take off onward with forecast cloud extending from 1,000 feet up to 12,000 feet. The freezing level was at 1,500 feet with icing conditions extending up to the Whitley's ceiling of 17,000 feet. Mixed in were thunderstorms and severe turbulence. The unreliable heating system and electrically-heated suits, for only a few members of the crew, soon reduced the crew to a dulled acceptance of their misery. Every action required considerable mental and physical effort to complete. Ejecting bundles of leaflets with a failing oxygen supply caused loss of judgement and nausea.

Failures of equipment, including engines, added to the pilot's control difficulties caused by ice building up on the wings and control surfaces. To add to the problems with a failed engine, the venturi tube that provided a reserve vacuum to drive the flight instruments was liable to ice up, thereby depriving the pilot of vital reference instruments. Even worse followed when the pitot head froze and the airspeed indicator failed. In a contemporary account in the press 'pitot' head became 'pilot' head. As one Whitley pilot remarked, who had struggled for six hours to maintain control at 10,000 feet in icing conditions, 'perhaps pilot head is right'

Although many of the Whitleys were reasonably well defended by three power-operated turrets, the operational records contain few references to being attacked by night fighters during the winter. Presumably the weather conditions that made life so miserable for the Whitley crews was equally hard on the *Luftwaffe*. The amazing endurance of the Whitley crews in the first winter of the war has been recounted at length in articles and books. Of concern to this study is the effect, or lack of effect, equipment, accessories and instruments had on the ability of RAF crews to reach, find and attack their targets even if only with leaflets. As suggested, the Whitley had few vices as a basic aircraft. The structure and major systems were up to the state of the technology of the time. However, like the missing nail in the horseshoe, the battle could be lost by the failure of a small item such as an electrically-heated flying suit, a pump, a pitot head or one of a thousand small items.

Where are we?

In nearly every de-briefing of bomber crews after sorties they claimed to have found their target. At the time it was not realised that in fact few crews had found their target. The mixture of deduction, art and luck which constituted the work of the navigator in the early months of the war was little different from that used in earlier years. Until the advent of electro-mechanical and electronic means of determining position there would be a significant difference in skill between the few experienced navigators and those just out of the Observer & Gunnery Schools.

It is worth considering in some detail the methods used to navigate RAF aircraft in the years before Air Position Indicators, Gee and radar were available.

If we take just one leg of a flight, say from A to B. A was the take-off point and therefore with little chance of error the entry in the navigation log was 'airborne from A at xxxx hours'. Prior to the flight the intended track towards B was marked on a Mercator chart. If the pilot then flew at a certain speed then a simple calculation gave the estimated time of arrival (ETA) at B. All this assumed a flight in still air. Unfortunately there were a number of potential errors and effects that worked against such a simple operation.

A likely and significant effect was the wind that might be blowing at an angle to thc intended course. Allowance for the effect of the wind was made using a simple vector triangle; either on the chart or on a mechanical device called a Course and Speed Calculator. The aircraft was then turned so that its head was pointing towards the side of the course from which the wind was blowing. The track being made good over the ground then coincided with the desired course: that is, as long as the navigator had applied the correct wind values of direction and speed. Before the flight the navigator noted in his log the direction and speed of the wind at various heights. However, they were only as accurate as the equipment used by the meteorologists.

As the flight proceeded the navigator would, if he could see the ground or sea, attempt to check on the direction of the wind. A drift sight would be used for this purpose. The grid wires of the sight were aligned so that objects on the ground, the waves or a smoke float or marker, dropped from the aircraft, appeared to move parallel to the wires. This gave the drift angle. It might coincide with that already in use or indicate a significant change in wind direction. Depending on how far they were away from radio stations the crew could request a 'fix' of their position from two or more direction-finding stations who obtained a compass bearing when listening to a continuous transmission from the aircraft when the wireless operator held the Morse key down. Butser in England and Dyce in Scotland were two of the radio stations used. Their reply either confirmed or confounded the navigator's calculated position.

The magnetic compass, of which there was usually only one, was subject to errors and effects which had to be compensated for by the pilot and the navigator. The compass reading had to be corrected for deviation and variation. The airspeed as indicated by the instruments on the panels in front of the pilot and the navigator were not very accurate. They showed 'indicated' speed and their readings had to be corrected for temperature and height to obtain true airspeed for use in navigational calculations.

The foregoing is an over simplified description of the navigational process known as 'dead reckoning'. The 'dead' was derived from the word deduced and referred to the fact that a navigator gathered a number of facts and observations, made some assumptions and then deduced the answers.

In good visibility position could be determined or verified by reference to geographical features. Targets on the coast or near readily identifiable stretches of water, particularly in moonlight, were easier to find. Other targets, hiding under the very effective blackout imposed over Germany, might only be hit by bombs through a lucky chance.

Astro-navigation, when practised by skilled navigators, could overcome the otherwise low standard of position-finding accuracy throughout Bomber Command. Unfortunately during the first few months of the war and well into 1940 there was shortage of navigators in general and those skilled in astro-navigation in particular. Although the Wellington 1A, for example, had a proper transparent plastic 'astro' dome, through which the navigator could sight his sextant, it was not a steady 'platform'. It often tended to wallow and progress along a corkscrew path. If the aircraft had an autopilot then the navigator's task was made a little easier. Although autopilots were a standard fitting in many RAF aircraft they were not necessarily fitted because of shortages of equipment. The Hampden, despite its intended role, did not have an astro-dome. Neither the Blenheim nor the Battle were suitable astro-navigation platforms.

Even if a bomber crew reached the target area, having successfully navigated with the benefit of radio bearings, astro-navigation and inspired dead-reckoning they had no specialised night flying target maps. Yet the need for special night target maps was foreseen during WWI.

RAF in France

Prior to September 1939 plans were drawn up for the movement of a force of Hurricanes, Battles, Lysanders and Blenheims to France. These were allocated to two separate commands: the Advanced Air Striking Force (AASF) and the Air Component of the Field Force (ACFF). The AASF was mostly made up of the Battle squadrons.

Bomb and stores parks were established during the summer under a cover plan that described the stores as having been purchased by the French air-force. However, despite the preparations to move a large part of the RAF to France, little was done to prepare a communications network comparable to that of the RAF in the UK. At the outbreak of war Air Formation Signals had not made much progress with the setting up of telephone and teleprinter circuits that would be independent of the French public service.

Plans for the Air Component were delayed in preparation or had to be changed because of political, not technical, considerations relating to the deployment of the British Army in France. The Air Component, as its title indicated, was operationally subordinate to the C-in-C British Expeditionary Force. As such it was in a similar chain of command position as the Royal Flying Corps in WWI. The Air Component's primary task was to act as the long-range 'eyes' of the C-in-C, Lord Gort. This role was allocated to the four Blenheim squadrons. Hurricane squadrons were included in the component in order to see off any German reconnaissance aircraft. Lysanders were allocated to divisions for army co-operation tasks. In addition to the two Air Stores Parks there were two port detachments.

Indicative of the lack of thought given to support operations by air was the use of Tiger Moths for communications flights and the need to impress civilian aircraft of many different ages and types to maintain an air link across the English Channel. As mentioned, the RAF was supplied with DH 89Ms (Rapide) for both training and communications roles. It was not until November that the National Air Communications service was sufficiently well organised and equipped to support the RAF in France. On the 15 November a motley collection of over 40 civil transport aircraft, escorted by 32 Gladiator fighters, transported stores, equipment and personnel to France. This massive, for its time, formation was not attacked

In general the move of RAF squadrons to France in September 1939 was not particularly well organised. There was muddle and confusion. The Air Component or, for that matter, any part of an air-force was far more than just aircraft, first echelon servicing and equipment. Pay, billets, food, medical services, airfield construction, communications, road transport and fuel were just some of the things needed to support air operations. As part of the Field Force, the Air Component was within the administrative area of the British Army and depended on the army for many supporting services. The airfields originally allocated were within the designated administrative area. Unfortunately on arriving in France the squadrons found that this was no longer the case. The majority of the airfields were outside the area and therefore the RAF could not depend on the army for supporting services. In the end many services had to be requisitioned from the French.

Radar in France

Radar was included in the list of services for the RAF in France. However in September 1939 there were no suitable radar sets available with which to form a detection screen around the perimeter of France. The Chain Home stations, which by then had become a familiar feature along the east and south coasts of Britain, were static installations requiring tall, oil-well-like, wooden masts. Robert Watson-Watt advised on radar cover for both the Air Component and the Advanced Air Striking Force. He recommended the rapid conversion of mobile GL (gun laying) Mk II sets that were originally designed for use with anti-aircraft gun batteries.

The first of the mobile radar units was positioned near Calais at the end of September in order to detect aircraft flying south-west along the coast of neutral Belgium. Another set was positioned to cover the approaches to the Field Force from the south-east. It was not until the end of December before all the planned sets were in position. However, it took even longer to overcome all the start-up problems that arose. In addition to the eleven GL sets, twelve MB type radars were allocated for use in France; three of which would be operated by French personnel. During the Summer of 1939 a number of French officers were given instruction in the operation of British radar equipment.

France had no radar defence system comparable to Britain's Chain Home, even though there were a number of research programmes and prototype installations for both aircraft and ship detection radar systems. For example, the David system, at about the same transmission frequency as CH, was set up in 1939 to protect important ports and the approaches from the north-east towards Paris.

A comprehensive reporting and control network, of the type established by Fighter Command for the defence of the United Kingdom, was not available for the RAF in France. The overall French air intelligence system, which included a network of visual observers and information centres, was considered inadequate by the RAF. Therefore the Air Ministry, in co-operation with the War Office, drew up plans for a network of visual observation posts in France similar to that of the Observer Corps in Britain. Some British anti-aircraft and searchlight units, such as 39 Squadron (AA) RE, were equipped with Mk IV plotters and telephone links to control centres.

A WAAF operator dummy monitoring the radar echoes on the CRT of a CH station. The large control knob to the left enabled her to determine both the bearing and height of a target echo. (GEC Marconi)

Receiver operator's station in Chain Home (CH) radar station. (GEC Marconi)

Radar investigated

In October 1939 Tizard chaired a committee investigating the working of the CH system. Two events contributed to the decision to set up the committee. One, already mentioned, the aircraft that approached the South Coast as Chamberlain made his historic broadcast on the 3 September. The other incident became known as the 'Battle of Barking Creek'. Fighters were scrambled to intercept an aircraft heading up the Thames estuary which was not transmitting the correct identification signal. Because of a fault in the CH radar station concerned the aircraft's position was incorrectly plotted. When the intercepting fighters came within coverage of the radar station they were confused with the target and plotted as 'hostile'. More fighters were scrambled. Eventually the reporting and control system became very confused and regrettably the RAF shot down some of its own aircraft.

Anti-aircraft guns

In addition to the Hurricane fighter squadrons in France the defence elements available to counter German air attacks consisted of only 96 heavy anti-aircraft guns, concentrated around the supply ports, 72 searchlights for the fighter sectors covering the sea approaches between Calais and Dunkirk and the magnificent total of six 40mm Bofors AA guns for the defence of all of 60 Wing's airfields.[12]

French aircraft

Of course the RAF was not alone in France. There was the French airforce whose personnel were determined but their aircraft in general were inferior to those of both the RAF and the *Luftwaffe*. The principal fighter the M-S 406 C1 was, like the Hurricane, of mixed metal and fabric construction: but there the similarity ended. The 406 was not large enough or sturdy enough to carry eight guns. It was also handicapped by having an engine, the Hispano-Suiza 12Y31, of only 860 hp. Of greater concern to France's ally was the history of political interference and uncertainty that far exceeded anything experienced by the British aircraft industry at the hands of government. Therefore the French airforce was not only below par at the sharp end it was without the backing of soundly established production facilities. A sustained air campaign proved the end of France's hope to stem a German advance.

Frozen guns

Once the Hurricane pilots started to use their guns above 15,000 feet there was no guarantee that they would fire. During the severe winter of 1939/40 guns were freezing at all altitudes. Essentially a machine gun was a high speed precision mechanism and therefore dependent on some, but not too much, lubricating oil for smooth operation. The oil also helped to prevent corrosion. There was nothing more abhorrent to an armourer and more likely to incur the wrath of superiors, than corrosion. Therefore to be on the safe side armourers applied a liberal coating of oil. Unfortunately in very low temperatures the oil congealed to an extent that could stop the action of a gun. A temporary cure was found by adding paraffin to the oil until there was just sufficient lubricating properties for the limited time a gun fired: but the special 'winter' mixture did not inhibit corrosion.

Another gun problem was that of moist air condensing on mechanisms and then freezing. One solution was to seal the muzzle with a cover; such as a piece of fabric doped over the aperture in the leading edge of the wing.

In addition to the above measures there was a - modification programme in hand for sealing the gun bays and feeding hot air ducted from the engine.

The manually controlled gun in the rear cockpit of the Battle was particularly prone to 'freezing up'.

RAF Barrage balloon with winch vehicle and trailer with hydrogen gas cylinders. (Aeroplane Monthly)

Chapter Eight

1940

The severe winter of ice, snow and record low temperatures eventually gave way to Spring. When and in what direction would the German army move once conditions were favourable for both a land and air war?

Early months

The lessons of the early months of war were learned the hard way. The loss of aircraft was serious but the loss of trained crews was even more serious. Why lessons had not been learnt during the air exercises of earlier years remains to this day a matter of speculation. Answers are available but they tend to contradict. For example, surely fighter camera-gun films must have highlighted the blind spots of the bombers' defensive armament? Or was it assumed that, although RAF fighters undoubtedly scored 'hits' during exercises, German pilots were not trained, equipped or had the *élan* to press home their attacks? Contributing to the lack of sufficient experience on which to base defensive tactics for bombers was the poor co-operation between Bomber and Fighter Commands.

During the first few months of war the monthly returns to the Air Ministry from HQ Fighter Command underlined the shortage of spare parts and the lack of specialised maintenance equipment. The paper strength of the RAF, like that of the *Luftwaffe*, was often at variance with the number of aircraft fully equipped and ready to go into action. Of the eighteen new fighter squadrons formed between September 1939 and February 1940, only two were fully equipped. Ironically these two squadrons operated Gladiator biplanes.

As late as April 1940 and with the knowledge that the Germans were likely to start an offensive at any

A Fairey Battle light bomber being prepared for a sortie during the harsh winter of 1939/40. (Derek James)

time, the Hurricanes of 73 Squadron in France, for example, had not all been fitted with variable-pitch propellers. With their fixed-pitch, two-blade propeller they were not able to catch a Bf110 unless they had the height advantage.

The types of aircraft available to the British and French airforces did not always match the needs of the two allies. The French army was the larger of the two armies and therefore the French airforce was expected to provide suitable aircraft, particularly for reconnaissance duties. In practice it was found that only the RAF's Blenheims were suitable and therefore they had to provide a service for both armies.

Hudsons hunting ships

By the end of January 1940 a number of Coastal Command Hudson crews had become familiar with ASV radar. Three aircraft were equipped with ASV in December 1939 and another eight in the following month. However the crews were not necessarily enamoured of the new electronic wizardry. E.G. Bowen and his team took only four months in which to advance from an experimental ASV radar to equipping twelve Hudsons by January 1940. Along the way some corners had to be cut with the result there were many problems to be overcome. The serviceability rate was only about 50 per cent so that during half the sorties either it was not installed because it was in the workshops or it failed soon after take off. Even when ASV was working its accuracy was not sufficient to guarantee detection. Adding to the problems was the vulnerability of the Yagi-type antennae which could easily be knocked out of alignment or damaged.[1,2] Despite the time it took to iron out the bugs, so that ASV became an effective hunter of ships, it was very useful as an aid to navigation because it presented a clear picture of coastlines and islands. Therefore it was an invaluable homing aid for crews returning from a long patrol during which time the visibility at their base may have deteriorated. The addition of transponder beacons at selected points near airfields further enhanced this secondary role. In-squadron service experience with the Mk I ASV (214 MHz) sets was applied to the development of the Mk II (175 MHz). The new set was more robust and designed for the mass-production of 4,000 units by Pye Radio and E.K. Cole Ltd.

Contemporary accounts of operations in the first half of 1940 refer to the practice of Hudsons flying in formation at night. Whether or not they used station-keeping lights or only flew in formation on bombing sorties on moonlit nights is not clear from the available records. The object of night formations was to ensure that all aircraft arrived over the target at the same time so as to saturate the defences.

Gyro sight

The angle of deflection or 'lead' needed to hit a target when it is moving across the line of sight was difficult to assess, even by an experienced pilot or air gunner. This was realised as early as 1917. Subsequently a number of scientists schemed automatic lead computing systems for use in aircraft. One proponent of the gyro-based sight was Dr L.B.C. Cunningham of the RAF Education Branch. In 1936 he suggested that a gyroscope be used to offset the line of sight from the gun line through an angle related to the rate of turn of the sight line.

Sir Henry Tizard and the Committee for the Scientific Survey of Air Defence had reported that the effectiveness of the Hurricanes and Spitfires in the 1938 air exercises would be improved if some means could be found to predict the lead angle when firing at an enemy aircraft that was moving across the line-of-sight. The inability to assess correctly the lead angle only came to light when the G45 16mm gun camera was fitted to some of the fighters and the films examined. In 1939, at the instigation of B. Melville Jones (later Sir Bennett), the RAE started to build an experimental gyro-gunsight that also incorporated the ideas of M. Hancock of the RAF's Fighter Development Unit.

An essential requirement for any precision equipment intended for the RAF was that of robustness. It was one thing to combine gyroscope, electric motors, potentiometers and an optical system and make them work on a test rig. It was another thing to design and put into quantity production a lead computing sight able to withstand the dust, extremes of temperature and vibration and G forces in the cockpit of a fighter aircraft or in the turret of a bomber

By October 1939 two experimental gyro sights were produced for evaluation in flight. One was fitted to a Hurricane and the other in the ventral turret of a Wellington. The principle of operation was proved and the Air Ministry proposed that production quantities be ordered, but the Gunnery Research Unit considered that the gyro-sight needed more operational trials. Also more time was needed in which to train pilots and gunners in how to make the most effective use of it. The Mk 1 gyro gunsight was ready for testing in June 1940. It came too late to affect the outcome of the air battles of France. Had it been available, the problem of consistent and accurate allowance for the relative movement of the target would have been solved.[3, 4, 5]

Navigational help

The limitations of dead reckoning procedures, described in the previous chapter, emphasised the need for automatic and semi-automatic devices both to simplify the navigator's task and improve accuracy.

As early as 1932 the RAE was considering the development of automatic navigational equipment. The gyro-based directional indicator was one of the instruments of the Basic Six panel. Its principal drawback was that it gradually drifted off the selected heading and had to be re-set at frequent intervals by reference to the magnetic compass. An experimental distant-reading compass was developed by I.C. Bygrave. A gyro unit and a magnetic compass unit were combined in a master unit installed in a location away from adverse magnetic effects. Distant-reading indicators were provided for the pilot's instrument panel and for the navigator's position.

Unfortunately, the Distant Reading Compass Mk I did not go into production until August 1940 and therefore it has to be classed as another essential item not developed to a production standard before September 1939. Also developed in parallel with the distant reading compass and also too late, was the automatic Air Mileage Unit from which derived the Air Position Indicator. These aids to navigation, had they been available to Bomber Command in particular, could have improved significantly the effectiveness of sorties during the first nine months of war.[6]

Radar Progress

The importance of radar, particularly the CH system of the late 1930s, has been remarked upon by many writers. The CH stations and the extensive

A typical transmitter tower of a CH station. This particular tower was erected at GEC-Marconi Great Baddow as a permanent reminder of the vital part played by the CH radar stations in the defence of Britain. (GEC-Marconi)

Transmitter control room of a Chain Home (CH) radar station. (GEC-Marconi)

network of communications, filter and operations rooms were virtually an airforce within and airforce. Ostensibly the expansion of the service from 1935 onward was related to the number of first-line aircraft and to the number of new air stations, maintenance and other support units and depots. The defence radar system had to be kept at the classification MOST SECRET even though its sensors, the tall towers and their webs of antennae, could not be hidden from spying eyes; any more than could the 'floodlight' pulses of electromagnetic energy at 30 MHz. be kept from an electronic intelligence gathering organisation, such as the *Luftwaffe*'s signals branch specialists in the *Graf Zeppelin*; that is provided their equipment was used correctly. The appellation AMES (Air Ministry Experimental Station) for the radar stations was intended to deter the inquisitive. Of course, there was strict security in the form of multiple barbed-wire perimeter fencing and entry could only be achieved by those trusted with the WATCHWORD that changed with each watch.

As mentioned, the most secret part of the MOST SECRET system was the way in which radar information was processed and used by fighter controllers to direct the interceptors to the most favourable position from which to make an attack.

Trials of AI radar continued throughout the winter months using Battles and Blenheims. None of the flights was allowed to fly over France. The interception of German aircraft at night over France depended on fighters co-operating with the searchlights whose basic method of detecting aircraft was still the 1918-type sound locator system; although radar for searchlight control was about to be produced. Stalking German bombers at night could be hazardous because the searchlights illuminated the fighter as well as the bomber, thereby giving the latter the opportunity to shoot at a well lit target.

In April there was an investigation into the 'leaking' of radar information. In May there were nearly fifty radar stations disposed around the coast of Britain. However, there were still gaps: notably north-west Scotland, part of the Welsh coast and the Bristol Channel. There were three principal types of stations: Chain Home, Mobile Units and Chain Home Low.[7]

End of 'Phoney War'

On the night of the 19/20 March Whitley crews of 77 Squadron were briefed to attack the German seaplane base at Hornum on the island of Sylt. They were part of a fifty strong force of Whitleys and Hampdens. For the first time their targets were not to be restricted to warships away from land. For the first time also a large force of Whitleys carried live bombs. The gloves were off. The international situation was changing, Germany was on the move again. On the 9 April Norway was invaded.

Gladiators in Norway

The decision to send a force of Gladiators to Norway in the Spring of 1940 was an example of political emotion dominating practical considerations.

On paper the idea of operating 18 Gladiator biplane fighters from an improvised airstrip on a frozen lake was intended to provide air cover for the army. Unfortunately those who prepared the operational orders and logistic requirements, were forced by their political masters to ignore some of the fundamental factors that govern the employment of aircraft. In general, RAF squadrons were dependent for their operational efficiency on large, well organised, support echelons. As an example, if the aircraft of a squadron were fuelled, armed and their engines started, then at a command they could be airborne and on their way to intercept the enemy: If there was an established reporting and control organisation then they could be directed to a favourable tactical position. On returning the aircraft could usually be re-armed, re-fuelled and serviced within thirty minutes.

In the 1940 Norwegian campaign RAF pilots flew their aircraft off an aircraft carrier (HMS *Glorious*) and then landed on the frozen, bomb-pitted, surface of Lake Lesjeskogen. The eighteen pilots and one armourer were the only RAF personnel: there were no fitters, riggers, aircrafthands or cooks. Although the eighteen achieved victories over the *Luftwaffe* the inevitable attrition from combat and mechanical failures steadily reduced the number of serviceable aircraft. Eventually the five aircraft that survived had to be destroyed.

On the 21 May a second squadron of Gladiators was sent to Norway. With the support of a complement of ground staff, they were more effective than those of the first venture. However, on the 7 June the deteriorating military situation forced their retirement. The Gladiators were then landed successfully on HMS *Glorious* despite the fact that the pilots, unlike some of their modern RAF counterparts, had received no training in deck landing. *Glorious* was sunk by a German battle cruiser and all but two of the Gladiator pilots were drowned.

A commentary on the RAF in Norway, written in 1942, made the point that:

> One of the truths about air warfare is that the least complicated thing in it is flying . . . . all branches of supply and maintenance must be adequately represented in the ground staff which even a small air-fighting unit needs to take with it for operation from a base abroad . . . . the bases they operate from ought, properly, to be strongly defended by anti-aircraft artillery.

German army starts westward

Every night throughout the ten months in France the Blenheim squadrons despatched one or more sorties that penetrated over the German frontier in order to give the field commanders information about the enemy's strength, dispositions and intentions. On average one Blenheim and its crew failed to return.

Night after night the Blenheim crews observed little activity behind the German front-line. But on the night of the 8 May a Blenheim of 70 Wing flying at 13,000 feet detected considerable activity. Two signals were sent giving the position, direction of movement and composition of an army that was moving westward along a winding road on the Luxembourg frontier. After the signals were received at Air Headquarters BAFF, nothing more was seen or heard of the aircraft. When the situation reports at AHQ BAFF (Eagle) indicated without doubt that German forces were massing in the Ardennes, the C-in-C, Air Marshal Sir Arthur Barratt, sought permission from Lord Gort's GHQ to use a greater part of his force in a mass bombing attack so as to pre-empt the German plan. For a number of reasons the operation did not take place. Group Captain Winterbotham, in his book *The Ultra Secret,* lists one reason as the lack of suitable bombs for use against armoured formations. If that was true then, once again, those who organised the establishment of the RAF in France appeared to have had no clear idea on how it should have been used.

Fighter control

As mentioned, the radar chain and reporting network from forward-looking radar stations back to filter and operations rooms in France was a replica of the UK based organisation. However, it was on a smaller scale and with a far less effective visual observer net. This meant that when enemy aircraft flew further and further into the 'radar' hinterland the system was unable to keep a continuous track of their movements.

On occasions fighters were scrambled towards an assumed track. Once airborne they had to rely entirely on visual observation to pick up their quarry. Reading accounts of operations in May 1940 emphasises the shortcomings of the reporting and control system. Pilots sat in their cockpits at readiness awaiting a scramble order. The sudden jerking of the control column as the airman standing at the wing tip moved the ailerons, to attract the pilot's attention, might have been the only indication of hostile aircraft. The airman would point toward the sound or sight of enemy aircraft. The lack of a continuous stream of information about enemy aircraft movements from the sector controller deprived the fighters of gaining a tactically advantageous position relative to the enemy. At 30,000 feet those Hurricanes equipped with a fixed-pitch propeller were at the limit of their performance. Close to the stall and at full power they lost speed the moment they fired their eight guns.

Expected or unexpected results?

The expected did not happen and
the unexpected did happen.

The Brook-Popham report to the Air Staff on the performance of the RAF in France contained many examples of failures of equipment and planning. These contributed to the RAF's inability to either attack or defend adequately as the Germans advanced from their 10 May start. As a simple statistic, squadrons that attempted to attack targets such as bridges suffered 50 per cent losses. At the same time the defending Hurricanes were unable to shoot down enough German bombers to affect the outcome of the land battle. Nevertheless, overall, the *Luftwaffe* was badly mauled during the Battle for France; particularly at the time of the Dunkirk evacuation when Spitfires joined in the battle. But irrespective of losses and courage in the air or at sea, it is the army that holds the most ground at the end who achieves the real victory.

The Hurricanes in France and those deployed from the UK, did not have a significant margin of performance over the Bf109s. The Blenheims and Battles were forced to attack in daylight and the night bombers did not have the systems or equipment needed for making accurate attacks at night.

Much of the technology expected from all the hard work and planning during the years of expansion did not arrive in time. If the Germans had postponed their advance to the west until 1941 then the RAF might have been able to strike with some effect against the rear areas and industry. That is provided there had been a great improvement in navigational skills, bomb-sights and bombs.

Cooks and Clerks

From 1914: '. . . that the corps (RFC), though it did its work in the air, had to live on the ground, and that its efficiency depended on a hundred important details.'

Sir Walter Raleigh p248

During the confused days from the 10 May onwards, as the RAF in France attempted a juggling act and tried to fight and regroup at one and the same time, distinctions of rank and skill were abandoned. Cooks and clerks, aircrafthands and transport drivers became impressed armourers, parachute packers and re-fuellers. All had to 'pitch-in' and service aircraft immediately they landed from a sortie. It no longer mattered to which unit an aircraft belonged.

Despite the sustained effort by unskilled personnel to keep the fighters in the air there were inevitable failures. The dispersal of skilled airmen away from the specialised parachute packing rooms often meant that pilots could not be sure of their parachutes. Like the MaeWest inflatable life jacket, the parachute provided a second chance to survive should the aircraft be crippled and, therefore, was an important psychological factor.

Vulnerability on the ground

One of the key tactics favoured by the *Luftwaffe* was the destruction of aircraft parked on airfields. However, despite intensive bombing and strafing attacks the RAF only lost about 25 aircraft from those causes. That was a small number compared with those shot down by fighters and anti-aircraft guns. The Blenheims of 114 Squadron were neatly parked in a line at Conde and suffered accordingly.

On the 11 May, 36 twin-engine bombers were 'borrowed' from Bomber Command. They landed on and dispersed around the edges of five connected airfields north of Arras. Each aircraft carried 2,000 lb of bombs. The crews stood-by to attack important tactical targets, such as bridges. Any inhibitions about a daylight operation in the face of formidable fighter opposition were put aside. Unlike Wilhelmshaven in December there would be no nonsense about avoiding damage to private property. The sabotage of communications and the confused situation in France and the lack of information about the enemy's movements left this large and valuable force sitting exposed on the ground from early morning to late afternoon. Only luck prevented them being destroyed where they stood.

By road

The report on the RAF's performance in France in 1940 includes a comment on the number of vehicles that squadrons considered they needed when re-positioning. A Blenheim squadron of 12 aircraft needed 26 lorries and 36 for 18 aircraft and a complement of 435 officers and airmen. A Battle squadron required 26 lorries and two buses when forced to move its base in a hurry. One Lysander squadron even claimed that it needed 77 lorries when re-positioning. Yet a Hurricane squadron settled for 58 vehicles.

The attention given squadron vehicle establishments, both expected and actual, was made in the light of the difficulties many units experienced after the 10 May in deploying out of range of the advancing German army. Apparently few squadrons had made any attempt to practise re-deployment; even though the planned advance of the Anglo-French left flank, in the event of the German army crossing into Belgium, would have required the immediate re-positioning of RAF formations.

Logistics on the move

It was not only the frequent re-location of squadrons that reduced the overall effectiveness of the RAF; the logistics also ran into trouble. Ammunition, bombs, oxygen, fuel, oil, hydraulic fluid and all the hundreds of other items needed to keep aircraft operational, were needed at all hours and at many different dispersed locations.

The breakdown of the communications net, through overloading and damage, meant that despite the huge stocks of materiél in the Air Stores Parks, spares and supplies could not be requisitioned. Even if ordered and loaded onto transports, the drivers could not always find the 'customers' because of the constant movement of units. Transport became scarce as empty vehicles were commandeered for other purposes. At one point in the Battle of France the supply of aviation fuel was halted. The RAF's road tankers were unable to uplift fuel from French railway tank cars because they did not have suitable pumping equipment.[8]

Mobility

It has been suggested that the *Luftwaffe*'s structure, particularly its support services, was extremely mobile and able to operate with a great degree of flexibility . The organisation was designed to match the fluid type of campaign waged by the German army. Squadrons were not intended to be dependent on fixed installations, such as the parent station organisation of the RAF. However, the *Luftwaffe* was not always as mobile as intended.

By the second week of the attack toward the west in 1940 many *Luftwaffe* squadrons outran their logistic tail to such an extent that they were rendered largely ineffective. In contrast, many RAF fighter squadrons in France were already operating away from fixed installations. In some respects the RAF sustained a fluid campaign for longer than the *Luftwaffe*. Only when forced to move faster and further, as more and more airfields were bombed out of use and ground staff were dispersed, did the squadrons begin to lose their effectiveness as an organised force.

As the RAF moved its ground facilities back and away from the advancing Germans the network of navigational beacons was no longer available for aircraft operating at night. Each of the beacons, of which there were many, flashed a Morse code letter to identify its location. The code changed every 24 hours; therefore a crew had to make certain before a night flight that they had the current beacon-map.

The criticism of the RAF by the troops waiting on the beaches at Dunkirk was eventually refuted. During the envelopment and evacuation the airforce prevented the *Luftwaffe* from executing wholesale destruction of men and ships. The Hurricanes and Spitfires gave good account of themselves even though they were operating at the limit of their range and of radar cover.

Ground targets

The report on RAF operations in France was critical of the long delays in taking action against 'fleeting targets'. These delays were occasioned by two factors: delays in tasking and protracted operational turn-round times. For example, four to five hours elapsed before Hurricanes reached the enemy's reported position. In that time the bird had 'flown the nest'. Similar delays occurred with the Battle and Blenheim squadrons. There were delays in rearming, refuelling and bombing up. A Hurricane took ten minutes to refuel and rearm. Operating from UK stations, Spitfires needed 15 minutes and Defiants ten minutes; provided the oxygen bottles did not have to be replaced. The Battle and Blenheim squadrons had the added delay of often having to change the type of bombs to match the target.

Among the few measures available to the French and British for slowing down the advancing German columns were low-level attacks against bridges and other bottlenecks by RAF Battle and Blenheim squadrons. To achieve accuracy they were briefed to attack as low as possible using delayed-action bombs. The Blenheims in France required twenty minutes between sorties for refuelling, rearming and bombing up. The critical factor was the loading of bombs. Placing a bomb onto the release mechanism, screwing in the fuse and connecting the arming link required skill and care. The average number of armourers available was usually only sufficient for bombing up three Blenheims at a time. If, for example, nine aircraft had to be loaded with bombs then it could take at least an hour. In that time a German armoured formation could be twenty or more miles further on from the last reported position. Three Battles needed only 20 minutes for refuelling and rearming. However the law of diminishing returns saw to it that it might take 90 minutes to re-fuel and bomb-up a complete squadron.

The currency and therefore the value of target information became overtaken by events because of the delays in transmitting enemy position reports. When a reconnaissance aircraft spotted, say, a column of enemy vehicles it had to send a WT signal back to a ground station. The signal was usually sent in code and therefore delayed in transmission. At the ground station it had to be decoded and distributed to the various operational headquarters for evaluation of the target's 'value' and then an operational signal sent, by whatever means remained open, to a squadron. At the same time elaborate and time consuming procedures had to be completed to ensure that all army formations concerned were aware of the intention and that none had any objections to an air strike.

On too many occasions the Blenheim crews set out for their assigned targets many hours after the Germans had first established a river crossing. In the time that had elapsed while the intelligence information was processed, the chain of command established, the crews briefed and the aircraft loaded with the correct type of bombs, a formidable ring of anti-aircraft guns had been installed round the target. The guns usually downed at least a third of each attacking formation. By the end of May the Blenheim squadrons had been cut down by over a half and virtually eliminated from the order of battle.

Both the Blenheim and the Battle were inadequate to the tasks set them. The Battle was not equipped for reconnaissance work at night and in daylight was a hostage to fortune whenever there were Bf109s around. The Blenheim was an order better than the Battle but by the time it went into the fight it was no longer the, as advertised, 'Fastest and most powerful medium bomber'. Accurate bombing of targets from an altitude out of range of light flak was not possible because of the ineffective bomb-aiming technology of the time. The only way in which the Blenheim squadrons could be certain of hitting a specific target was to go in at low level and suffer crippling losses.

The Blenheim, like other types, was the subject of many modifications and additions during the first six months of war: particularly after some hare and hound chases over France during which they were caught from below by fighters if they flew too high or by light flak if they flew at tree-top height. Some of the things that had to be done to improve survivability included the fitting of self-sealing fuel tanks, armour plate below the turret and below the pilot and observer positions. Some Blenheims were equipped with fixed guns firing aft from the engine nacelles and the majority were fitted with a single or twin 7.7mm Browning gun pod firing aft aimed by the observer.

Bomber Command – UK

The Whitleys, Wellingtons, Blenheims and other aircraft based in the UK exerted maximum effort against targets in the Netherlands, Belgium and France in an endeavour to slow the German advance toward the west and south. The lack of navigational aids for finding point targets, such as a bridge or concentration of troops, particularly at night, negated much of the effort. Number 77 Squadron of Whitleys experimented with an early form of target indicating or pathfinding. Crossing the coast at the easily identifiable Spurn Head the crews set course for Rotterdam. When within 100 miles they could see the intense fires of the bombed city on the horizon. A time and distance run was then made from overhead Rotterdam to the known position of the target. At the end of the run each aircraft released a flare and fired a red Very light to assist the others and to confirm the required position. Any flares well away from the majority were to be discounted. Although the visibility was good none of the crews was able to see the flares or Very

An example of twin-Browning 7.7mm guns on a flexible mounting in the rear cockpit of a Lysander. (R Wallace Clarke)

lights of other aircraft. Although this is an isolated incident it serves to highlight the problems that had to be solved if Bomber Command was going to make concentrated attacks.

Communications

During the winter months, that had curtailed operations to some extent, a comprehensive signals network was eventually established in France. As in the UK, a proportion of the required lines were part of the public utility. Therefore, as the RAF's communications network began to disintegrate from the middle of May onwards, units found that they could no longer pick up the telephone to give or receive orders. Also they found they could no longer communicate with other units by teleprinter. Therefore they reverted to wireless telegraphy (WT) but then found that many WT operators had not maintained or acquired sufficient skill.

In the UK during 1940 the RAF was building up a comprehensive Y Service that listened to German RT conversations. This information was used to build up a file of *Luftwaffe* dispositions, personnel and intentions. It was known that the Germans had a similar service, yet on too many occasions in France RAF airfields were referred to in messages by name and not by code.

Army Co-operation

The Lysander used for army co-operation work required care to be exercised by the pilot when attempting landings in a confined space. A balked landing required even more care to be exercised by the pilot. When the throttle was advanced to go-around, the negative 'landing' incidence setting of the tailplane meant that it was difficult to hold the aircraft level during the time it took to re-trim. The WT set in the Lysander only had a range of about 70 miles. The range could be increased by flying higher. Flying too high prevented accurate observation of troop movements. Flying too low risked coming close to a light flak battery and at all altitudes there was always a Bf109 pilot on the look out for easy pickings. As a tactical reconnaissance aircraft it was at a disadvantage if pounced upon by enemy fighters because its defensive armament was only one, sometimes two, guns operated by the observer. When the German advance started the observers were not provided with cameras to record enemy dispositions. Air Headquarters had to send someone to Paris in a hurry to buy as many Leica 35mm cameras as possible. By then the Lysanders had been withdrawn from the order of battle. Their surviving pilots then 'borrowed' the first available Hurricane. Unfortunately they too were downed by the very effective German light flak or by the guns of 'trigger-happy' French and British troops.

Airmen loading a parachute supply container onto the bomb rack under the starboard stub-wing of a Lysander. (James Goulding)

In retrospect it is clear that too much reliance was placed on the superiority of aircraft as a weapon against ground targets and on immunity from anti-aircraft gunfire. The *Luftwaffe*'s flak guns in support of the army were both mobile and effective. The awareness of some and the unawareness of others of the chances of low-flying aircraft surviving against flak was made against the optimistic statement in the *RAF Manual of Air Tactics* January 1939 that read: 'Low flying bombers would enjoy comparative immunity from anti-aircraft fire'. One of the strangest comments to come out of Air Headquarters France in 1940 related to bombing accuracy: 'The accuracy of bombing is as accurate on active service as it was at pre-war practice camps'. An interesting observation in view of the generally low accuracy in the years before the war. Or, perhaps, it reflected the daring and often suicidal low-level attacks adopted by aircrews trying to stem the German advance.

On the 12 May Defiants went into action for the first time. During the following two weeks they shot down sixty-five enemy aircraft, mostly bombers. They were withdrawn from the order of battle at the beginning of August having suffered irreplaceable losses once the *Luftwaffe* overcame its initial surprise. Perhaps there were voices in the Air Ministry saying 'We told you so'.

Human fatigue

The policy of having only one aircrew allocated to each aircraft sufficed for the normal routine of operations during which each crew was given sufficient time in which to rest before the next sortie. However, from the 10 May onward, when the demands on squadrons became increasingly more frequent, greater utilisation of the few available aircraft would have been achieved had there been two crews for each aircraft. Pilots and aircrew became fatigued to a level that began to impair their judgement. The fatigue of the aircrew was matched by that of the ground crews. A typical fighter pilot's log book entry after the 10 May showed that in 13 days he had flown 65 hours. In other words five hours in the air every day; and that did not include the time spent sitting in the cockpit waiting for the 'scramble' order. A typical bomber aircrew log book recorded 90 hours flown in 21 days.

Fighter problems and modifications

The Hurricane's combination of a metal structure with fabric covering was better able to withstand the rigours of operations from French airfields than the Spitfire. The all-metal Spitfire, other than special flights, was not based in France. Among Dowding's objections to the demand from the War Cabinet that he base more fighters in France was that in the less sophisticated environment they would be far less effective than when operating from the well-equipped airfields of Britain.

The report on the performance of the RAF in France contains few criticism of the engine and airframe of the Hurricane. Of the many large and small problems that beset the RAF during the Summer of 1940 in France and one of the least expected, was the choking of carburettors with grass seed. The Merlin engine of the Hurricane was particularly prone to this.

On the 9 June, in the midst of all the airforce's problems of fighting a rearguard action, Flt Lt McGarth suggested that it was possible to try out a constant-speed propeller on a Spitfire 'without a lot of paper work and fuss'. It was done. Seven thousand feet was added to the aircraft's ceiling and its performance overall so transformed that the Air Ministry immediately authorised the modification of all Spitfires and all Hurricanes. A tremendous effort on the part of industry, particularly by de Havilland and Rotol, resulted in a total of 1050 aircraft being re-equipped by August. Without the modification the outcome of the Battle of Britain might have been different.

Hawker Hurricane eight-gun fighter with three-blade, constant-speed, propeller. (Peter Ottery)

History is full of 'ifs'

When Bomber Command was released from the restraints imposed during the first six months of war it was free to attack inland targets in Germany. At the time a combination of propaganda, wishful thinking and inability to observe bombing results clearly engendered a false sense of success. As we now know, the effectiveness of the command was an illusion. In 1941 D.M.B. Butt made a statistical assessment of the results. Those results can be applied retrospectively to Bomber Command operations in 1939 and 1940 and, more importantly, can be applied to September 1938. If, in 1938, the command had attempted to strike an effective blow at Germany it would not have had the means to do so effectively. At the time many realised this fact but their warnings were suppressed.[9]

Even with Bomber Command 'let off the leash' in 1940 it was still deficient in five respects:

1. Range and bomb load.
2. Ability to resist and overcome enemy defences.
3. Ability to find the target.
4. Ability to bomb accurately.
5. Effective bombs.

These criticisms must be considered against the fact that the RAF was not the only airforce that concentrated on developing a bomber force while at the same time neglecting the essential provision of navigators and navigational equipment. The US Army Air Corps in the 1930s concentrated on building up a long-range bomber arm but virtually ignored the need for navigators.

'The operationally feasible dictates the strategically possible'. These words of Harris succinctly highlight the impossibility of Bomber Command fulfilling the wishes of the War Cabinet in the first two years of the war.

Torpedo-bomber technology

On the 21 June 1940 Beauforts of No 42 Squadron attacked the *Scharnhorst*. This was the first time Beauforts were used in action against an enemy warship. Although they were designed as torpedo-bombers, for this operation they carried two 500 lb bombs. The attack did not sink the ship. A third of the Beauforts were shot down by the escorting Bf 109s. The action against the *Scharnhorst* serves to introduce the technology of the Beaufort and similar aircraft, such as the Blenheim, in relation to advances and sometimes no advances, made in aircraft design and performance since 1935.

We do not have to look any further than *AP 1580 Pilot's Notes* for the Beaufort I. Because the Taurus engines did not provide sufficient power the Notes contain a number of warnings; particularly those concerning engine failure. For example: if an engine failed during take-off at 3,300 rpm or with the flaps partly down then there would be a rapid swing and roll. The roll could not be stopped and within three seconds would pass through the vertical and the aircraft would crash. The only chance the pilot had of recovery was to cut the good engine and crash-land straight ahead. If more than a quarter throttle was used on the good engine and with flaps and undercarriage down the pilot had great difficulty in preventing a violent swing and roll. At full load the aircraft would not climb on one engine.

En route engine failure in the Beaufort and with many other RAF aircraft types, presented the pilot with a Catch 22 dilemma. In the event of having to continue flying on one engine and the cooling gills were opened, to keep down cylinder head temperatures at high rpm and low airspeed, then drag would increase. With even lower airspeed the cooling flow over the cylinders could not keep down the temperature: therefore the gills had to be opened further and so on in a vicious circle.

Technology in general in 1940

How far had the RAF in 1940 progressed in technology since the start of the expansion programme? Were any important technical lessons learnt from the first six months of war?

The answer to the first question depends on the particular rather than on the general. The new were superposed on the old. Perhaps the most significant change was also the most obvious to the visual observer. This was the near total abandonment of the biplane configuration for first-line aircraft: although one or two fighter squadrons were still operating biplane fighters in 1940: and the Walrus continued to serve in the RAF on air-sea rescue duties and with the Fleet Air Arm; as did the Swordfish and Albacore to the end of WWII.

As for the second question: a number of important lessons were learnt. They included:

Existing bombs and bomb aiming equipment had to be improved.

A range of automatic and semi-automatic systems and equipment was needed to improve accuracy of navigation.

The daylight battles between bombers and fighters emphasised the need for self-sealing fuel tanks and armour plate protection for vital areas.

Variable-pitch, constant-speed, propellers were essential if fighters were to retain air superiority.

The importance of well organised and well-equipped training programme for all skills.

More air-sea rescue launches were needed.

Surprising was the failure to provide enough high-speed, air-sea rescue launches for the recovery of aircrew forced to bale out over the sea or take to a dinghy after 'ditching'. Surprising because the RAF had had marine craft units for the support of flying boat operations for many years. In 1932 the C class seaplane tenders were introduced. These had a top speed of 27 knots. They were not only used at seaplane bases but would take station as rescue launches along the route of long-distance flights. Their design and development owed much to T.E. Lawrence, alias Aircraftman Shaw. In 1936 Scott-Paine received an order for 64ft marine craft for marine rescue duties. In 1938, in anticipation that aircraft would be operating over the sea for much of the time, the number of high-speed launches on order was increased to meet the demands of Bomber Command. However the needs of Fighter Command in that respect received less attention. Possibly because it was anticipated that the fighters would be operating over land for most of the time. As the Battle of France came to an end and the Battle of Britain started, many shot down RAF fighter pilots were drowned before they could be rescued from the English Channel. Until the RAF Air-Sea Rescue service was fully organised in February 1941, recovery of downed pilots depended on the availability in the area of lifeboats and Royal Navy ships.

Perhaps the most important lesson learnt from the first six months of war with Germany was the value of radar to Fighter and Coastal Commands. Despite the erection of high wooden towers, similar to oil rigs, at numerous places around the coast of Britain and strange arrangements of pipework sticking out under the wings of aircraft, the purpose and functioning of this most advanced science was known to only a few in the service.

Things to come

By the time the expansion programme started, illustrators for magazines and books were visualising the aircraft shapes of the future. In the 1936 film *Things to Come* the aircraft of the future were elegant and streamlined. There was also a helicopter. The few helicopters flying in 1939 were ungainly and their control had yet to be perfected. In practice there was a wide gap between what could be schemed on paper, using smooth shapes and gentle curves, and what could be manufactured. Many of the racing single-seat monoplanes entered for the King's Cup in Britain and for the closed-circuit air races in the USA were compact, low-drag shapes. The marked difference between racing and service aircraft emphasised the practical considerations of designing, operating and maintaining air-force machines. An early exception must be the Spitfire. When compared with its closest rival, the Bf109, it resembled a racing-machine. In contrast the Hurricane's lines owed much to the Hawker biplanes, such as the Fury. Its details reflected the needs of uncomplicated production processes and ease of maintenance, therefore it lacked the graceful lines of the Spitfire. Interestingly the comparatively graceful, smooth lines of the early marks of the Spitfire only gave it a marginal advantage in speed over the Hurricane and over the Bf109 with its

Martin-Baker MB-3. Although it did not fly until August 1942 the specification to which it was designed was issued in 1939 when plans were being made for a new generation of fighters with heavier armament. The MB-3 would have been equipped with six 20mm guns. However its progress towards a production contract was ended by the continuing problems with the Napier Sabre engine. (Martin-Baker)

Miles M.20 eight-gun low-cost fighter intended as a simple easy-to-produce replacement of Spitfires and Hurricanes being lost at the time of the Battle of Britain. It was based on a 1938 project. (Adwest Group plc via Julian C. Temple)

angular geometry. Further development of the Spitfire, as more power became available from the Merlin engine, enabled it to attain speeds significantly greater than those of other fighters.

As noted in Chapter Five, James Martin of Martin-Baker designed a fighter as a private venture. He was of the opinion that he could do better than Camm's Hurricane. His primary design target was ease of maintenance. The metal panels of the steel tube fuselage were easily detachable. One handle opened the access panels to all eight wing-mounted guns. The undercarriage was fixed. The fuel tanks could be removed quickly from the fuselage and great attention had been made to the detail design of every component. When the MB-2 was evaluated at Martlesham Heath the test pilots found it uncomfortable to fly and it was a poor gun platform. The ailerons needed improving and there was not enough rudder area. The MB-2 was not accepted for production and therefore serves only as an example of the gap between good intentions and practical flying that characterised so many well-meaning attempts to try something different.[10]

Design direction

As mentioned in Chapter Two, too many aircraft designs in the 1930s were compromised in the end because of uncertain specification writing and because of subsequent changes in operational requirements; both of which were symptoms of a lack of direction. Some of the better types of air-

Cockpit of a Bristol Beaufighter. Apart from the small radar CRT display unit, this photograph is representative of a 1940 aircraft. It emphasises the massive increase in instruments and controls consequent on the advancement of aircraft technology and lethality in general since 1935. (Crown Copyright)

A typical Spitfire production line. (Vickers Archives – Cambridge University Library)

craft might have been in service a year or two earlier had there been clear direction given to the aircraft industry. As an example of a lack of direction: the Typhoon might have been available in 1940 had the Air Ministry not persisted in sponsoring an engine, the Napier Sabre, whose unreliability took sometime to cure. However, in the absence at the time of effective air-to-ground weapons, the Typhoon was not necessarily the best size and shape for the air war of 1940. Another example was the DH Don trainer of 1937. Neither DHs nor the Air Ministry appeared to have any clear idea about what a three-seat, two pilots and a gunner, trainer weighing 6,500 lb, with an engine (Gipsy King) of only 525 hp, was intended to achieve. The lack of direction was confirmed when the original order for 250 was cut to 50 with the gunner's position deleted.

Other possible examples of a lack of design direction were the Halifax and Stirling; particularly when compared with the Lancaster. These two heavy bombers became the subject of much criticism in 1942 by the C-in-C Bomber Command. Air Marshal Arthur Harris considered that both types had too many shortcomings and overall their production was adversely affected by poor management. He managed to get Stirling production resources diverted to the building of more Lancasters.[11]

One aspect of aircraft design of the late 1930s for which there are few records or comments is that of airframe lives. As it happened, RAF aircraft rarely achieved 'high mileages'. Some first-line aircraft logged 300 hours but the majority far less because

A typical Vickers Wellington production scene. c.1940. (Vickers Archives – Cambridge University Library)

of accidents and losses in action. Therefore the potential dangers of fatigue failures from old age were of little importance in time of war. For example, with hindsight we know that the Wellington had a built-in 'time bomb' in the shape of limited-life components. Many Air Staff specifications concentrated on speed and rate of climb for fighters and speed and range for bombers while neglecting some of the practical matters related to operating and maintaining aircraft.

One potential improvement in the design of aircraft not achieved in the years of expansion was standardisation of the shape and position of controls and of secondary instruments. Aircraft design offices throughout the world and not just in Britain, relied heavily on the adaptability of the human pilot. Pilots, as a species, were expected to put up with being either too hot or too cold, having to reach and contort to operate wheels, levers, knobs and switches. The cockpits of the RAF in the 1930s and 40s were no exception to the design practice of positioning cockpit equipment to suit the associated rods, shafts, cables and electrical circuits rather than considering the needs of the human pilot.

Now and then a pilot, particularly one who flew many different types of aircraft, would write about the subject of cockpit design and argue for a greater degree of standardisation in the position and shape of controls. As one ferry and test pilot wrote, 'Pilots became accustomed to accustoming themselves to different cockpit layouts' as mentioned in Chapter 3, the RAF's Basic Six panel of primary and essential instruments was an exception to the general lack of thought given to cockpit design.

North American B-25 Mitchell medium bomber. One of the many American aircraft types which eventually took over from the Blenheim. (Peter Ottery)

Conclusion

The re-equipment programme involved many different aspects of airforce operations including: the defence of the United kingdom; an effective long-range bomber force; coastal and ocean patrolling: and, of equal importance, training and support services. In 1936 the Air Staff had to make certain assumptions about the equipment and tactics of the potential enemy. In retrospect, they got most of the answers right. But when they came to Bomber Command they did not get all the right answers. Eventually wrong decisions were abandoned. The breathing space afforded by the character of the opening campaigns of the war, gave time in which to put a number of things right. All the events that might have happened together in September 1939 were spaced out over the following eighteen months: mass assaults from the air on Britain were delayed until the Summer of 1940 and full-scale bombing of Germany did not start until 1941.

The RAF did its best with aircraft and equipment that was not always equal to that of the enemy. Had Bomber and Coastal Commands been given the right aircraft in sufficient numbers, and the means to strike with accuracy and effect, then Germany might have hesitated over venturing towards the West. Army co-operation tasks, one of the primary reasons for the RAF presence in France in 1940, were not given high enough priority in the years leading up to the war. This was despite the valuable experience gained during WWI when aircraft worked closely with the ground forces. The Blenheim and Battle squadrons were deemed 'expendable' in an effort to attack tactical targets. These operations, in retrospect, were 'hostages to

Whittle WR2/700 jet engine. Had greater support been given to the project in the 1930s, the RAF might have had a jet aircraft by 1940 rather than 1944. (Rolls-Royce)

fortune' because they were rarely given an escort of fighters. Even when escorts were allocated the lack of training and communication between bombers and fighters along with poor visibility weighed against success.

Bomber Command needed improving in many departments and the politicians and the Air Staff needed to pay more attention to the scientists when it came to selecting targets. For example, sending a squadron of Blenheims to attack a seaplane base was a waste of crews and aircraft. Even had the base been obliterated it would have been only a 'pinprick' to the *Luftwaffe*'s order of battle. It also had to realise that at night the *Luftwaffe*'s flak organisation was not only well equipped with target-finding and gun-laying-radar it was formidable in the number of guns and searchlights deployed. Until the Germans perfected their night-fighter radars the guns were the greater threat.

One particular task was accomplished with much success by Bomber Command in 1940. This was the mining of enemy waters by Hampdens. Air Vice-Marshal Harris, AOC 5 Group, convinced the CAS and the Admiralty of the contribution the RAF could make to the war effort when other commands were locked in the stalemate of the 'phoney war'.

Harris not only contributed a number of ideas which advanced the technology of the service as a whole he also was one of the principal instigators of synthetic training equipment and devices.

Fighter Command entered the Battle of Britain with a a reporting and control system of radar, observer posts, filter and operations rooms that enabled it to prevent the *Luftwaffe* achieving its objectives in daylight. At night the command was less well prepared and it took a few more months for the radar-equipped night-fighter force to achieve dominance in the night skies over Britain.

The American contribution

At the beginning of the year the recently formed Purchasing Board organised orders for 11,000 American aircraft. Part of the deal with the then neutral USA covered paying for the building of complete factories. The Hudson having proved suitable for Coastal Command the military version of the Lockheed Lodestar Model L-37, the Ventura, was selected and an order for 25 placed.

In June 1940 the service acquired 50 Martin Maryland twin-engine bombers that had been part of an order from the French airforce. The Hudsons and Harvards ordered and delivered before the war would be joined from 1940 onward by Catalinas, P-40s, Bostons, B-17s, B-24s, B-25s, Venturas and other American types. Such a diverse collection of aircraft types imposed an additional strain on support and maintenance services. However Britain in 1939 and 1940 was in no position to do other than get what aircraft it could from where it could. By the end of the war there would be virtually two RAFs: one equipped with British aircraft; the other with American.

In the six years of change that started in 1935 the RAF not only expanded in numbers of aircraft and new technologies, it metamorphosed. Starting in 1935 as a predominantly bomber force it expanded to the advantage of the bomber lobby. However, by 1938 it was realised that the concept 'The bomber will always get through' applied equally to Britain as to Germany. Therefore fighter production was given greater priority. In six years radar was advanced from a radio phenomenon to an essential, all-purpose, system for detecting aircraft, terrestrial features and ships. After 1940 the RAF had to expand globally as the war spread outwards from the original confined area of north-west Europe. That required the provision of fighter, coastal and bomber squadrons and improved technology for the RAF in North Africa, the Middle East, India and the Far East as well as for the airforces of the dominions. Also after 1940, Fighter Command no longer acted purely in a defensive role. Fighter sweeps and escorting bomber sorties over France took the air war to the enemy.

The decisions taken in the years of expansion enabled the RAF to grow in size and to embrace new technologies even faster after 1940. By the end of WWII there were over one million serving men and women and it had been supplied with over 130,000 aircraft and the Germans were wishing they had never taken up the profession of war.

NOTES

Notes are referenced to books in the following Bibliography and denoted by author. Others are referenced to files in the Public Record Office and are indicated by 'AIR' and by 'AVIA' and to the Air Historical Branch of the Ministry of Defence by 'AHB'.

Notes for the Preface

1 Richards, Portal and Terrain, p. 37.

Notes for Chapter One

1. Boyle p 689
2. Spaight p 90 Ordering procedures.
3. Terrain p 38
4. Her Majesty's Balloon Factory of the 1890s became the Royal Aircraft Factory (RAF). In 1918 the name was changed to the Royal Aircraft Establishment to avoid confusion with the present RAF. Today Farnborough is part of the Defence Research Agency having lost, like so many institutions, its royal appelation
5. James p 217
6. *AIR 2* code I/2 2062 36-37
7. RAE Report No H.1111. on gas turbines.
8. Swords. p 71 *et seq:*
9. The electro-mechanical system was based on a number of Strowger selectors of the type used for automatic telephone exchanges.
10. Dean p 61
11. Dean p 81

Notes for Chapter Two

1. Correspondence with D.H. Middleton
2. Dean p 139
3. Night flying on some HP 0400 RNAS/RAF airfields in WWI was controlled from a 'bandstand'-like structure. Electric lamps were used to indicate the take-off and landing area and direction.
4. Bulmore p 9
5. Wallace p 25
6. The War Office was primarily concerned with army matters and was not, as in some countries, a ministry of defence responsible for all arms.
7. The word 'cannon' came to be applied to automatic guns of 20mm and above. However this trend was one of doubtful semantics rather than logic.
8. Parnall merged with Nash & Thompson in 1936
9. British Patents. Group XXI Nos 541,991 and 494,248
10. *AIR 2* 1381
11. *AIR 2* 1569
12. Boyle p 705
13. Hartcup p 236

Notes for Chapter Three

1. Lewis p 270
2. Slessor p 157
3. AIR 27 650
4. Gunston, *Encyclopedia of Combat Aircraft* 1976 p 213
5. *AIR* Code B 2023
6. Lewis p 275
7. *AIR 2* 8536
8. Townsend p 154
9. The pilot was Sgt Naish and the scientists Bowen and Wood.
10. AP 1530A
11. *AIR 27* 882
12. Correspondence with D.H. Middleton
13. Wallace-Clarke p 151
14. Barnes p 374
15. *Through the Overcast* by Assen Jordanoff was one of the most comprehensive guides to instrument flying available in the late 1930s.
16. AHB Box 2 Folder 7: Ludlow-Hewitt letter of the 10 Nov. 1937 to the Air Ministry
17. Barnes p 383

Notes for Chapter Four

1. Chapman p 33 et seq.
2. Middleton p 63. H. Wynn, in letter to *Aeroplane Monthly* 10 March 1984, refers to 31 aircraft companies and 14 engine companies in 1945.
3. Swinton p 119. On the 17 May 1940 Beaverbrook, the Minister of Aircraft Production, transferred the Castle Bromwich factory back to Vickers .

4. Spaight p 95
5. Dean p 75
6. Lovell p 7
7. The initial production batch of the Beaufighter had to have Hercules IIIs of 1,400 bhp pending delivery of the more powerful VIs.
8. *AVIA 6* 3393
9. The geodetic form of structure was first used in aviation for the Schutte Lanz SL-1 dirigible of 1911.
10. Wallace-Clarke p 120 mentions the habit of the FN 17 turret creeping down which suggests that the up-locks were a later modification.
11. Hastings p 62
12. *AIR 27* 1383
13. ASDIC The Allied Submarine Detection Investigation Committee of 1917 initiated the development of a sonic detection system. This was the precursor of modern SONAR.
14. Dean p 151
15. Penrose p 210 records that the order was worth £5million.
16. Dean p 80

Notes for Chapter Five

1. *AIR 27* 1383
2. Spaight p 75
3. Dean p 58
4. The fifth fixed gun was the standard wing-mounted 7.7mm Browning
5. *AIR 2* 3265
6. Dean p 58
7. Upward-firing guns were evaluated at the A&AEE in the early 1930s. The object of the tests of both the Vickers 7.7mm and the COW 37mm gun was the design of aiming equipment for 'no-allowance' sighting. No-allowance sighting took no account of gravity, range or relative movement of the target.2
8. Williams p 832
9. Erwood p 470
10. Bowen p 61
11. Mason *The British Fighter* p 277
12. Millar & Sawers p 76 *et seq.*
13. Mason, *Hawker Aircraft Since 1920* p 254
14. Middleton *Test Pilots* p 88
15. The Imperial Airways C-Class/Harrow operation, using the 'looped hose' technique, required up to seven minutes to make contact and connect the hose and then one minute for every 100 gallons of fuel transferred.

Notes for Chapter Six

1. Dean p 76
2. *AIR 2* 3265
3. The standard Merlin of the Spitfire in 1939 developed 1,000 hp at 3,000 rpm with a boost pressure of 6.5 psi using 87 octane fuel. In March 1939 an He 100 was flown at 463 mph. In April the Me 209 reached 469 mph; a record which was unchallenged for thirty years.
4. Wallace-Clarke p 57
5. Goulding p 117
6. In 1916 F.W. Lanchester derived an expression which stated that: the strength of a given force should be considered to be proportional to the average effectiveness of each unit times the square of the number of units employed, provided each unit is able to fire on any or all of the opposing force.

   Gestalt, in the psychology of perception, includes the concept that we tend to perceive the whole as greater than just the summation of the parts.
7. Nicolson p 74
8. Clark p 203
9. Blackett p 103
10. AP 1881 (1940)
11. Nicolson p 70
12. Dean p 96
13. Bowen p 127 *et seq.*
14. *AIR 27* 1383
15. Masefield, Sir Peter *Aerospace* Oct 1990
16. Wood & Dempster p 19
17. Scanlan p 183
18. Hartcup p 122 *et seq.*
19. Harris pp 98 & 184
20. Baker p 309
21. Hartcup p 110
22. Wood & Dempster p 169

Notes for Chapter Seven

1. Townsend p 188
2. Collier p 78
3. Terrain p 689
4. *AIR 27* 788
5. When *The Lion Has Wings* was released Sqn/Ldr H.M.S. Wright was credited as RAF adviser.
6. HMSO. *Laboratory of the Air* p 23
7. Dean p 169
8. The author's recollection is that some Tiger Moths were equipped with light-series bomb racks.
9. The pitot head was an open-ended tube facing into the airstream. The dynamic pressure of the air was applied to one side of the airspeed indicator mechanism. The other side was exposed to the static air pressure detected by holes which were not facing into the airstream.
10. Boyle p 713 The leaflet raids were, to Trenchard's mind, a monstrously ineffective means to a useless end.
11. The author's recollection is of an ominous blackness stretching to the horizon.
12. *AIR 2* 4227

13. Dope: a compound of nitro-cellulose or cellulose acetate base applied to fabric in order to waterproof, strengthen and tauten it.

Notes for Chapter Eight

1. Joubert de la Ferte p 142
2. Price *Aircraft versus Submarine* p 55
3. HMSO *Laboratory of the Air* p 16
4. Turnill & Reed p 55
5. Wallace-Clarke p 165 *et seq.*
6. HMSO *Laboratory of the Air* p 16
7. Wood & Dempster p 146
8. *AIR 2* 5251
9. D.M.B. Butt's *Bombing Report of 1941* included the following conclusions:

Of those aircraft recorded as attacking their target, only one in three were within three miles. Over the French ports the proportion was two in three; over Germany it was one in four and only one in ten over the Ruhr.

At full moon, the proportion was two in five, whereas at the new moon it was only one in fifteen. In the absence of haze, two in five were within five miles and in thick haze only one in fifteen .

An increase in anti-aircraft fire reduced the number of aircraft getting within five miles of the target by 30%.

10. Bowyer *Interceptors for the RAF* p 35
11. Saward. *Bomber Harris* p 390

RAF 73ft. High speed rescue launch designed and built by Vosper. (Aeroplane Monthly)

Glossary

A&AEE	Aeroplane & Armament Experimental Establishment at Martlesham Heath Suffolk.
ABC	Automatic Boost Control: the system which held engine boost pressure to a selected value.
ACM	Air Chief Marshal
AI	Airborne Interception radar.
AM	Air Marshal
AMC	Automatic Mixture Control: the system which automatically adjusted the mixture ratio to match the engine operating conditions.
AMES	Air Ministry Experimental Station (A cover name for a radar station)
AOC in C	Air Officer Commanding in Chief
ASV	Air to Surface Vessel radar.
auw	All Up Weight
AVM	Air Vice-Marshal
bhp	Brake Horsepower
BAFF	British Air Forces France (1940)
CAS	Chief of the Air Staff
CG	Centre of Gravity
CH	Chain Home: the chain of radar stations around the coast of Britain.
CHL	Chain Home Low: the chain of radar stations used to detect low flying enemy aircraft.
CinC	Commander in Chief
Collimated	An optical system which gives a parallel beam from a point source; as used in the Aldis and the reflector gun sights whose aiming marks were focused at infinity.
CS	Constant Speed: a CS propeller held engine rpm to a selected value irrespective, within limits, of aircraft manoeuvres.
DF	Direction Finding radio.
DH	de Havilland
DTD	Directorate of Technical Development
EHF	Extremely High Frequency
FN	Frazer-Nash: the designer of powered gun mountings and Nash and Thompson (NT) the manufacturing company.
HF	High Frequency radio.
K gun	Abbreviation for the Vickers gas-operated 7.7mm machine-gun which replaced the Lewis.
MAEE	Marine Aircraft Experimental Establishment at Felixstowe.
MAP	Ministry of Aircraft Production
MRAF	Marshal of the RAF.
MHz	MegaHertz: millions of cycles per second.
RAE	Royal Aircraft Establishment: now part of the Defence Research Agency.
PRO	Public Record Office
RT	Radio Telephone
rpm	revolutions per minute
USMC	United States Marine Corps
VHF	Very High Frequency radio
Vne	Never to be exceeded speed.
Wet wing.	One in which the wing structure and skin contain the fuel: an alternative to separate fuel tanks.
Yagi array.	A radar antenna similar to a modern television antenna.

Bibliography

Adkin, F. *From The Ground Up* (Airlife 1983)

Baker, W.J. *A History of the Marconi Co* (Methuen 1970)

Blackett, P.M.S *Studies of War (1962)*

Banks, R.O.D. Air Commodore *I Kept No Diary* (Airlife 1978)

Bowen, E.G., *Radar Days* (Hilger 1987)

Bowyer, M.J.F. *Interceptor Fighters for the Royal Air Force 1935-45* (Patrick Stevens 1984)

Boyle, A. *Trenchard* (Collins 1962)

Brook-Popham, Sir Robert, ACM *Report on the Performance of the RAF in France.(PRO)*

Bulmore, F.T.K. *The Dark Haven* (Cape 1956)

Chamberlain, G. *Zeppelin* (Dalton 1984)

Clark, R.W. *Tizard* (Methuen 1965)

Collier, B. *The Defence of the United Kingdom* (Her Majesty's Stationery Office 1957)

Coombs, L.F.E. *Cockpits of the RAF* (Series in *Aeroplane Monthly* 1983)

The Aircraft Cockpit (Patrick Stephens 1990)

The Expanding Years (Series in *Aeroplane Monthly* 1985)

Dean, Sir Maurice *The RAF and Two World Wars* (Cassell 1979)

Erwood, P. *Back Track* Vol 9 No 9 (Atlantic 1995)

Exupéry, A. de St-. *Wind Sand and Stars* (Heinemann 1939)

Flint, P. *Dowding and Headquarters Fighter Command* (Airlife 1996)

Goulding, J. *Interceptor* (Ian Allan 1986)

Gunston, W.T. *Avionics* (Patrick Stephens 1990)

Encyclopedia of Combat Aircraft (Salamander 1976)

Night Fighters (Patrick Stephens 1976)

Plane Speaking (Patrick Stephens 1991)

Harris, L.H. *Signal Venture* (*Gale & Polden* 1951)

Hartcup, G. *The Challenge of War* (David & Charles 1970)

Hastings, M. *Bomber Command* (Pan 1982)

Her Majesty's Stationery Office *Laboratory of the Air* (1948)

James, D. *Gloster Aircraft* (Putnam ?)

Jackson, R. *Before the Storm* (Arthur Barker 1972)

James, J. *The Palladins* (Futura 1991)

Jordenoff, A. *Through the Overcast*

Joubert de la Ferte, Sir Philip. ACM *The Third Service* (Thames & Hudson 1955)

King, H.F. *Armament of British Aircraft 1909–1939* (Putnam 1971)

Lewis, P. *The British Bomber Since 1914* (Putnam 1980)

Lovell, Sir Bernard. *Echoes of War* (Hilger 1991)

Lumsden, A.S. *British Piston Aero-Engines* (Airlife 1994)

Mason, F.K. *The British Fighter* (Putnam 1992)

The British Bomber (Putnam 1994)

Hawker Aircraft since 1920 (Putnam1961)

McClure, V. *Gladiators Over Norway* (W.H.Allen 1942)

Middleton, D. *Test Pilots* (Guild Pub. 1985)

Miller & Sawers *The Technical Development of Modern Aviation* (*Routledge & Keegan Paul 1968*)

Neale, B.T. *CH–The First Operational Radar* (GEC Journal of Research. Vol 3 No2 1985)

Nicolson, N. *Sir Keith Park* (Methuen 1984)

Penrose, H. *The* Ominous *Skies* (RAF Museum 1980)

Price, A. *Aircraft Versus Submarine* (Kimber 1973)

Instruments of Darkness (Macdonald & Janes. 1977 ed.)

Raleigh, Sir Walter. *The War in The Air* (Clarendon 1928)

Richards, D. *The Royal Air Force 1939–1945* Vol 1 (HMSO 1953-54)

Richards, D. *Portal of Hungerford* (Heinemann 1977)

Saward, D. Group Captain *The Bomber's Eye* (Cassell 1959)

'Bomber' Harris (Buchan & Enright 1984)
Scanlan, M.J.B. *Chain Home Radar–A Personal Reminiscence* (GEC Review Vol 8, No3, 1993)
Slessor, Sir John, MRAF, *The Central Blue* (Cassell 1957)
Spaight, J.M. *Expansion of the RAF 1934–1939* (AHB/II/116/17)
Swinton, Lord. *60 Years of Power* (Hutchinson 1968)
Swords, S.S. *Technical History of the Beginnings of Radar* (Peter Peregrinius & IEE 1986)
Terrain, J. *The Right of the Line* (Hodder & Stoughton 1985)
Townsend, P. Group Captain *Duel of Eagles* (Weidenfeld & Nicolson 1970)
Turnill & Reed. *Farnborough, The Story of the RAE* (Hale 1980)
Verrier, A. *The Bomber Offensive* (Batsford 1968)
Wallace-Clarke, R. *British Aircraft Armament* Vols 1 & 2 (PSL 1993)
Wallace, G.F. *Guns of the Royal Air Force* (William Kimber 1972)
Williams, T.I. *A History of Technology* Vol VII Part II (Oxford 1978)
Wood & Dempster *The Narrow Margin* (Hutchinson 1961)
Wright, M.D. *Most Probable Position* (University of Kansas 1974)

INDEX